SPIRITS ALIVE!

Dennis Jim Trish

Thanks for
opening the Door.

SPIRITS ALIVE!

CONFRONTATIONS WITH THE SPIRITS OF BRAZIL

Dennis J. Trisker

VANTAGE PRESS
New York

Copyright © 1996 by Dennis J. Trisker

Published by Vantage Press, Inc.
516 West 34th Street, New York, New York 10001

Manufactured in the United States of America
ISBN: 0-533-11852-2

Library of Congress Catalog Card No.: 95-91044

0 9 8 7 6 5 4 3 2 1

Dr. Dennis, your work will be surrounded by success because your country isn't free yet from dogma, superstitions, and fanatical religiosity. Your people still do not understand respect for transcendence. Be assured that your work will be very well accepted, since you labor seriously and are not given to banalities and superficialities. For this reason your work is progressing perfectly and will be well accepted.

—Pai Guillerme, a spirit, Sorocaba

Contents

Introduction

It is related that one day they came upon Majnun sifting the dust, and his tears flowing down. They said, "What doest thou?" He said, "I seek for Layli." They cried, "Alas for thee! Layli is of pure spirit, and thou seekest her in the dust!" He said, "I seek her everywhere; haply somewhere I shall find her."
—Baha'u'llah, *The Seven Valleys and the Four Valleys*

It is almost traditional when introducing a work of this type to begin by saying that everything reported is the "absolute" truth. The truth is that nothing is absolute, nothing—neither the contents of this adventure nor even my own existence upon this planet. What are herein given are perceptions of experiences—of entities and events—as I observed them. They were my realities; they became my truths during the time in which I ventured through Brazil.

I perceived that the spirits and I confronted each other for a period of six human months. They, for the most part, obviously found it fun to instruct me. They cajoled me into experiencing other levels of consciousness in which the fantastic became the ordinary and in which the ordinary was never routine. They showed me how in their world our logic only exists as a fleeting attempt to solidify a time and space continuum that is defined by its immensity, bordered by limitlessness. They often scoffed at the way human reason attempted to categorize the world into neat little packages. They warned me not to fall into the same trap. "Humans," they told me, "do this for security. You earth incarnates are afraid of allowing yourselves to flow into the emptiness and the unstructured." Sunyata, the void, the goal of Zen training, I tried to experience. But certain of the higher disincarnates tried forcing me to experience this state in which all things flow each into another.

They were forcing me to! These spirits wanted me to move fully into their world which is less solidified than our own, less bounded by rigidity, more fluid, full of potential and creative impulses.

Some wiser spirits warned me not to reveal my invisible sources, which might become dependencies for others. Many were playful and taught me through spirit games. I had to walk with caution and discrimination at times as well, because spirits are not always wise or closer to liberation and might easily lead one into blind obedience to their will. In fact, the great majority of spirits are not awakened beings and often confuse their astral existence with their earth relations.

Most people lack experience in this area, and adequate discernment is therefore nearly impossible. I have found this to be generally true in psychic and spiritual circles. Faith is generally misplaced, placed in the spirit guide and not in self. A person who receives a spontaneous healing of some physical disease is automatically disposed to accept the healer's wisdom about life. Yet is it necessary for a human surgeon to have wisdom outside of his field to practice surgery? Must a massage therapist, dentist, or botanical healer be automatically wise in all areas because he can rub a body, pull a tooth, or recommend an herb?

In Brazil I did meet some mediums who performed phenomenal wonders and functioned on many levels. Some did have wisdom, but not many. I met others who did none of these spectacular things and yet were known as repositories of great knowledge. Sometimes, but rarely, the two came together in the same person.

Reflecting on the words of the Apostle Paul, some higher spirits who taught me well warned me "Believe not, O brothers, every spirit . . . " They pointed out to me not to automatically accept all that the disincarnates might relate to me as "true." Those of us from the western world tend to have unconscious religious programs, even if we do not formally attend a church. These programs emphasize the need to "believe" in and "have faith" as the way to salvation. In fact, many people presently jumping into the New Age movement without any previous preparation are refugees from overbearing religious philosophies. But they are what they flee!

They take with them the need to identify with and believe in something. They tend to grasp and believe in the new with the same sort of fanaticism as that which their parents believed in the old. Everything that they read or experience becomes "gospel truth." They are, in other words, putting new wine in old winesacks. Much of the channeled spirit scripture on the commercial market is assimilated by masses of people who are otherwise innocents in the spiritual field. They believe, and with faith to move mountains.

I struggled to maintain a spiritual balance, not to automatically deny or accept anything I heard or saw. One metaphysical leader told me in Panama, "I can't say for sure if these people are sincere or true or not. I don't want to make initial judgments. Let's listen and then test them out." I found that this attitude was the wisest to follow.

Great wisdom is needed. In normal life we often come across people who appear to be sincere and noble, only to find out later that they were quite dishonest in their dealings with us. The same applies to many spirits and their mediums. One Brazilian spirit related to me the following: "Many human beings believe that death confers some type of sanctity and wisdom upon discarnate souls. This, unfortunately is not true. Liars in your world often continue to be liars in our world as well. Very little changes. There is much loneliness here among the sick souls. They will do almost anything to get the attention of people in your world!"

Learn to discriminate, understand. Sift through the excitement, the theatrics, and the verbosity to find the truth or falsehood of a situation. In such way might one have the privilege of finding one's highest reality.

A São Paulo Subway Experience

I wandered for some two weeks around São Paulo and its spiritist institutes to orient myself. I spent nights attending seances and sessions, my days interviewing mediums and conversing with other investigators. Nothing clicked; nothing made sense. They turned out to be a jumble of aimless wanderings. I was being entertained and nothing more.

Then one day, in the subway, two stories below the center of São Paulo . . .

I was frantically running from one station to another. It was rush hour, the worst time to meander through the city streets. The inhabitants of this city, who are at other times warmhearted and civilized, turn into pushy and unruly animals, just like their cousins in Washington, D.C., New York, Paris, and other large cities that have subway systems.

With people streaming around me, shoving, bumping, and obstructing my access, something happened to me.

It was like being in Zen meditation, completely immersed in the activity of being still, and then having a fellow monk hit you on your shoulder with his bamboo staff. Only it wasn't another monk. I was hit, grabbed, paralyzed, and finally forced to grab hold of a railing to steady myself. Something within me fell ten floors. At least, that is what it felt like. I was transported—there is no other word for this—into another "place." The sounds, the trains, the crowds, and everything else became shadowy images, distant and noiseless. I was suddenly surrounded by an awareness of "another," a non-part of myself, yet in direct contact with me. It gave me to understand that I should stop everything and be still, listen with my whole being. As the energy began to penetrate my brain, I felt strangely animated and forced to write what was coming through to me.

Imagine, if you can. There I was during the evening rush hour, with thousands of people swirling around me, not unlike the schools of fish streaming through the Amazon River. I was sitting on the floor of the station, for there was nowhere else to sit, oblivious to everything around me, feeling drunk and stunned, writing feverishly on some scraps of paper. These notes would later become the book that you are reading.

I was being instructed to proceed with my own investigations, to develop a little bit more humility and a lot more patience so that I would recognize help from the other world when it was proffered.

Later on I received tremendous cooperation from those still incarnate as well as spirits active on the other side, reminding me continually to keep my mind open. I observed that help was readily rendered and was led to those who could supply necessary information and experience that would assist me in my own spiritual growth. Especially important was a feeling of respect for the invisible and a remembrance of the Oneness of all life, which was the lesson toward which the higher spirits were leading me.

The spirits confronted me whenever they desired. They wouldn't leave me alone. They wished to constantly stimulate me on my search. At times they immersed me in events that would change my thinking and expand my consciousness.

A Blanked-Out Mind or a Case of Teleportation?

After my initiatory subway experience, I began to doubt what had occurred. I asked my mind (for where else should I ask?) for some confirmation of the event. Every day thereafter I would walk to the center of São Paulo to the Spiritist Federation Building. It was a short mile or so from my own apartment in Libertade, the Oriental sector of the city. This day however, my body was aching and tired. I really wished that I didn't have to walk the distance through crowded streets and neighborhoods.

I left the apartment, turned in the right direction, and began to walk. I passed the usual subway entrance. But then, in the next moment, I found myself standing inside the main entrance of the Federation offices. I couldn't remember anything else. My mind had blanked out for over half an hour—or had it? What other explanation could there be? My legs trembled as I sought a chair to sit on. My mind again began to fade in and out as dizziness and fear began to paralyze me. I remembered the previous day's subway occurrence and my search for a confirmation. Apparently, I had received it. But how?

Further discussion with mediums still left me vague in this. Had I been transported or had I had a mental lapse? If it was the latter, if my mind had lapsed for a half hour, then it was miraculous that I had been able to cross three main thoroughfares, bustling with traffic, and arrive safely at the Federation. What's more, these neighborhoods were not the safest even for the locals. I still have not found a satisfactory explanation for this phenomenon. Oh, how weak the mind in its struggle to explain; how well the veil of ignorance obscures, which doesn't permit clear understanding.

*   *   *

I subtitled this book "Confrontation with the Spirits of Brazil." I did this with a special reason; I went to confront them. They in turn took it upon themselves to confront me. We mutually tugged, slapped, and taught each other. They were often eager to learn from me. More often I met egotistical souls who only sought an audience. They are the dangerous ones. Supposedly superior, they have little desire to listen, only to "teach," a trademark of a true nonmaster. They are also very powerful and impressive to the nondiscriminating soul who makes first contact with them.

I was confronted on several levels; I came into contact through many demonstrations of what I would call creativity. This creativity, manifested through spirit phenomena, challenged many of my own limited beliefs. My inner mental structure was rapidly dismembered in the face of this startling reality, and I fell into conditions of mental anxiety and fear. This, more than anything else, provoked rapid changes within me. More than anything else it created psychological space that continually emptied the nooks and crannies of my mental cabinet. Old mental structures were swept away like a rickety boardwalk under the enormous force of a tsunami. Little was left and even that, too, was eventually destroyed!

Nights found me huddled under my covers trying to avoid confrontation with the spirits. I became strung out as my sensitivity evolved; I could hear the gabble of those on other planes of existence.

Initially I thought that I was not ready. But they thought otherwise. My time had come, and I am glad that they persisted in awakening me.

What I present in this book is a condensation of notes and tapes of those experiences, interviews, and encounters. I relate my adventures for those who know that truth may be found outside the confines of their national (and personal) boundaries, but who may not be as mobile in lifestyle as I. While I have strived to share the energy of my pilgrimage, one must realize that putting it down in words is a job for a supremely talented writer. Alas, I must say no more.

My Search to Sacred Brazil

My mind was racing as the Varig stewardess announced our immediate arrival at São Paulo International Airport. I was aching to get off, having been confined for half a day. My body wanted contact with solid ground. The flight from Bogotá, Colombia, to this southern industrial city had been extremely long and tiresome.

I'd slept little during the flight, wondering what lay ahead and how prepared I was for it. Could I learn Brazilian Portuguese quickly? Doubts assailed me; thoughts crowded in. But finally, as I passed through customs, I was glad that I was in Brazil. The moment of my pilgrimage had arrived. My heart was pounding strongly, my breath irregular as I realized that I was here.

I had made pilgrimages before to other lands: Iran, to seek out the Sufi and Baha'i origins; to Machu Picchu, in order to make contact with the old native culture; to Israel, to seek out my own spiritual roots in the only Jewish nation in the entire world.

There were other adventures as well: the quests into Buddhism, into Hinduism, the time spent with various spiritual masters, and my many years living in Central America and other parts of the world, seeking, always searching, for understanding, growth, and knowledge of myself.

Ten years earlier, the wife of the then Brazilian ambassador in Panama invited me to visit her country. I didn't go. Years later, my dentist in Costa Rica returned to Brazil for specialization. He and his wife also invited me. Still, the time was not right.

Later still, a young friend of mine, Ian, invited me to wander with him through that subcontinent. I felt compelled to go but didn't listen to my heart.

Finally one day, while planning a trip to the Far East, I received two letters that had been mailed a month apart from another friend, Marvin, telling of his experiences in São Paulo. My heart cords began to vibrate. Now was the time. Within five days I had all of my life rearranged to travel to Brazil.

I sent Marvin a telegram immediately after deciding to head southward to Brazil:

Marvin, Don't know where you are. Don't go anywhere. Will arrive Brazil soon. Be informed. Dennis.

But this was not to be a tourist trip. I went to the embassy and explained my reasons for going. I was going to participate as deeply as permitted into the mysteries of the mediumistic religions. I told them that I would return by land through the Amazons.

They were understanding and even touched that I viewed Brazil as a special nation. They even waived certain prerequisites, such as a return ticket. They spoke with the head consul, who approved my visa, and off I went.

I had sent telegrams all over Latin America, with a poor delivery average. I decided to wait for the Colombia-to-Brazil leg of my trip to wire Marvin again:

Marvin. Arrive Monday, Sept. 4, 8 AM, São Paulo. Dennis

Then, suddenly, there I was, setting foot on Brazilian soil, without a clue as to how I was to begin my walk, not even knowing where I would stay. But I had done this many times. Somehow, things always worked out far better than I could have ever imagined. Like a good idea whose time has come, I could not be stopped.

I was quickly passed through immigration, and as I entered the arrival lounge I saw a blur moving towards me. Stepping out of that blur was my friend Marvin, who had received my two telegrams.

Marvin was all cheers and smiles as he ran up to me and gave me a big embrace. After all the chit-chatting was over and we caught up on the news of the past year, we took a bus into São Paulo.

*　　*　　*

I decided to visit Brazil because it entranced me; Brazil has a large spiritistic culture, which shares its daily living space with the spirit world, recognizes a common kinship with the "others," and lives with the understanding that the boundary between the incarnate and disincarnate is permeable.

Mediums in the United States are often obligated to live in two worlds, alternately turning one on and the other off. They consort with spirits in meetings and seances then live in the "practical" world. But in Brazil, there is an accepted intermingling of the seen and unseen. Their spirits, orixas, exus, caboclos, and others walk the streets, sit in the parks, attend meetings, and converse together whenever they want. Conscious mediumship is practiced twenty-four hours each day. There is witness to this at the street-corner shrines of the Quimbanda and Candomble, as well as acceptance by a large part of the population.

I was committed to understanding the phenomenon of *incorporacao,* the way in which mediums interface with the spirit entities. I am not sure why I was so motivated.

Perhaps it was due to some mystical childhood experience, perhaps to my close encounter with death due to cancer.

I had been introduced to spiritualism and the works of Edgar Cayce studies by an aunt of mine who purported to be a medium herself. She talked endlessly about it at family gatherings. While most of those present mocked it as her special type of insanity, I listened with fascination.

In my travels to distant countries, I always made contact with people who felt confident in reporting to me their spiritual encounters. Even those who opposed spirit manifestations told me about their encounters with demons and evil spirits. It began to appear that a significant number of people around me had had contact with something beyond the limits of normal, routine experience.

Do spirits exist? Something speaks through the mediums; some energy motivates them to perform unusual works. Religious traditions all over the world speak of spirit worlds, and some revelatory phenomena involving the spirit world is prominent in many of them.

Just what was I looking for? I believe I was seeking ways in which human potential could be released and creativity expressed. Were these extrahuman creative wonders produced by transhuman forces called spirits, or are these psychic powers inherent in all of us and emerging from the deepest dimensions of the human mind? What is the nature of these urges? Are they personal or nonpersonal? Could the human mind be so powerful as to create a psychological and spiritual space into which this supercreativity could be projected as an extension of the deepest aspects of self? Could it then be endowed with special powers and sufficient energy so that it might appear to be separate but isn't?

The suitable question, dear reader, is this: is the spirit really a spirit? Is it a product of our own supercreative mind, yet undiscovered in its capacity? These are important questions to keep in mind when reading this book. I, for one, have not resolved them.

First Thoughts

A medium is a person who can tap into supercreativity while claiming that it is not the conscious self, but "another" working through him. Did not Jesus, for example, deny his own capacity, citing "the Father" who worked through him? Consider the prophets, who claimed their work was not by their own ken but by the revelation of the god, goddess, or God that sent them. Perhaps they were also mediums.

I learned, through studying with the Kardecist (Spiritist) school that a medium is a person who has the capacity to enter into the worlds of invisible spirits. Theoretically, all people are mediums, but most, because of one or more reasons, do not presently have access to the invisible, extradimensional world of the disincarnates.

A medium is a transformer of energies, an instrument by which otherworld entities communicate with incarnates for various reasons, the principal one being the enrichment of the life-death experience.

A medium is the vehicle of spirit revelation. One might compare mediumship to ordinary photograph development. The paper upon which the image is impressed is the medium. The image, which is the interconnectedness of information between planes of existence, is the spirit. The spirit appears to be an image; it is perceived as an image by the medium and subsequently "revealed" through the incarnate's more conventional means of communication. It may be equally true that the spirit is an energy pattern that is reconstructed through the sensitive and adaptable mechanisms of the incarnate medium.

The practice itself may be the product of endless inner work, the result of brain evolution, or the result of reincarnation. No one is quite sure, though most Brazilian mediums have their own ideas. In Spiritist lingo, the process of impression and revelation is called "incorporation." However, naming it doesn't explain it, the same way that diagnosing cancer doesn't cure it. The process remains essentially unknown and poorly understood. I do know, however, that it is real.

I observed dozens of spirit manifestations and am willing to state that something, be it a powerful urge, belief, or spirit, impresses itself upon the medium's mind. This makes for some very powerful and impressive demonstrations. I saw no perceptible fraud in any of the cases I observed; the mediums worked in well-lit rooms, wore short sleeves, and were constantly in view. The results of their work were intelligible and tangible; they were visible, tactile, odiforous, or otherwise identifiable through the senses.

I noticed, as well, a certain definite psychological sensation, an expectancy, the energy of something quite extraordinary occurring. The Spiritists assured me, however, that what I perceived as unusual was quite ordinary for them. I often felt fidgety, the room was often warm;

my own skin and that of my invited guests prickly, as if something was touching or biting it. In some seances, I would tremble or shiver uncontrollably. Without doubt this can be attributed to my own psychological state; a football game produces similar responses in its aficionados. But a "football atmosphere" must exist for such a reaction to occur. Similarly, an appropriate atmosphere must have existed which would account for my shivering. But, like the excitement of a football game, it is not visible to the eye.

Little Investigation Available

There is little psychological research available concerning spirit-induced personalities. A few cases of "possession" have been studied from the Western psychiatric viewpoint, which regard the receiver as a deranged personality. In the Western perspective, spirit influences couldn't possibly exist in such cases because spiritology doesn't fall properly within the limits of current psychology.

Religious studies of possession tend to affirm such Spiritist anomalies but define them in negative terms. In the religious view, possessed individuals are occupied by destructive spirits, demons, or His Infernal Highness. These all seek to claim human territory and corrupt the immortal soul. The subject is always an involuntary and helpless victim (or a fool) who invited a spirit to enter the body, thus causing a harmful situation in which the spirit is at war against God and humanity. During the battle, those who are peripherally close to the victim, such as family, are also hurt. Not a very inviting scenario.

The possessions ("incorporations") which I observed were voluntary on the part of the medium and served such enriching and creative purposes as service to others through healing, counseling, and artistic and musical endeavours.

Few serious studies on positive possession have been undertaken beyond the notes gathered by psychical societies concerning spiritualistic phenomena in the last century. Western psychology has, until recently, ignored paranormal activity in general and possession specifically. Even American parapsycholology has shunned this area of study, preferring to relegate itself to the "psychic" rather than the "spiritualistic." To most psychologists, spirit possession, benevolent or otherwise, has been considered "hallucination" and "escape mechanism" and deemed unfit for serious study by proper scientists. Most psychologists do recognize the pathology of multiple personalities as well as hallucinatory effects in which the "psychotic" sees, hears, tastes, smells, and feels the presence of other "individuals" near or inside of himself, be they demons, intrusive spirits, or others. Until recently, however, these have been regarded as signs of mental collapse or disorder.

Brazil's mediums have, in fact, been tested and compared to nonmediumistic individuals. They tend to be normal in every measurable way, except when in the trance state. They are as ordinary as anyone else, as happy or depressed, as creative or boring. I met many mediums personally and know that they can certainly be as egotistical or simple as any others!

In Brazil and other nations, there are mediums who experience these "hallucinations" regularly. These so-called illusions do not appear to interfere with their normal daily functioning (R. Lucio et al, 1991). In fact, these individuals do not demonstrate any type of deviatory or "pathological" behavior outside of auditory, olfactory, visual, or tactile contact with these "spirit beings" (C. A. Perandrea, 1990). On all other accounts they are completely ordinary and unremarkable.

My personal interaction with many of these mediums leads me to conclude that they can be as open-minded or as intolerant as anyone. They seem to be no more or less moral than members of other religious groups. Many claim never to have had contact with a demon, neither do all of them even believe in the existence of hell and its dominions. Their one significant difference is that they claim to enter into trance states and access information not usually and consciously obtainable to "normal" individuals.

Most religious traditions do accept certain types of mediumship in which a spirit world populated by beings may interact with the human faithful in different ways. Some accomplish this through dreams, others in substance-produced experiences. Still others present themselves during ecstatic visions and meditative trances, such as angelic visitors, voices, and prayer answering. The Koran speaks of the angels and jinni, the Torah of angelic messengers and the "still inner voice." The Hellenistic tradition is filled with demons; the Christians have hierarchies of demons, angels, and powers. The Hindus have their gods and devas; the Zoroastrians have Ahrimane and Ahura. The Tibetan Book of the

Dead offers its Bardo entities, such as the Bodhisattvas and Buddhas. Whether among native peoples' religion or among the most sophisticated, there are tales of spirit relationships and intervention, messages from the invisible world to ours, and stories of prayers and supplications being answered by the saints. In fact, every religion tries to unite the worlds of the invisible with that of our own.

Dr. George Meek, famous investigator and visitor to Brazil, asks the following question:

> By the same token, when all peoples in all parts of the globe, at all times in recorded history, have instinctively postulated somewhat similar beliefs in "spirits" and in an individual afterlife, might it not be worthwhile for science to at least examine such a possibility? (2)

Indeed, this is a propitious time to study the phenomena of spirits. Serious books are being written about the spirit-incarnate relationships called channeling. Transpersonal psychology and consciousness work are beginning to make some inroads into the structure and nature of thought. This will shed much light upon spiritual work in general.

Still, much of the work is being conducted in the closet. Mainstream psychology and religion are continuing to ignore the evidence, that is piling up. For the most part, modern religion has ignored the type of mediumistic phenomenon which produced its birth: prophecy, seership, voyants, and revelations.

Those sectors of present day religious practice that do take note of spiritistic activity usually classify it according to the focus of their philosophy, as in the case of Charismatics and Pentecostals. These factions assume that any phenomenon occurring within their sanctuaries is the work of the Holy Spirit, while any occurring among spiritualists or other groups is, more often than not, the activity of the archfiend. Perhaps the major exception to this is the work being carried out by the Spiritual Frontiers Fellowship, which recognizes the value of spirit and psychic activity in religion.

Little Understanding on the Part of the Mediums

These "mediums," as they are called, serve as focal points for energies that they themselves do not always understand. They call them spirit entities, or light bodies, depending upon their training. Many of these mediums manifest phenomena that cannot as yet be explained by our Western scientific paradigm.

For example, when these mediums enter into either light or deep trance, they can materialize objects, create honey, flowers; they can paint, write, sing, or practice surgery, all of which, in normal consciousness, they appear to be unable to achieve. Mediums are people who "provide an environment in which healing can take place." We can also say that they create environments in which wonders are manifested. Mediums have " . . . the capacity to enter into contact with energies beyond the normal." (2)

Creativity, spirit-induced or otherwise, is fascinating. Visible creativity is the outward expression of inward state, be it mental, intellectual, spiritual, or any other. Creativity enriches our passage here on earth. As I viewed these creative manifestations of inner urges, I wanted to know more about the "environment" which served as the witches' cauldron. This phase of mediumship is overlooked by the researchers of more scientific training, who were busy measuring brain cells, trying so determinedly to assert that it was psychic and not spiritistic phenomena that was occurring. They were focusing their work on "how" manifestations were enacted, a sort of ABC of psychism.

I perceived a psychological environment, a creative and fruitful area, a phenomenological "space" in which a creative force could be generated and produce the necessary amount of energy and a blueprint for miracles to occur. There was nothing written about this "space," called "incorporation" in Brazil. This word, translated from the Portuguese *incorporacao*, is a space rather than an action. It includes the area in which contact, the intermingling of energy, and the mind of the medium is made. Here, both elements cooperate, and the waves which produce manifestation follow. If this definition is vague, it is because the process is also vague. Though much conjecture is presented by the spiritists and observers alike, no satisfactory explanation of incorporation has yet been produced.

The incorporation environment is the space in which a medium creates prodigies. Without it, there could be no manifestation; mediumship would be reduced to some type of focus meditation. When asking the mediums directly about this state of consciousness, I found that they had little insight into their experiences. Most felt assured by repeating standard doctrine.

What I observed was this: the spirits didn't teach the mediums very much. Most of the mediums I encountered and observed would be unconscious and not know what was going on. They remembered nothing of the information they channeled. A majority conceded that they were just as unaware of the workings of the process as I was. As one medium told me, "The truth is that we know as little about it as you do!"

The Bible speaks of the Acts of the Apostles, how they worked "miracles," such as spiritual healing and speaking in various tongues. Jesus appears to be one of the greatest of psychics in the Bible. Allan Kardec declared Him the finest medium in history. The Torah of the Jews is not lacking in wonders either. In it, Prophets foretold the future, healed the sick, transported food from long distances, stabilized the sun, and brought plagues upon Egypt. All of this is very impressive paranormal work. Even so, the scriptures fail to explain how such marvels could be enacted. It wasn't until my visit to Brazil that I could actually believe that such works are possible.

Challenges and Confrontations to My Mindset

As I pilgrimaged inwardly as well as outwardly across the mystical Brazilian landscape, I began to develop certain conclusions and made related decisions. I was privileged to witness many phenomena, and my logical mind was forced to open, even to push, itself beyond its oftentimes comfortable limits, challenged to take in this new data and process it. By the end of the second month, certain cracks were appearing in my old belief system. My entrance into this strange land produced a mental crisis. Gone were the niceties of life, the feeling of protective normalcy and routine.

Reading about others' paranormal accounts from an isolated intellectual tower was one thing. But my own present interaction with these forces stirred up many new and strange feelings. I soon reconsidered my sheltered lifestyle. My crisis was one of adaptation only. Once it passed, I was able to move freely from one world to another.

To truly investigate, I believe it necessary to feel, to intimately savor the subject and its experiences. Otherwise it would remain only within the dry domain of the intellect. But to consume it, to be consumed by it, then later on to separate from it and analyze the totality of the experience is a valid approach, one which I have chosen to do. It is one thing to "observe" and another to "see." Both have validity.

On how many "normal" occasions do I have the opportunity to see a medium plunge a scissor into the abdomen of a willing patient and see the person survive? The "victim" felt no pain, she said, because the "spirits" were administering anesthetics.

How many of us can produce bee honey (much less without the bees) in our hands? How many can drink strong liquor in a trance and show no sign of inebriation when the trance ends? How many can paint worthy art forms with our eyes closed, using our feet, mouths, or other parts of the body, and at such velocity that the possibility of prior contemplation is eliminated? In "real life" most of these mediums can't paint at all.

By the end of my third month, I experienced a shift in consciousness, fermented by the constant bombardment of these marvels. I began to hear, feel, and see spirit entities myself. I would experience them night and day. I would lie awake in my bed at three in the morning, sweating and trembling, because I perceived a host of beings in my room. I became physically and mentally disoriented—boarding the wrong buses, forgetting my name or the way home, using the wrong currency. I was an active participant in the disintegration of my programmed ego.

It was finally necessary to isolate myself for a few days in order to assimilate all these new experiences. My personal sensitivity to "influences" around me was expanding. My normal, everyday nervous system was not prepared for the inclusion of other worlds!

What was occurring: other ego-natures invaded my own persona. I was not comforted by this theory. It also implied that much of the creativity was not produced by living people but by wandering souls from other worlds which used us! Benevolent or not, they were outsiders seeking territory, my territory, within my own space. An entity, similar to myself, but now deceased, was going to take over my mind and use me as it wished! I could be psychically raped!

The Mediums Themselves

As I traveled the wide expanse of Brazil from São Paulo northward to Manaos, I visited many mediums. Some refused to see me for reasons unknown, others shied away from publicity, and still others who worked wonders were very dogmatic in their manner of seeing the mediumship model. Often I asked deep and perturbing questions to this last group and found that they had little or no knowledge of how they functioned. There were also those who assumed that I would accept, on faith, any explanation at face value. I didn't, and this often created friction between us. I wanted to understand what the medium saw and also experience some of his reality. At the same time I had to accept the medium's own limitations: poor education, religious fanaticism, imprisonment (like most of us) within certain thought patterns.

Still there was that other side of them, and I had to honor it. These people produced wonders. They could operate in a space and on levels which I couldn't. They exercised an unconscious ability to enact feats, few of which can be observed among U.S. mediums since the great Spiritualist movement of the late 1800s. For example: if I stuck a scissor into a person, I would kill him and be arrested for manslaughter. If I rubbed a rose between my hands, I would produce wrinkled petals. If I held a paint brush between my toes, I might get a few strokes out. More likely I would suffer from leg cramps. I daresay that any of my friends would end up the same as I would.

Claiming that it was not they but extra-mind consciousness, called spirits, they would duplicate, hundreds of times over, their miraculous works. While Jesus called the doer the "Father," while the Prophets of Israel claimed that it was Jehovah, these mediums affirm that they have little to do with these phenomena, that it is not a state of evolution but simply a cooperative relationship with disembodied spirits who do the work.

Two Views on Communication

Spirit entities appear to communicate in two basic styles. Some are able to transmit messages, imprints through time and space, thus influencing the minds of the mediums. Others control some parts of the nervous system and work an isolated arm or other body part as if it was their own. Still others take control over all the essential nodes of communication in the body.

"Incorporation " assumes an intimate relationship between the medium and the spirit entity. In most of the spiritistic schools, it is held that the spirit does, in fact, physically (if such a word may be used with an ethereal being) enter into the medium's person in the same way that a person may enter an automobile. This is denied by the Kardecists, who believe that information is projected from the spirit to its human vehicle. This last concept is held also by the majority of North American and European spiritualists, as very well expressed by the famous medium Betty and recorded by E. S. White:

> The invisibles have no direct powers to manipulate our physical substance though at times they may appear to do so. Their ability to levitate tables, for instance or to move a pencil in automatic writing, or to appear to speak by direct control of another all depend on their ability to impress an idea on a portion of the station's [medium's] mind. That portion . . . so manipulates the necessary physical mechanism as to approximate the result desired. This rule I conceive to be invariable. (3)

It amounts to this: a message is received at a psychological distance; that is, from another psyche, and it impresses itself upon the mind of the receiver.

While these two concepts appear to be far apart, both are accepted by Brazilian mediums. Both types of mediums can and do perform the same dramatic acts. Again, while the Kardecists deny that the medium becomes invaded by the spirit, the Candomble and Umbanda traditions affirm this to be so. They affirm that the spirit is joined in a temporary cooperative union with the instrument and shares the mental and physical space of the medium. The degree of that unitive experience depends upon whether the medium is willing to go unconscious or wishes to maintain some threads of awareness.

I did, in fact, confront several "spirits" on this theological divergence. Some disclosed to me that they were indeed within the medium's body while others flatly denied it, claiming that these other spirits were poorly informed and uneducated. They also reminded me to make no assumptions about all spirits and that many on the other side were as ignorant of the mediumship process as those on our side.

So What Are We Dealing With?

What is the purpose in all of this? Does this have any value to anything practical, a query asked of me upon my return to the States. I feel that there are some insights to be gained by questioning the mediums. Visit our asylums and observe how many of its inmates are obsessed by misplaced (or displaced) personalities. I use this term quite literally. And although from our point of view, many of these people suffer from multiple personality syndromes and hallucination, from the Brazilian view they are suffering from possible intrusive possession.

Though this may go against the "scientific" viewpoint of the U.S. psychiatric community, there are many serious Brazilian professionals in the same field who believe that this is so and do not hesitate to offer their patients spiritual therapies. They also tend to meet with success.

Many of these therapists informed me that pathological illness might be, in many cases, undeveloped mediumship. These psychologists have ample people to study, since the Spiritists own and operate about sixty percent of the psychiatric institutions.

In the field of education, what would be the affect of creative impulses upon our world? Creativity may come from various sources: the genetic code, the inner mystical side of humanity, and discarnate entities on the other side. According to mediums, these disembodied geniuses wish to continue sharing their wisdom, art, and science with humanity, thus enriching and educating our planet. Our educational system would advance through the employment of these invisible teachers if ways could be discovered to contact and channel them mechanically, as though on video and television. It is not outside the realm of possibility. At present we can transmit conferences from one side of the planet to the other. Perhaps in the future, we will be able to pick up these "urges" from other worlds, translate them into an understandable language, and utilize them for educational purposes. Human mediums can do that already. Perhaps mediums should be invited into the classroom, enter into trance, and teach courses dictated by their spirit guides.

I cannot convince the reader that spirits exist. In my investigations I decided to accept the Spiritist mindset that they "probably" do. Otherwise I would be accepting the opposite, a viewpoint that is generally accepted on faith by disbelievers. Still, I remain a healthy doubter, not swallowing the entire fish. Even seeing so much, I still find it hard to be totally convinced, like the Apostle Thomas.

If, in fact, extraterrestrials (spirits are extraterrestrials, too) exist, then studies like this may open up common ground for sharing our experiences. I refer to mutual communications, not the one-way street assumed by so many channelers. I have often wondered if, in the invisible spirit realm, there are also mediums who channel earthly intelligence! One thing appears obvious to me; the spirits who communicate with us seem to need our help as much as we need theirs. Let us make no assumption that they are "higher" or liberated because they are dead!

Nor may they be more compassionate. Anyone, be they advanced or not, may use a telephone. If these entities exist, then we might together discover a common platform for gathering and sharing creative energies. The universe would be seen through another window, one which would show us a world populated by a myriad of other beings. Deceased beings possessed of superconsciousness, of talents like those of geniuses who have passed away and might continue to feed our cultural and educational life. Imagine the possibility of evoking the wisdom of the great minds of the past, to dip into their experiences. To say the least we would obtain more knowledge of the possibility of continued survival of consciousness. Would that this become scientifically demonstrable; the spiritualization of the planet would take a vast leap forward.

Some Obstacles in My Search

I had many difficulties in this work; I didn't speak the language of the mediums. I spoke the language of the heart, yes, but of the tongue, no. I had to satisfy myself by communicating with spirits and their mediums in Spanish when they spoke Portuguese. I also had to review literature written in that language. Mediums are human beings, and that in itself presents difficulties. They weren't always so easy to see, to gather, and to administer tests to. I had to meet them one by one on their own turf and time. Whenever they incorporated I tried to ask them questions, tape their answers, and film their actions when I had some help to do so. Not always easy.

Try dealing with the dead! It is even more difficult than with the living. Some of the spirits were evasive in answering, not wanting to demonstrate their ignorance, trying to cover it up with long-winded explanations devoid of meaning. Some told me that it was not permitted to give me such information, most of which can be read in any ordinary Spiritist book. Some were rude and uncouth. Obviously the dead were as uncultured as the living. Many of these spirits were addicted to compulsive behaviors and habits and took to smoking and drinking as soon as they could control a body. Some of the more enlightened spirits told me that there were more confused souls on the astral plane than on earth. I can well believe it!

The reader may discover some interesting speculations within this book. You may begin to question the origins of your own thoughts. Are they original or are you unconsciously incorporating entities which think through you? Who are the real dreamers here? Are you already a channel on the earth plane through which other "selves" may occasionally reveal their identities and commune with each other? Are you essentially a telephone that others use to make calls? Are you even possessed? Disquieting thoughts, indeed, to contemplate. But I wouldn't worry too much about it; you have gotten along over the years without any answers!

I am reporting events that I lived and fully experienced. I make no claim as to higher understanding or mediumistic know-how. I traveled, I saw, I listened, and now I am transmitting those experiences to you.

It is important to view the experience through the eyes of Brazilian mediums, because the judgments we tend to impose stem from different cultural and religious points of view. As I presented some of my movies in Spiritualist churches in Virginia, there invariably was biased comment about Brazilian mediums being demon-possessed. The Christians, of course, make the same claim of the Spiritualists.

We cannot judge the working mind of a Brazilian medium from the experiences of our own culture—though we often do! What may appear to us as primitive, from our cultural stance, may be an enormous lesson for us. It was necessary for me to develop a sense of humility and reverence in order to see beyond the ritualistic aspects of the cults. I had to learn patience and to let things progress as they flowed through that culture and not to intervene nor control the situation by imposing limitations comfortable to my life experience, as one normally does.

Many investigators fall into this trap. They isolate the individual experience from the macrocosm, whence it emanates. They take pictures, analyze brain waves, and then try to insert their findings as evidence into the psychological, religious, and physical models of the universe which fit into their comfort zones. If it doesn't fit snug and smug, verifiable experience is rejected or dismissed.

I could not do this. I would not do this. I personally felt the energy of the mediums I observed and wished to present the information through their perspective. I aggregate my own experiences with it, as I also entered into the spiritistic culture of the "psi-nation," as mediumistic Brazil has been called.

I made the pilgrimage because I wanted to. I wandered through Brazil joyously, and within a few days, it seemed as if I had always been there. Every street was a mystery to be investigated, every person a shining entrance into adventure. I have nothing to prove, but much to share, for not everyone is called to walk upon the same path, to skip so lightly across the same stones of life. There are many pilgrimages; but I was called to do this, in the way that others are called to work, to make right relationships, or to create a timeless something from nothing.

In a university course, a very special instructor repeatedly told me that what appears to be pathological behavior in one culture may be considered an elevated and mystical experience in another. This has been borne out in my observations. I offer you the product, as it was seen, felt, and heard, for your contemplation.

SPIRITS ALIVE!

Chapter I
Spirits in the Bank

Spirits I was to discover, had made previous arrangements for me to locate them. I, unfortunately, was unconscious of their plans.

I wandered the environment of São Paulo for over a week, surrounded by Spiritist centers and yet failed to make the acquaintance of even one medium. The worst thing that one can do is to open up the directory to Spiritist institutes: one is confronted by an exorbitant array of endless locations named after founders, spirits, and distinguished laborers of the vineyards.

I was feeling the frustration of being a tourist in a strange land. I was not, however, in any way suffering through my visit to this beautiful, enormous South American city. The subway system is clean, efficient, and safer than several that I used in the United States and Europe. The central subway station where the east-west/north-south lines cross is two stories underground. It would take me everywhere. Unfortunately, I had no idea where to begin.

São Paulo is graced with the extremes of wealth and poverty but also contains a large middle class that is enthusiastic about the Umbanda and Kardecism. Sitting at the very center of the original city is the Roman Catholic cathedral, built in the French gothic style. In front of the principal doors, as in all Latin cities, lies a large formal square, usually filled to the brim with vendors of all types and descriptions. One also finds there snake charmers, native *Capuera* wrestlers, Christian evangelical preachers, and herbalists.

I noticed later that there was a Yoga center, several vegetarian restaurants, and numerous stores which peddle to the needs of the Candomble, Quimbanda, and Umbanda followers. These stores are

1

filled with the statues of the saints, candles, incense, holy objects, and any other apparatus needed for occult practice.

The banking district lies at the foot of the square, its twenty or so banks dominating the promenades that make up the old business center. The banking center is old and sedate, quite distinct from the sections of the city around it where beggars vie with vendors and youthful Capuera dancers for the attention of passersby. Capuera is a native form of martial arts developed by young African slaves who were prohibited from carrying weapons on their persons. As there were many opportunities for being set upon in old Brazil, some type of defense was needed. As practiced today, Capuera is a combination of postures and movements akin to those of Tai' Chi and Tae-Kwon-Do, a dance routine that has its own tradition of chanting and music. I later discovered in Salvador, Bahia, that many academies teach distinct lineages of the dance. Walking about the old city, I often found myself visiting with boys sitting on the porches with their drums and stringed harps, singing their martial dance songs. I found it quite inspiring to watch the movements of the lean young men who danced to its music.

Today, I noticed none of this as I hurried through the square directly perpendicular to the cathedral's main portal. Today was to be the beginning of my mystical journey through Brazil. I couldn't imagine the banking district, with its bricked over streets, to be in any way related to making contact with the spirit world. Often we imagine chapels and ancient ruins to be the hideouts of the invisible and their earthly representatives.

I was directed to a certain bank which offered me the convenience of having branches not only in the cities of Brazil, but most of the cities of South America as well. I entered the Lloyds Bank through their solid doors and found the inside to be quite a contrast to the outside noise of the city. Everything was quiet and proper. I chuckled, thinking that I was neither quiet nor proper in my own life. How proper would it seem for someone to have taken off from the university to travel around Brazil seeking spirits? I wasn't even a member of any psychical society.

After the proper introduction and presentation of my letters, I was finally ushered to the international department, where my funds would eventually be received. It was the manager of this department who attended me quite willingly.

Mr. Scorpio (real name withheld) was perhaps younger than I. Most

2

of his coworkers were in their middle to late twenties. Through a most improper use of the English and Portuguese tongues, we began to discuss business, eventually turning the discussion around to Brazil and my reasons for being there. After the typical procedural discussions, our talk took a somewhat personal direction. Something inside informed me that this fine person was one with whom I could speak frankly. I told him of my desire to imbibe the spiritual side of this country, having a special interest in the mediumship religions.

As I spoke, Mr. Scorpio sat looking at me as though something was troubling him. For a moment I was afraid that he was a devout Catholic who perhaps detested the Spiritists, or maybe he was a middle-class snob who considered such themes as outside proper realms of consideration.

When I finished speaking, we sat for a moment in silence until this suited, bespectacled, and very proper-looking bank department head informed me, "I am a medium. I am a Kardecist and study at the São Paulo Federation. I would be pleased to arrange an interview with the head of the society."

I was joyous. an inroad was finally made. "I should be very grateful to you," I beamed back. "That would facilitate my research greatly."

"Can you meet me tomorrow at the Federation Building? I will introduce you to Dr. Julia Nezo, head of the Spiritist training program. Here is her office number. I will meet you at 7:00 P.M."

The next day I anxiously awaited my banking contact at the Federation Building, which turned out to be only one kilometer from my apartment. I walked and found a large complex fronted by a bookstore. Walking through the gate, I saw an old building, three floors in height and two floors beneath ground level. This housed the Spiritist Federation of São Paulo, one of the largest and most active federations in the nation. I found out later that there were at least one million declared Spiritists in this state alone and that they were very well organized into groups of lecturers, assistants, volunteers, teachers, and other functionaries. There was another Spiritist organization, which monitored associations that didn't want to be as tightly controlled by a central organization. There was also a Spiritist high school, as well as many service organizations.

The building that I entered might have passed, in another twenty years, as an appropriate setting for a horror story. It was immense, with

3

an auditorium on the upper level, classrooms on the lower levels, a library, cafeteria, and service rooms. The building was always occupied by hundreds of students and workers, those seeking aid and those dispensing it. Within the next few years, this building would be abandoned for a new modern skyscraper that was being erected in the heart of the city. What the building lacked in decoration, it more than compensated for in personal warmth.

Upon entering the building, I soon located the office of the directoress and waited until the 7 P.M. rendezvous. When my friend didn't arrive by then, I decided to give him another fifteen minutes, as he had training class that night. By that time classes had already begun, and I decided that he wasn't to show. I was left in a quandary, one of many during my Brazilian trip. I decided to try to communicate in Spanish, a brother language to Brazilian. With or without a formal introduction I would meet this directoress and convince her to open the doors of the entire Federation to me. Most of all, I needed a translator.

I entered Dr. Julia Nezo's office, which was a hub of activity. People were coming in and going out, what with her being the head of the training section of the Federation. Finally I got a chance to speak to her secretary, who at that moment was not in the best mood. When she heard my terrible Portuguese, she shouted back an answer, which I, of course, couldn't translate. Not willing to leave, I sat down in front of the door of the office. Finally a calmer secretary came to me, and we spoke a minute. I was invited back into the office and told to wait.

Dr. Julia is a Japanese Brazilian. There are about two million Japanese living in São Paulo. I was living in their ghetto, the streets decorated with Japanese lanterns. There were also several temples and other cultural indications of their presence. My building had a majority of Japanese tenants. They were always very courteous to me, and I have always felt comfortable with the Oriental mind.

The doctor was behind a partition in the small office. I was told that as soon as she could, she would be glad to attend me. Presently, she came out.

She invited me to sit down and gave me about an hour of her time. This was quite generous, as she was obviously a very busy person. As we finished our conversation, she asked me to visit her again on the following day during the midmorning, at which time she would have two hours in which she could set aside her work. At that time she would

4

begin to orient me in the art of medium hunting. As I took my leave, she enriched my person with far too many pamphlets and books—all in Portuguese. Mr. Scorpio didn't show up, but with a map and the name of Dr. Julia, I had made my first contact. I might add that I still didn't speak very much Portuguese.

The next day I arrived, being ever the punctual North American, at the appointed time and place and found Julia, as she insisted on being called, quite eager to converse. I found her to be a warm and caring individual who seemed just as interested in becoming friends with me as she was in my research.

She began to guide me in my studies concerning the Spiritist religions and Spiritism especially. We often met in the cafeteria over herbal tea and chocolate cake, and any time I happened to pass by the Federation, she would find time to attend to me.

The library of the Federation was small but well stocked with old books about the Spiritist teaching. Between discussions with Spiritist officials and mediums and library references, I soon began to acquire a rudimentary knowledge of a religion that was based upon the teachings of the spirits.

Spiritism is the best organized of all of the mediumistic religions in Brazil. It is also an import, not a native Brazilian religion. Spiritism, or A Espirita, had its origins in the latter part of the 1800s in France, through the spiritual adventures of Allan Kardec, from whom the religion takes its second name in Brazil: Kardecism. Allan Kardec was the pen name which he adopted at the urging of his spirit guides. Kardec was of scientific temperament and, as a young man, had questions, then lost, much confidence in the traditional Roman Catholic faith. Subsequently, he sought teaching which might satisfy both his heart and his mind.

The 1800s were a time of spiritual awakening in the United States. Far off from France, new religions were being born in the fertile soil of the New World. The colonies' revolution against the mother nation, England, had also produced new revelations by the dozens. A multitude of new sects and movements began and became worldwide in scope.

The New England states had been dominated, since their founding, by a Puritan philosophy, which was theocratic as well as extremely strict, unbending, and based upon a literal understanding of the Bible, when convenient. The Puritans tended to see themselves as the only bastion of light in a sea of satanic darkness. As a revolt against this, the transcendental movement with its Oriental influences soon produced its first children: the Universalist and Unitarian churches.

In New York State, a one-time atheist, William Miller, got religion and began to proclaim the near coming of Jesus Christ. The Millerites, as they were referred to, declared that the millennium was at hand and cited the time of 1843–44 as the time for the expected theophany.

In the northern state of Maine, a young watchmaker began to experiment with hypnosis. His enterprises led him to formulate what became the basis of the New Thought movement. One of his students, Mary Patterson, later known as Mary Baker Eddy, founded her own church, which she called the First Church of Christ, Scientist, or simply Christian Science. One of her own students, Helen Curtis Hopkins moved to Chicago, where she was later excommunicated by the fiery Mrs. Eddy and taught her own type of New Thought to such famous students as Charles and Myrtle Filmore, Ernest Holmes, and the Brooks sisters, who founded, respectively, the Unity, Science of Mind, and Divine Science churches.

Still, the 1800s continued to spew forth new religions. In upstate New York, a young man named Joseph Smith asked the "Father" which church represented the true faith. Upon that answer he was soon to found the Mormon church.

A group of people called the Russelites were meeting in New York City, where they also called themselves the Followers of the Millennial Dawn. They later changed their name to Jehovah's Witnesses.

It was not only among the Christian churches that changes were being felt. A Russian immigrant, calling herself "Madame Blavatsky," met with Colonel Olcott In New York City to present a series of revelations that she had received from invisible Tibetan masters. Colonel Olcott was convinced of the lady's integrity and soon cofounded the Theosophical Society, which declared itself the recipient and disseminator of universal truths.

Last, but not least, some strange occurrences were being reported in Rochester, New York. Rochester was, in the early 1800s, a small rustic town, somewhat isolated from the world. Early one morning, the Fox sisters heard some rappings on the wall. It was soon discovered that they formed patterns and communications. When an answer was asked, the raps would signify a latter of the alphabet. Soon messages from the spirits were traveling back and forth as a new movement was formed, Spiritualism. This movement soon became independent from the Fox sisters, who appeared to be very problematic individuals, and mediumism, as it became known, was reported by hundreds of individuals who claimed to be having messages from spirit guides. Spiritualism soon took on a religious veneer and established thousands of societies, churches, and chapels far beyond the borders of its native land. The movement spread to the European continent and rapidly grew in Great Britain, Russia, and France.

By this time Allan Kardec was a young man with a mind waiting to discover some great truth. He became an adherent of the new faith. With his questioning mind, he began to visit hundreds of "spirits," asking them questions regarding afterlife, reincarnation, personal growth, and other spiritual themes. Gaining answers and insights, he wrote. His books were soon published: *The Book of the Spirits, The Gospel According to Spiritism, The Book of the Mediums.* Soon he had a large following among the Spiritualists, who began to call themselves "Spiritists" because they adhered to the teachings of the spirits.

Spiritism was brought to Brazil, a country already watered in the belief in spirits, angels, demons, and invisible saints by its Roman Catholic and African heritages. The questioning youth, who studied in France, brought back, not only French language and customs but the teachings of Allan Kardec. This movement, called Kardecism, spread rapidly and secretly among the members of the upper middle class without drawing any undue attention. Soon hundreds of thousands were attending seances, and Kardecism became quite the thing, though Church and class opposed it. For a time people were both Catholics and Spiritists. But among the younger generations today, they are firmly Spiritists.

I had no idea that Kardicism was so well propagated and organized until I went to Brazil. Certainly there is little notice of Allan Kardec and his books among U.S. Spiritualists and trance mediums. Quite the sad opposite. I have discovered that a large majority of our mediums are quite provincial in the spiritual education, not ever hearing of Spiritism or having investigated the great books of Kardec. The contrary was true in Brazil.

According to the Spiritist teaching, the basis of true Christianity was mediumship as exercised by both Jesus Christ, the medium par excellence, and his apostolic successors. But the Christian faith had, after a few hundred years, degenerated and lost most of the "gifts of the spirit" which were the gifts of mediumship.

Jesus Christ, the supreme model and master medium, foresaw this situation and promised that in the future, at the time of the end, a "Spirit of Truth" would come into the world and redeem the Christian faith. The Spiritists believe this to be the energy which engendered the Spiritualistic Spiritist movements. These represent restored Christianity, purified and redeemed to its original simplicity, its gifts again practiced. Allan Kardec is thus seen as a messianic figure, though not a personal Messiah, who instrumented the restoration of the great truths and is reverently referred to as the Codifier of the Third Revelation. The first revelation was that of Moses, the second of Jesus, and the third of the spirits.

An enlightened form of Christianity, as taught by the Spirit of Truth, had come into the world. It did away with structures and dogmas and substituted a few basic teachings, universal in scope, and commanded its followers to use their intelligence. It was not only faith, but a faith experimented, which would set the stage for the "new revelation." The Spiritist religion would also offer many proofs of the powerful Doctrine which it espoused. It taught a living gospel, which would not ever be spread by the sword, but by the power of human reason, love, and the visible fruits of spirit participation.

Before going to Brazil, all that I knew of Spiritism were the negative comments of a Catholic priest, Father Oscar Quevedo, who tirelessly attacked this religion whenever possible. Also the word "spiritist" as used in Central and South Americas is a term the Catholic church uses generically to embrace all types of spirit and mediumistic religions. I had no idea that a Kardecist (Spiritist, or Espirita) religion existed with an extensive library, scientific investigations, and service projects, the equal of which I have never seen among other religions.

The more I associated with Spiritists, the more intense became my interest in their work and in the "homeland of the living gospel," as they called Brazil.

The Spiritist religion has about seven million enrolled members, but probably as many unofficial ones. There are movie stars, congresspersons, literary and intellectual luminaries, as well as the middle and upper classes.

The official doctrine of Spiritism may be summed up from some of its principles: First, despite the accusations of opposing ecclesiastical organizations, the Spiritists assured me that they believe in a god, or deity, as they wish to call Him, which is "completely good and powerful." They often speak of it in terms of "light" and "spirit." Their conceptions are very similar to metaphysical conceptions except that their Supreme Deity appears in its creation, yet is not the same creation. To clarify the point, I asked leaders of the movement if Spiritism accepts a pantheistic god, meaning that God and Creation are the same. They very emphatically answered no. They affirm the existence of individual souls which are reflections of, but not the same as God.

Second, Spiritism teaches that a universal law called Karma governs all life. Whatever actions or thoughts that are undertaken today will influence your future life. Therefore, personal responsibility in all things is a prime necessity. I have never resided in a country where so many people are not afraid to say that they believe in reincarnation. The Spiritist religion affirms the belief that all souls will continue to return to the earth plane until they are perfected. I asked them why, if reincarnation was a reality, was mediumship a necessity? The souls who communed with earth and humankind are beings who had evolved highly enough to become "angels of light." They had no reason to reincarnate upon earth.

Third, perhaps the concept of service as the vehicle to salvation is the greatest of all Spiritist beliefs. Service is the expression of love in outward form. Any kindness done to another without expectation of spiritual or material compensation will advance the soul upon its eternal path. Any hurt to another will have a retrograde effect.

The Spiritists are very active in social work and, as I will mention throughout this book have raised schools, hospitals, clinics, orphanages, and many other institutions to help the social order.

Whenever one thinks of Spiritism, one must also think of mediums. This is because one of the tenets of this religion is that communication and cooperation between spirits and residents of other planes of existence will enrich the spiritual culture of each. Spirits in the invisible or spirit world incorporate into mediums in order to aid humanity in its quest towards the Kingdom of God. Therefore this relationship is beneficent for both groups. Additionally, the Spiritist concept of brotherhood includes not only humankind but spiritkind as well.

Spiritist teaching states that there is no punishment, no hell, no eternal suffering, no demons, and no day of Judgment. Evil is the confusion resulting from the misunderstanding of God's law. Heaven and hell are merely conditions of spiritual clarity and confusion and can be changed by service, love, and awareness of one's karma.

Man has a triune nature, which means that each individual consists of a unique individual soul, reflecting the Divine nature but not that nature; a body which is composed of chemicals and an "energy envelope" that surrounds the two and moves information between them. This is the perispirit, often seen by sensitives as the aura. There is much written upon this theme in the psychological articles of the Spiritist Medical Journal. We will talked more about the perispirit later.

I realized that I was not dealing only with mediumship and spirits, but an entire theological system based upon certain principles embedded in the Spiritist Doctrine. How did these principles come about?

Allan Kardec traveled to hundreds and even thousands of mediums of his time and questioned the spirits which spoke through them. He found them to be consistent in certain areas and dissident in others. The consistencies became "The Doctrine" and serve as the religion's foundation. I was assured by members of the Federation that this took many years to complete and that during that time Kardec was attacked by the Catholic church. But with steady persistence, his teaching, which is defined as a religion, science, and philosophy, has spread around the world and embraced millions of adherents. I am often surprised that the most organized of mediumship religions is little known to the mediums, channelers, and New Agers in the United States. I must attribute this to a general lack of Spiritualist education and religious provincialism. The Spiritists are quite up on who's who in U.S. circles and are also quite disappointed by what they are hearing from these circles.

Invariably, as I talked to mediums, I was first asked if it was true that mediumship had become a commercial pursuit in the United States. I assured them that it had become a very good business to be in, perhaps second only to the televangelists. This disheartened them. You see, mediumship in Spiritism is a sacred trust, and mediums feel it cheap and spiritually degenerate to "peddle" their talents. The spirits warn them against going commercial, and the federations will not license mediums who go Hollywood. This is why many of the famous Brazilian mediums who become wealthy in the United States are not members of the Federation. They are delicensed. Mediumship, as part of the ancient apostolic tradition of "true Christianity" is an extremely sacred gift of the Holy Spirit. They are carrying on the apostolic responsibility to heal the sick, preach the Gospel, and serve without compensation.

Another question which mediums frequently asked is why is there so much talk about negative forces, demons, and devils in the United States. Spiritists acknowledge evil-appearing beings, but these entities are vengeful and malevolent against humanity because they are confused or suffering in their spiritual blindness. They are not inherently evil. It is a temporary situation. The medium's work includes the evangelization of those lost souls, which means that they teach those souls the Gospel of the Spirits until they awaken and know their true selves. Then they are saved. In fact, this is an important task carried out in all Spiritist centers. A troubled soul is brought to a medium who then makes contact with that spirit and teaches it. There are sessions for disincarnates who are not essentially evil, only bereft of the truth.

Another surprising attitude I found was the willingness of the Spiritist institutions to allow questioning of the mediums. They invite scientific investigation and are tolerant of those who do not think in the same way. While there certainly exist several personality cults around some mediums, the federations try to discourage this.

Six days after making the initial contact with the São Paulo Spiritist Federation, Julia invited me to attend a weekend seminar featuring a renowned spirit artist from Salvador, Bahia. The proceeds would go to the Federation's social action funds. Would I like to attend?

Of course I would. That is why I was there!

Chapter II
Spirit Painting

The Spiritist religion prohibits the sale of mediumistic talents for personal economic gains. This point has been argued back and forth in their assemblies, and it is one upon which they will not yield; however, they do allow their mediums to accept donations and to participate in activities that would allow their talents to benefit social service projects.

The first Saturday after making contact with the Federation, there was arranged a demonstration of spirit artistry for the benefit of one of the orphanages which needed help. Usually when some social service agency needs funds, one or several mediums get together and put on demonstrations, asking those present to make donations. In this case, the mediums would be painting. All of the paintings would be sold and the money given to the orphanage.

I was told by Dr. Julia to arrive early in order to get good seats. The star of the day was Jose Medrado, an upcoming young medium of whom I knew little.

I arrived with a friend, a lapsed Spiritist, at the Federation about one hour before show time. We found about one hundred and fifty people forming a long line which began at the gate of the institute's property, then up the long stairway to the top floor, where the auditorium is located. At first we joined the line but found it much too difficult to stand in.

I told my friend that there was a back stairway to the main auditorium. We sauntered in, looking like we owned the place. I found one of the dividing doors open, and up we walked, first, second, and third floor, onto the stage of the auditorium. By the time we entered, it was almost filled. I was wondering where I could get a good seat, when

I spotted a row of vacant chairs right in front of where the medium and his assistants were to perform.

Never having been a respecter of seating anyway, I walked up and plunked myself right down in the best seat of the house. Within a few minutes an usher came up to me and said, in Brazilian, that I cannot seat myself there as these are reserved sections. When one is a foreigner, one can pretend that communication is almost impossible! I raised my hands in the air in a questioning gesture and answered something in English. He was obviously puzzled at my reply and sought out someone who could speak my language. I settled down comfortably, knowing that it might be easier to change the magnetic poles of the earth than to find someone at the Federation who spoke English.

Luckily, whom did they locate, but my friend Dr. Nezo. She knew that I could speak Spanish; however, before coming to me, she had asked and received permission from the Federation for me to sit there, in view of my work.

She explained to me that trained mediums were to sit in the seats I had stolen, in the front row around the working mediums, in order to supply them with needed energy and protection. They would go into trance during the presentation and keep the air clean, so to speak, against any invasive spirits.

My friend and I were ensconced in a comfortable position when Jose Medrado entered. He was tall and thin, and in his way quite a handsome young man, with some effeminate airs about him. I met quite a few male mediums, and it seemed that a significant number of them were effeminate, if not altogether homosexual.

Never being one to skirt an issue, I asked a group of Federation board members about the high level of homosexuality and femininity among male mediums. It was a passing question, not asked from a prejudicial viewpoint, but more from a clinical interest.

Julia was shocked that I could even imply such a thing. I thought that perhaps she hadn't understood my question and asked more bluntly if a majority of mediums were gay. I thought that she might have an attack of apoplexy!

I did not mean to cast aspersions upon the character of Mr. Medrado, a very dedicated and gifted medium with a series of social product endorsements to his name. However, several other board members, one a psychiatrist, told me that he had wondered about the same thing. He felt that it had to do with the development of what he called the passive or feminine side of the brain, which allowed the spirits to take command.

This is not to imply that all famous mediums are homosexual. Such a claim would, in fact, be quite unjust. There was, however, a high percentage of gay men among the "famous" mediums I met, perhaps only the ones whom I met. Several of them, of international fame, were openly gay. Others were openly quite romantic with the ladies.

The Brazilian Spiritists are, as a group, quite tolerant of sexual differences, especially as it applies to homosexuals. I saw several books, accepted as spirit messages, warning heterosexual men against condemning gays. These books explained homosexuality as an incomplete migration of the personality from one incarnation to the next and reminded readers that this is not an isolated occurrence. In fact, it said, among the hundreds of incarnations that each person has, "macho" males were at one time females and, therefore, should have more tolerance of differences. In a scientific world that cannot as yet give a good explanation of homosexuality, it may be that the Spiritist understanding is closer to the truth than some of our psychotherapeutic explanations.

The presentation began with Mr. Medrado and about ten other spirit artists standing in front of tables filled with painting supplies. The purpose of this session was to bring the genius of past painters into the present, channeling famous artists from the other side who wished to demonstrate their artistry.

This is some confusion as to the use of the words "psychic" and "spirit" regarding mediums. They are often utilized interchangeably. However, in Spiritist Brazil there are differences. A psychic medium is a person who does wonders and produces phenomena, utilizing powers of the mental, or mind, level. A spirit artist uses his mind not at all, but he channels a spirit which is of a completely different mentality.

Most, if not all, of the spirit artists had no inherent talent for painting whatsoever. Mr. Medrado said that he was merely a typist. In the talk following his demonstration, he said that when quizzed by North American scientists as to his educational level, he did not know how to answer. They asked him what diplomas he had attained, and he answered in his self-deprecating style, with a laugh, and told them that he had a certificate in typing.

The lights were lowered. I was sitting right behind one medium spirit artist, and Mr. Medrado was about five feet to my left. I had a good view of his work. On his table to his right was an abundance of painting needs: tubes, oils, and palettes. There were also brushes and materials for cleaning his brushes.

The audience recited the Lord's Prayer and offered an invitation for the spirits to approach their mediums.

All of a sudden, Medrado's body began to shake as his head was violently thrown back and forth. He then relaxed and, with his eyes closed, began to paint. But he didn't often use brushes.

He had plastic gloves on his hands and dipped them liberally into a mess of colors, which he smeared onto the canvas that lay flat on the table. His head was hanging forward and he worked rapidly, having no obvious intention of what was to be painted. First a smear here and there with his palm. Then a few daubs with his fingers or cotton pads. Then he might pick up a brush and add a stroke or two, all without obvious premeditation. He was painting like a madman—all while his eyes were closed.

I was watching the painters work; there was instrumental music in the background and the audience was hushed. The lights were dim but not enough to allow for trickery. The Federation does not allow any medium to work in the dark. They want no accusations of fraud.

Something quite marvelous occurred; out of the daubs of paint certain forms began to appear—trees, faces, skies.

An inner voice questioned me. "Is this merely my imagination?" "Am I under some type of spell?" "Am I a participant in group hysteria?"

I ask my companion what he saw, and he validated my own impressions. The green blobs of paint appeared to take on the form of background objects. The medium finished a painting. He signed it as a Manet or a Renoir, I was not sure, but it was whisked off to the back wall to dry in full view of the public.

Next, no, I couldn't believe it. He kicked off his right shoe and began to paint with his foot, holding a brush between his toes. His head was thrown backwards in sleep, and he was stretched out on his chair, not even looking in the direction of the next canvas, which was being supported by an assistant. He smeared on blobs of paint and began another countryside picture. On and on he went until the painting

15

appeared to finish itself. It was the darndest way of painting that I had ever seen.

"If the fellow is not painting through spirit intervention," my inner voice remarked at that moment, "then he is a genius." I had to agree. Most painters must meditate or contemplate an idea for days before they can put it down on canvas. Also, in the act of painting, they seem to follow a plan, if even a momentary one. Not Medrado. He jumped from one part of the canvas to another with abandon, almost without any apparent direction. He smeared on oils like there was no tomorrow.

Definitely so, if he was not a medium, he was an extraordinary painter. Is this spontaneous creativity the hidden potential of his mind? If so, it was a privilege to witness. I wondered what I can do to open up my own potential to write in the manner that he paints.

Within a period of two hours, Jose Medrado produced at least ten paintings. The other mediums, of inferior status, painted several each. They were new and under his training. At the end of the session, we were able to view the paintings up front and then purchase them if we wished, the money going to the support of social service projects. Most of the works were quite accomplished and sold rapidly. I wished that I had a wall to hang one on.

As my first introduction to him was after the presentation, we had a little time for an interview. It is easy for North Americans to interview mediums, because many mediums think that we are investigators who will take them to the States and introduce them to famous movie stars. Unfortunately for him, I was merely an investigator without connections.

In the short five-minute interview that followed, I was invited by the medium to Salvador, Bahia; I decided to visit him in a few weeks. I went, but every time I went to his center or called his house, he was never there, so we never had a chance to sit down and chat about spirit adventures. I was informed later that he has other gifts besides spirit artistry and that he was to become perhaps the most gifted medium of his generation. At the time that I met him, in 1991, he was a medium for only three years. His gifts at present include healing, prescribing remedies, some telepathy, communication with the dead, and of course psychographics—a fancy way to say spirit artistry.

Jose Medrado makes no claims to using his own brain power to create his works. He works as an unconscious spirit medium, one who is completely unaware of what is coming through him; thus he is a perfect instrument for his spirits. He turns over his mental apparatus to whomever chooses to use it. However, as was explained by another medium in Salvador, there is a negative side to unconscious mediumship; the medium as a soul doesn't learn anything of benefit to assist him in his evolution. The medium told me:

Anyone can serve as a telephone. Most people are under the direct or indirect influence of spirit(s) without ever knowing it. What is the personal benefit derived? Nothing. The purpose of mediumship is to enrich the life of the planet and the life of the individual as well. If you don't know what is occurring and don't participate consciously in the spirit/human relationship, then there is no personal growth involved.

Conscious and unconscious mediums are at battle over this point. It is obvious, however, that the phenomenon of unconscious mediumship is more spectacular than that of conscious mediumship.

Someone Hears My Prayers

During the demonstration I felt myself identifying with the energies of the room. I felt my own pulse beat quickly as the painters raced around me (I was sitting only about one foot behind one of them) and worked even faster and faster. It was quite exhilarating for me to observe.

Suddenly I had a sad realization. I forgot to come prepared for this event. Why didn't I buy a video camera while I was in Panama? They were much too expensive in Brazil. Here I was witnessing spirit work, or at the bottom line, remarkable creativity, and I had no way to document it. In that moment of sadness a powerful thought welled up from inside of me: *If only I could have a movie of this.*

As I was watching the medium in front of me and thinking how important it was to record this occasion, something strange occurred. This same medium, his eyes opened, turned for a moment, and, looking over his shoulder, stared at me. I felt that whatever he was looking at, he had picked up some energy pattern of mine. He stared as if to say, "Please don't annoy me with your human requests. I'm much too busy channeling Mr. So-and-So."

I still had the strange feeling that my request was being relayed. My attention was then drawn to a very attractive woman who seemed to be running up and down with something in her hand. This person turned out to be Sheila Avellar, an architect, Spiritist, and medium in her own right. What she had in her hand was a video camera. She was filming the proceedings! I told my friend to get a hold of her, that I needed to talk to her.

As soon as the session was over, I caught up to her and, in a flurry of Spanish and English, introduced myself. I told her what I was doing and why and requested that she sell me a copy of her tape. She told me that she would be more than happy to give me a copy but she was filming for the Federation who *never* gives or sells these records. "Never?" I thought, grinning inwardly.

I had other connections, visible, as well as the invisible spirit who appeared to be aiding me; surely he would put in a good word for me. I then asked her if perhaps I could have bits and pieces of the film, just enough to present at the university. She thought about it and decided that I would not be betraying her commitment to the Federation, which had granted her special permission to film. She gave me her telephone number with the idea that we should discuss it later.

The next evening I called her, and she assented to my wish. She would also be next on my list to interview, for she was a functioning medium working through a local Spiritist institute. As things ended up, I received from Sheila not only a large amount of tape footage documenting the event, but also her guidance and friendship as well. More on her later.

The next day, Sunday, I returned to the Federation hall to see yet another gift of the medium Medrado. He was apparently able to diagnose and recommend treatment for illness in people he did not know. I was especially interested in this, as I had been attending Atlantic University in Virginia Beach the year before at the Association for Research and Enlightenment, also known as the Edgar Cayce Foundation.

Edgar Cayce, as most people in spirit and psychic circles know, was one of America's best and most sincere instruments. As he entered into trance he made contact with a higher Source and was able to diagnose illness and ailments and prescribe remedies, some of which were very rare and unknown to even most pharmacists of his time. This stimulated me to drag myself out of bed and march down to the Federation to see how Mr. Medrado worked.

The people of Brazil surely love their mediums. The session began with a lively and entertaining talk by the medium, one such as only a person who likes the attention of huge audiences could truly appreciate. Then the Lord's Prayer was recited by everyone present, about two hundred people. Finally, with a shake of his head and a forward push of his body, Medrado, the medium, entered into trance.

Those of the general public who wished to receive a diagnosis and remedy for an ailment were asked to fill out a form stating their name and address, but not their problem. These papers were gathered by ushers and placed face down on the table. Mr. Medrado, who appeared to be unconscious, then began to write at a rapid pace without looking at the papers on the table before him. When he finished one, his assistant took the answer and stapled it to the page on top of the request stack and returned it to the person whose name appeared there.

It was assumed that his spirit guide would see the name on the paper and transmit the diagnosis and prescription to Mr. Medrado, who apparently had no need to even look at the requests. The answers were forthcoming immediately.

It was quite marvelous to watch. I had no way, however, to follow up with any of the patients to see who had an accurate diagnosis or recovered from the treatment.

Another Spirit Painter

At the close of the Sunday affair there was an open house in the classrooms of the Federation, where one could meet and talk with others as well as purchase some of the artistic works and drink some coffee. Though I do not drink coffee, I decided to head down to the rooms before the crowd got there. As I was walking around, nibbling on a piece of cake, I realized that a very nice lady with a kindly smile was looking at me. As I smiled back at her and greeted her in my broken Brazilian tongue, she noted immediately that I was a foreigner and was delighted to find out that I spoke Spanish, a language which she claimed was prettier to the ear than Portuguese. (I, incidentally, feel that Brazilian is a lovely language, more romantic than Spanish.)

We began to discuss several things. She introduced herself as Cleobe Brandao, a lesser-known psychographic medium. Cleobe is a conscious medium. This means that she maintains herself partially observant to the process. While she may go off into a sort of haze while creating, she doesn't relinquish all of her awareness to the spirit using or sharing her faculties.

Brazil is filled with top quality mediums, many of whom receive little or no publicity and wish to keep it that way. Cleobe is one such person, a teacher who works with mentally retarded children and loves her work.

When I first saw some of her creations I was little impressed. Then she passed me a miniature of a little girl. I looked at it closely (I was given a magnifying glass) and was surprised to see that in the little iris of the eye was a replica of the entire girl, an intricate and fascinating piece of work.

Chapter III
My First Preto Velho and Cabocla

Like most newcomers to the spiritistic scene, I was immediately surprised to find that there are different traditions within the great mediumship umbrella. Most visitors tend to group all of them under one name, Macumba. That is a great error. I hope that by the end of this book, the reader will be able to differentiate among the various strains of religious thought and practice within the Brazilian milieu.

The Umbanda is one of the largest and strangest of these movements. There is so much to say about Umbanda that I could dedicate several chapters to it without exhausting my information.

After returning from my first conversations with Dr. Nezo of the Spiritist Federation, I was telephoned and invited to visit another friend, Catia. She and her husband had been my gracious hosts during my arrival week until I located a small apartment in Libertade that I could use during my stay in the city. Something compelled me to visit them, but the traditional excuse of lack of time had held me back.

Without wasting a moment extra, I took the subway two stops up the line and walked the remaining five blocks to their small home. As I stepped through the door, Catia jumped at me, grabbed my hand, and led me to their dining room table, where I would have to eat her delicious food, every morsel of it, before we could even talk.

"I was hoping that you would show up. I have a contact who will introduce you to an Umbanda Mai, here in São Paulo," she said.

I was soon to discover that a significant quantity of Umbandistas are Euro-Brazilians from the middle class. Many are university graduates and take Umbanda quite seriously.

Within an hour we were sitting in the attractive living room of Miguel

21

Bersani, a young Italian-Brazilian, very typical of the type of person now practicing Umbanda in São Paulo.

Miguel, who like most others in the spiritistic religions, was born into the Roman Catholic church. He was dedicated in his early years, but just didn't find the Church's teachings to be relevant to his life. He wandered through many religious groups and discovered in this particular Umbanda group what he felt he was lacking.

Later, he introduced me to other members of the Umbanda. I discovered most of them to be quite similar to him, spiritual seekers from solid middle-class homes.

We sat in the large stone-walled living room, sipping Brazilian coffee and talking about many spiritual things, my own question and search as well as his. Like most young mediums-to-be, Miguel is quite amiable; we soon became friends, and he often contacted me to attend many of the different types of spiritual sessions. By night's end, Miguel decided that I could be presented to his *tenda* and spiritual "Mai" ("mother") the following evening. I would also participate in my first Umbanda seance.

Tenda ("tent," "shelter," or "store") refers to a place where Umbanda is practiced, such as a sanctuary or a consultation office. Within the tenda is a *terreiro,* or holy place, where spirits mingle freely with the living mediums.

On the evening of May 10, I readied myself to attend a healing service at the Umbanda tenda of Mai Neusa, Miguel's spiritual directoress and the head of the Caraon Umbanda institute. Mai Neusa preferred to use the more modern term of "spiritual director" instead of the traditional Umbanda *Mai do Santo* ("saint's mother"), the ordained priestess of the teaching, within a certain lineage. A Mai or *Pai* ("father") must study for many years, living a disciplined life and passing spiritual tests and proofs before ordination. As with other professions, the study is long and arduous, often taking up to fourteen years. Many of the Pais and Mais are feared for their powers, though the Spiritists pooh-pooh the ritual and priestcraft. It is a title not taken lightly in Brazil; it is quite respected.

In her daily life, Mai Neusa is a publicity agent which, she admits, she does only to maintain her spiritual activities. She feels that it is her responsibility to modernize the Umbanda, to eliminate many of its nonessential aspects which are tangentially related to mediumship practice. She has plans to open a mediumship training school and also a drug rehabilitation center, within which she would employ spiritual therapy. Mai refuses to live off of her religion and won't charge for any of its activities. Her disciples, however, make contributions for the apprenticeship work in which they are involved.

In appearance she is an attractive, rather youngish grandmother and very down-to-earth on most subjects. When I met her, Mai Neusa was training ten future priest-mediums and was quite strict in their education.

Her chapel is small, as Umbanda centers go. It contains a meeting room and an office where she tends to the public. Some tendas are cathedrallike and very elegant, on the scale of many Catholic churches. Others, like hers, are quite simple.

I arrived early to see what the ritual chapel was like and, to my surprise, found a plain, rectangular room divided in half by a white transparent curtain and rope. The uninitiated sit on one side of the chapel, not venturing to the other side unless invited by the spirits or the priestess. In the center of the sacred area, separated by a barrier from the seating area, was a white cross, which dominated the entire area. Along the wall on both sides of the cross were symbols of African and Brazilian heritage, indicating that this Umbanda sect was still related to its traditional African roots. There were also yellow and white candles in many places, signifying the veneration of certain archangels, or *orixas,* some of whom we will meet later.

On a wall on the left side of the sanctuary, there was a painting of the presiding spirit, a *caboclo* ("native Indian") who is the patron saint of the center. It is he who teaches the students through the medium Neusa.

The entire chapel was painted white, the color worn by Jesus Christ and the acolytes. High priests and priestesses all wear that color as well. In fact, everyone practicing Umbanda dresses in white. I found that when I walked through towns dressed in white clothes, people would stare at me, thinking that I was a Pai do Santo. I must admit I did nothing to discourage their perceptions.

As the initiates enter the curtained area, they prostrate themselves before the cross and other sacred images. They then meditate in silence for a while. At some point, Mai Neusa, dressed in white robes, enters and greets the guests, priests, and spirits. After the ritual songs, or *pontos,* are performed, she enters into the spirit-trance necessary for incorporation.

During my first visit, she incorporated a *preto velho,* an old black slave who lived in Brazil during the days of the Portuguese conquest. It is believed that some of these slaves achieved sainthood because of their intense suffering, which reportedly caused the development of the spiritual qualities necessary for their elevated station.

There obviously are various ways in which a medium may go into trance, but this is what I observed at Mai Neusa's chapel:

The acolyte-priests established an environment of expectancy by singing and dancing around her. The pontos were simple and repetitive, and induced a type of hypnosis. At some point Mai Neusa's body began to tremble as though attacked from the outside, and she fell unconscious upon the floor. Her husband and others were usually present to catch her and lower her gently in front of the cross. Before long, she rose; when she did there was something different about her aspect.

I made some quick notes about these differences:

Neusa, during normal consciousness blinked her eyes regularly, and her stare was not always direct. During trance her stare was very hard. Her eyes were completely open, and her eyeballs appeared larger than normal. She did not blink at all. Her stare was very direct and maintained itself fixed, that is, without the eye movements associated with normal sight. She adopted the stare of a blind person during incorporation and walked with a straight military spine. Her voice was considerably deeper than usual.

The spirit who spoke through Mai Neusa, a *preto velho* ("old black"), was a slave using a curious dialect which dated from two hundred years ago. I still had serious comprehension problems with modern Brazilian dialects, let alone an antiquated dialect no longer in use. However, I was more interested in how the spirit worked through Mai Neusa. He barked orders at the assistants, played around with them, poking them in the arms and chests and making the sign of the cross over everyone.

He was soon offered a cigar and whiskey, traditional for this spirit, in a rather ritualistic and eucharistic manner. He puffed on the cigar and had a dandy time drinking the whiskey, a few glasses, all the while dispensing counsel and doing his healing work.

Soon people were filing up to speak with the preto velho and ask for boons and favors. I felt that any communication would be impossible during the rituals and decided to remain in my seat, despite the prodding of Miguel and other acolytes.

I observed that the spirit used a large piece of chalk to run over the body of the supplicant during and after the interviews, which lasted from a few to maybe ten minutes.

My inner voice egged me on: "Try an experiment with these people. Ask for the piece of chalk mentally and see if the medium can read your mind." Sounded like a plan to me. I decided to do it.

I was seated in the first row, men on one side and women on the other. I was the only foreigner present in the small crowd of about fifty people.

I lowered my head, staring at the floor, and willed in my mind that Mai Neusa give me the chalk at the end of the session. I prayed for about three minutes, until I felt satisfied that I had made enough mental noise to be heard. When I looked up, *Mai Neusa had stopped her work and was staring at me.* She held her gaze a few moments and then went back to work.

At the very end of the session, as the spirit was about to depart from Mai Neusa's body, he called over an assistant and spoke in a whisper, handing him the chalk. The assistant then approached me and told me that this was a gift from the spirit, that I should take it with me as it holds the energy imbued in it. The spirit then waved at me, said something, which I didn't understand, and disincorporated.

After the seance I asked Mai Neusa about the chalk. She responded that she didn't know what I was talking about. She said she never knew what occurred in the sessions, as she is unconscious for the duration. She often laughs at the things that people tell her she does during incorporation. I noticed that she didn't appear tired at all and that the smell of alcohol which hung around her during the seance was not present.

She answered that her mind goes to a different "place" where it rests and is reenergized. Subsequently, she never feels tired after a session. Of the alcohol, she said of course not, since the preto velho drank the whiskey and not her.

I was surprised and delighted with the gift of the chalk and that my experiment was successful. It sat on my table for several weeks and traveled with me for some time until I used it up.

On May 15, I attended a second session at the tenda where Mai Neusa presides. This night a different spirit-helper, a cabocla called Liria do Campos, was incorporated. Mai Neusa's personality went through an even more startling change as Liria incorporated.

In normal life, Mai Neusa is rather dominating in the way she moves and organizes those around her. She is viewed as a person not to be crossed. In this trance, however, she spoke with a native Indian accent and expressed herself with very feminine, flowing, and gentle gestures. Her eyes were again pronounced and intent, and she joked a lot with the students.

As the preto velhos, she was pushy, telling everyone what to do and how to sing the pontos correctly. As a cabocla, she treated the patients with maternal attention and tenderness. Again, I had no wish to speak with the spirit, as this time her dialect would be even more confusing than before. But I did decide upon another confrontation.

I felt a great desire to be touched by Mai Neusa as she channeled this cabocla. I wondered if a spirit's touch differed much from human touch. I had been touched by her under normal conditions and wanted to see if there might be a significant difference. Admittedly, this was no scientific experiment. I couldn't attach her to a machine to verify any change. But as a massage therapist, it seemed an enticing idea to prove. Was there some type of spiritual energy which might be felt through her hands?

After about three minutes, the spirit Liria rose from her chair and walked up to me. I was sitting again in the front row. She stood on the other side of the sanctuary barrier looking at me. She did not cross over. She began to speak to me, very quietly, in her Indian dialect, which, unfortunately, I did not understand. Even so, I was moved by her words. There was something of love in them, very maternal, very goddesslike. Then she lightly touched me on my forehead, over the pineal gland. I felt what I can only describe as an energy slowly fill up my head and expand within me. I experienced a lot of inner pressure from the expansion of energy, as if the parietal bones of my skull were moved apart.

At that moment I experienced what can only be described as a wetness spill from my forehead. I thought that there was a water or something on my head, but when I touched myself, I was dry. The wetness was on the inside and it spilled down, ever so lightly, into my mouth. My body trembled lightly and dizziness spread through me. She spoke softly to me, and though I couldn't translate, I knew they were words of reassurance. "Don't be afraid," she whispered within my skull. "You wanted to feel my touch. Well, here it is."

This was not the first time that I had this experience. I had been initiated by several spiritual masters, including Thakur Singh, who touched my head "to create contact between my self and God." I had also studied with a Shaktipat master from India who produced a similar feeling.

I took the medium's hand and pressed it to my lips and kissed it. My lips felt anesthetized, I could feel nothing in them for about twenty minutes and had difficulty in speaking. Also the front of my face reacted in the same way. I could squeeze my cheeks and feel nothing.

Later, at other times and places, I was to come into contact with other mediums—and spirits—embracing them, kissing them, and having all types of physical responses while in contact with them.

I knew that telepathy existed because I had direct and personal experiences with it while I lived in Santa Fe, New Mexico. At that time I decided to take a course, where I met a very spiritual and attractive woman whose name remains forever in the deepest recesses of my mind, a simple soul, a mother, and a wife. A compassionate woman, never seeking publicity or celebrity for her gifts, she came to the school I was attending and spoke about a course that she would give.

I wasn't interested in the course, but something within me wanted to be with her for a while. I asked if I might attend the first three sessions, and my request was granted. By the end of the third session, I noticed that there was something "different" about this woman. I came to the unusual conclusion that she was able to read my mind. When this hit me, it was like a revelation. I looked up at her and she looked down at me knowingly. She smiled at me and merely said, "Of course!"

This surprised me even more. Then I quickly received a thought and wrote it down. I thought to her, "See if you can write this down, too." She responded by writing something down and handing it to me. It was the same sentence that I had written down! The rest of my final class was taken with the understanding that I could communicate with her silently. I did.

Several months later, while still in Santa Fe, I had a similar experience, this time with the Hindu with whom I was studying. I had just had an argument with one of my massage teachers and was feeling quite saddened by it. I decided to attend meditation class with Sri Krishna K. and ask him for a *mantra* (a power or a focusing word) which I might use as a vehicle for curbing my temper. I arrived as meditation began.

Among the thirty or so people present, I sat in the back of the room. Suddenly Krishna opened his eyes, looked at me, and giggled silently. He then touched his wife on the shoulder and pointed at me. She smiled, kindly as usual. He asked her for a piece of paper and a pen and wrote something, all of the time looking at me. Then he folded the paper and put it in his pocket. I was curious, but at the end of the session the students crowded so much around him that I gave up any hope of being able to converse with him.

As I got to the door to exit the room, a hand tapped me on my back. I swung around and saw Krishna, smiling at me. He said, "Here's your mantra. Now repeat it one thousand times. That should keep you busy enough so you won't fight with your teachers anymore."

Telepathy exists. My question in Brazil was whether the medium's attentiveness to me was a response to my telepathic wish. Was it the medium herself or the spirits with whom she incorporated who responded twice to my telepathic message? Could the spirit look inside my mind and read what was there, like the Hindu gurus claimed? Could we, incarnate humans, do this as well? Was this spirit communication?

Chapter IV
A Brief History of Umbanda

Having put the proverbial cart before the horse by first relating my encounter with two Umbanda spirits during the seances at Mai Neusa's tenda, I choose now to enrich the reader's knowledge of that religion, unknown outside of Brazil.

Umbanda, I found as I wandered around and through it, was very similar to a gigantic iceberg. Deceptive in its overt appearance, it was very often fluffed off as a superstitious conglomeration of rituals, songs, and confusion. But, like the iceberg, the larger portion of it lies beneath the surface. This, I found, was by no means a little sect, but a full-blown religion, complete with rites, holy days, priestcraft, and churches. It merits even deeper investigation than that which I am presenting here.

I completed separate research on the Umbanda and wrote it under the heading, "Umbanda: A Second Look," some of which is presented in a digested form in the appendix to this book. It makes for interesting reading, especially to students of religion.

The polemics surrounding the origins of Umbanda have been under debate for some time. Still a vast majority state that it is a progressive outgrowth of the Candomble. Many of its priests claim that it is a fragment of an ancient nature religion which originated in the Far East. while others claim that it is only an evolved form of a Brazilian religion known as Catimbo. Still others claim that Umbanda was formed in the village of Niteroi in 1908 by Zelio de Moraes.

Perhaps the most sensible explanation is that the roots of modern Umbanda are in the ancient cultural and religious heartbeats of the African peoples, especially of the Bantu, Malo, Sudanese, and Yoruba tribes. These people experienced several religious cultures through the efforts of Muslim and Christian missionaries long before slave trade with the West began. As the slave trade took hold, these tribes became the largest source of revenue in Latin America; it is natural that their languages, gods, and customs would predominate in what would one day be known as the Afro-Brazilian Syncretism.

It is of special interest that the Malo and, to a lesser extent, some smaller tribes such as the Male and the Houssa, were under Islamic influence when slaving became a profitable enterprise. People of these tribes later became the Bahiana people, and certain Arabic words and Islamic customs may still be detected in Capuera music and among the customs of Umbanda—the use of long, white clothes, dresses,and turbans. These have now become the ritual clothing in the practices of Umbanda and are reminiscent of early Muslim influences. Other predominant African cultures are the Jeje, Bantu, and Nagoes, which practiced fetishism and were animists. Practitioners of animism believe that typically inanimate objects are imbued with souls or spirits and are therefore alive, especially as demonstrated by the forces of nature, with polytheistic propensity for spirit or demon worship.

It was difficult for them to move away from this polytheistic sense of the cosmos towards the Roman Catholic ideal of monotheism, which was forced upon them by eager catechists. However, they disguised their tribal gods and forces under the names of the multitudinous array of Christian saints and were thus able to parade their religion before the eyes of patrons and bishops without reprisals.

The Afro-Brazilian Syncretism is based not only upon racial heredity and tradition. In the New World, as mentioned, the African peoples accepted the Catholic faith, some by force, others by design. A minority accepted out of the desire to assimilate the new culture. It was difficult enough for the various tribesfolk to mix among themselves, since in Africa they were organized as separate peoples. Now there was a white Portuguese culture to deal with as well. The Church offered a step towards social acceptance and some limited legal franchising. This acceptance took hundreds of years to accomplish and to this day is still not complete.

Catholicism offered an array of ritual, practice, and nomenclature, which was rapidly assimilated into the African religious experience. Many of the ancient deities were adapted to the saints' images, and modern Umbanda, like its predecessor, the Candomble, contains many Roman effects in both its art and rituals. Thus, the history of Umbanda began in Africa and was transmitted through the Candomble orixa tradition, which was firmly established in the first national capital of Salvador, Bahia dos Santos, and then to the south in the city of Rio de Janeiro.

The Spiritism of Allan Kardec, the French mystic, was the next notable influence on the scene. It arrived in Brazil through visits of traveling lecturers and citizens who had studied in Europe. It then landed on Brazilian shores and found the country quite receptive to it, despite the official opposition of the Church.

In the coastal cities, many devotees of the Candomble and another fraternal sect, the Macumba, began to read its literature and absorb its ideas. All of the African religious cults that migrated to Brazil contained concepts of mediumship, reincarnation, and spirit worlds. These elements were necessary to pave the way for the Spiritist expansion throughout the area.

Kardecism lent a doctrinal basis and practice, as well as a more unified teaching to many of the beliefs extant. This "codification" allowed groups to present their teachings in a more organized procedure. Kardecism contributed the use of magnetic passes, magnetized water, and the *palestras* (spirit lessons) to the public. Some Candomble sects appeared to be more Spiritist than African in nature, as they began to prohibit alcohol and cheroot smokes, both essential in African ritual.

These reformed groups began to call themselves Spiritist Candomble, or Umbanda Spiritist institutes. It is here in these fragmented groups that many modern Umbanda federations had their beginnings.

The cultures of the Amerindian of Brazil, many of whom were enslaved and tortured during the European conquest, contributed deeply to the new synthesis. Several of the native deities soon became models for Umbanda cosmology. There are scores of Indian spirits called *caboclos* and even two orixas, Damien and Cosme, who are gods of indigenous Brazilian origin, worshipped in the Umbanda.

Finally, with the ascent of occultism in Brazil, primarily through the efforts of the Theosophical Society and the Rosacrucian orders, certain cabalistic elements were added to Umbanda ritual. The *pontos riscados* (magical seals) drawn upon the floors of the terreiros, which identify and invoke the powers of the presiding spirits, come from the esoteric *yantra* traditions.

Umbanda is an ongoing process of cultural and religious syncretism, a living experience representative of the Brazilian people. I have no doubt that it will continue to reevaluate its symbology, quietly abandoning certain symbolic representations while acquiring others. The U.S. New Age movement, for example, is already invading certain Umbanda temples in Brasilia and São Paulo. Certain of their centers no longer use the African *Pais do Santo* preferring instead the titles of "religious director" or "reverend," in an attempt to modernize the movement.

Others have simplified the altar and replaced the African symbols with crystals, flowers, and natural representations of their deities. Some Umbanda sanctuaries appear more like Pentecostal churches than Afro-Brazilian centers; in Brasilia, some of the centers have even eliminated the sacred dances.

A popular claim by the majority of Umbandistas, especially among the well-to-do institutes in the southern states, cites the origin of Umbanda as extending far back to the ancient Hindus. They claim that Umbanda is older than Judaism and is, in fact, part of an ancient chain of knowledge.

One famous Umbanda priest states that the present name of "Umbanda" is a derivative of the sanskrit word *Aumband* and that the names of the principal deities are degenerate forms of ancient Hindu gods. He views Umbanda as the ancient natural religion of humankind that suffered transformations in its external forms and rituals due to its meandering across the planet. The African rituals only represent the migration of Umbanda across the African continent. But Umbanda is not limited only to black peoples of Africa, but has roots in ancient Egypt, Palestine, and other countries of the fertile crescent as well.

Tancredo Da Silva, founder of the Umbandista congregation, in his book says that the development of Umbanda can be traced back to the beginnings of the world, when it was revealed by great spiritual avatars, or messengers such as Moses, Christ, and the orixas. He envisions an apostolic succession of Umbanda teachers who will connect the wisdom of the ancient schools to the present form of the religion. He interprets Umbanda through a theosophical, rather than a specifically African approach, though he does not deny its newest roots. His version of Umbanda is often called "Esoteric Umbanda" and has many followers, especially among the well-educated upper classes.

Another theory is that Umbanda is of divine origin. According to

32

this theory, the revelation of Umbanda emanated in all its purity from the invisible realm. In this way, Umbanda was "not created by the work of man, but simply by the inspiration of the Higher Uncreated . . . revealed through mediumistic work. . . . " (4)

It appears, however, putting aside theological considerations, that modern Umbanda was organized, or reorganized, by Zelio de Moraes, in the early part of the present century.

During his youth, de Moraes, who was of Catholic upbringing, had a series of powerful mediumistic experiences. In 1908, at the age of seventeen, Zelio was stricken with a strange paralysis that no doctor was able to cure. One morning after breakfast, he announced to his family that tomorrow he would be cured. He arose from his bed the next day, as predicted, and walked as if nothing had happened.

He had been destined for a naval career. His uncles, who were Catholic priests, were surprised at his strange recovery but could shed no light upon it. A family friend suggested that he visit a nearby Spiritist center for answers. It was at this meeting that the young Zelio participated in his first seance.

Zelio was reportedly possessed by a very strong force that made him say, "A flower is lacking here!" From that moment on, he channeled the spirits of black slaves and native Indians, spirits which were considered to be quite out-of-place in the more established Spiritist centers of that era; these entities were considered to be low spirits, not illumined ones.

Zelio questioned the leaders of the Kardecist center for explanations about why the work of these spirits wasn't allowed. They explained that these were retarded entities, not suitable for any real spiritual work. The young medium blurted out, as if possessed, "Tomorrow I will be in my house to initiate a religion in which these Blacks and Indians will be able to give their messages, and also to fulfill the missions that on the spiritual plane were confided to them. It will be a religion in which even the poor will speak, symbolizing equality, which ought to exist among all brothers, incarnated or not. And, if anyone wishes to know my name it is this: Caboclo of the Seven Crossroads, because none will find any doors closed to them." (4)

The next day, November 16, 1908, the first Umbanda seance was held. As practicing Catholics, his family was amazed and quite fearful, but at 8 P.M., members of the Spiritist center arrived to prove the truth

33

of the statements made the day before, and the same entity came through Zelio the medium. This spirit declared the form of the cult service, named Jesus as the spiritual head, announce that people of all social classes and colors were welcome, and that charity and fraternal love should be characteristic of the meetings. He also announced the name of this new religion, *Umbanda,* which means, "God is with us."

In the days that followed, the town of Neves was in turmoil. The sick, the blind, the paralyzed, all came in search of cures.

Thus, the fifteenth day of November is held as the official date of the birth of Umbanda. By 1935, there were seven temples, one for each of the seven Umbanda lineages. By 1939, there were dozens of temples and a new federation was founded. By 1975, there were approximately thirty million Umbanda adepts, according to the Brazilian Institute of Geography and Statistics.(4)

Chapter V
Principles of Umbanda

Umbanda is a religion in the throes of evolution, but, unlike other religions, has very little in the way of organic doctrine.

Its federations and institutes, call "tendas," have attempted to establish a universal catechism, but without much success. Spiritism, which contributed certain elements to the magical worship rituals, also lent to Umbanda the Kardecian Codification, was called by its own loyal devotees, "The Doctrine."

Umbanda accepts the Codification, more or less officially, as its "Ten Commandments"; however, no priest or member of the religion is obligated to accept every dot and letter as literal, or limit his beliefs to it alone. On the contrary, every Pai and Mai, the priests and priestesses of Umbanda, possesses full authority to speak ex cathedra on doctrine and ritual practices. Thus, each member is unencumbered by any formal codification other than that of mediumship, appeal to the spirits, and ritual magic.

This, of course, tends to create a certain amount of confusion upon presentation of the concepts of Umbanda to the general public, not to mention significant disagreements between federations and centers as to what constitutes authentic teaching. Nevertheless, the Pais remain the sole interpreters of doctrine. They are the link between the *axe* (ashay), or grace, of *Olorum* and their incarnate congregations! When they declare, subjects pay the utmost attention.[1]

The culture and education of the priests greatly influence the presentation of Umbanda concepts. Should the priest originate in the southern states, populated by the descendants of Europeans, his tendency will lean toward a more Christian type of understanding. If a

Pai or Mai is well educated, that may play a role in fusing traditions of Rosicrucianism, Yoga, and Theosophy with his teaching.

As I wandered from one tenda to the next, I questioned many Pais on their beliefs. Not one of them could agree with another. Not only did they disagree as to the origins of Umbanda, but could not even unite upon catechistic statements. After much questioning, I discovered that, to most of them, sectarian beliefs were less important than the spiritual values, which should be lived, and the work, which must be carried on in cooperative venture with the invisible world. Some of the Umbanda institutes are more Kardecian, while others retain more of the Afro-Brazilian flavor. The aforementioned Kardecian Codification, acquired from the Spiritists, forms the basis of Umbanda theology. Sectarian philosophy is gleaned from Talmudic and Midrashic interpretations of sacred texts.

These interpretations are often revealed by the Pais in a state of mediumship and are attributed to the spirits themselves. It is here that doctrinal confusion most often occurs. Many of the ideas become vague and uncertain. It is because of this uncertainty that each individual is given the freedom to explore cult precepts, which most do. It is therefore not the philosophical foundation of Umbanda that attracts the average member, but the specific need(s) which it may fulfill in his life.

Certainly the Umbanda of São Paulo and the south, demographically more Christian and white, is different from the Umbanda of the north, which is more African. An American parallel is the differences between Baptist churches of the north and south. Similarly, the Esoteric Umbanda of Brasilia is quite different from its siblings in other parts of the nation.

Umbanda is divided into many subsects, each with its own special emphasis. Each subgroup is called a "lineage," and is similar to those Catholic orders that emphasize specific characteristics of Christian doctrine, such as the Franciscan order and their vows of poverty. Each lineage contains its own beliefs and rituals, all appropriate to its principal *orixa* (o-ri-shah), and encompasses a hierarchy of incarnate beings, also orixas, but of less importance than the principal orixa, who stands as supreme hierophant of his particular mysteries.[2]

The orixas, who number from twelve to as many as twenty-five, possess vast amounts of axe which they distribute through the falange in descending order, to their supplicants. Axe can solve problems; it can heal and bring peace and order to the discordant notes in the lives of those who seek succor. Each falange upholds its own rituals, colors, and initiations; each is a mystery school, containing its own secrets, inviolate to all save its initiates.[3]

The principal orixa never incarnated on earth. It is pure spirit, the primordial creation of the great God Olorum; it has power, grace, manna. It is impersonal and yet works through personality; it is proto-typical, archetypical, archangelic, aeonic, and divine, similar to the gods of ancient Rome and Greece, though less substantial.

The lesser orixas are considered representatives, or individual incarnations of the leading Power. Each is similar to the Tibetan *tulka,* who are incarnations of the ephemeral Bodhisattvas, or the Hindu, Sat-guru, who has attained the realization of his ideals and thus becomes the living ideal on earth. These orixas are revered in cult worship as worthy spirits who incorporate and therefore grace devotees with the ecstasy of their presence.

The function of the falange is to transmit axe from the gods to humankind. I was instructed that, through receiving and living in this state of grace, all truly spiritual beings have the opportunity to evolve to orixa, though they may not become a primal orixa.

Umbanda exists on two levels: an esoteric level, for the initiated and the priests, and an exoteric level for the majority of those who visit its temples. While there are some very educated and radical Umbanda priests, the majority are quite circumspect in their spiritual and philo-sophical education.

This is one of the major reasons for the continual failure of the myriad Umbanda sects to reach doctrinal concordance. As previously mentioned, there is a general acceptance of basic doctrine promul-gated by the Kardecian Codification: reincarnation, karma, service, the triple nature of human beings, and spirit communication. These, however, do not define the entirety of Umbanda experience. The cultural, educational, social, and religious backgrounds of the popular members all produce factors that influence the understanding of Um-banda and effectively contribute to the distortion of any unifying system of belief.

However, there are some fundamental universal notions held by all the Pais of the cult, a major one being the "Law of Karma." According to Umbanda and not unlike most Oriental teaching, the universe in its entirety is governed by karma. It results from actions which were previously committed on either conscious or unconscious levels—that is to say, acts of commission or omission. Such acts must be reconciled so that true spiritual progress might be attained.

A true being is manifest as a neutral soul, neither good nor bad, neither to the left nor the right. He is colored by his actions. A true being, very much like the Taoist "perfect man," is a flowing individual in which all energies function in harmony and balance. The true being has perfect axe. Illness, possession, destruction, and suffering result in a loss of axe. All humans who are presently in physical incarnation are the manifestation of a soul which was and is affected by energies, which either cause it to expand or contract. The soul has passed through many stages of the mineral, vegetable, and animal kingdoms in order to become a human being and is still vulnerable to the effects of spirits and energies. This will continue until it becomes an orixa. Officially, I was informed that two Brazilian orixas, Cosme and Damien already are recognized.

I should interject that Umbanda does not teach that the soul becomes an animal, though some Pais may believe so. The soul must pass through these worlds and experience the characteristics of minerals, animals, and vegetables, while maintaining its basic human integrity. It experiences identification with the life and vibration of the different kingdoms, an association of experience with the energies of each kingdom, rather than a transmigration of each.

As the soul travels through these kingdoms, where much confusion and many dangers exist, it is most vulnerable to the most terrible of all, the possibility of entrapment. Guides and teachers are therefore needed. When the soul finally and completely incarnates as human, the entrapments, according to the Law of Karma, still wield power. The karma of the present life may be used to blot out these entrapments.

Some, known as preto velhos, or the black slaves who suffered the cruelty of their enslavement, seemed to rise above their condition and attain some levels of enlightenment. These have entered the ranks of the falanges. The caboclos, a generic term for the indigenous population who also endured great suffering, are also in the falanges.

There is a certain parallel to this belief with that of popular Christianity, in that Jesus obtained his eternal dominion through his suffering and death upon the cross.

These advanced souls serve as active guardians for the benefit of less evolved beings. They impart the higher knowledge known to some priests of Umbanda as "the internal principles given in the Astral Current of Umbanda." Their teaching assist the soul in regaining its original purity.

W. D. Mattos Silva, along with other Umbanda Pais, has suggested that the ritual of *fumigacao,* subjecting of the faithful to the smoke from burning incense, represents the fundamental belief of Umbanda. In this rite, sacred herbs are burned in a brazier. Each devotee is approached and surrounded by a smoke cloud. The devotee makes a full turn in the cloud, which then dissipates. The incense cloud represents the unfolding of the soul, moving from limited congestion towards free expansion as it dissipates evenly throughout the universe. To most observers this is simply a purification rite; however, to the initiated, this is the symbolic baptism by fire; the smoke which envelops us, expands through space and time, becoming one with the substance of the universe. This is the deepest purpose of the Umbanda.

God and Spirits

God is the Supreme Force and the Spirit of absolute perfection. God is eternal, uncreated, One and indivisible, self-extant. In Umbanda, God is the supreme transcendent consciousness that directs the world and the cosmos, called *Olorum,* God Almighty. God is the Creator of all laws that control the universe.

Unlike the gods of most world religions, Olorum did not enact the Creation. In his perfection, Olorum could not create a being which would be imperfect, suffering, and eternally ignoble. Spirit angels created the substantial forms in harmony with the karmic plan from the preexistent etheric.

Spiritual beings, both astral and incarnate, are of a high spiritual vibration. They do not disintegrate as physical bodies do. They are coeternal with Olorum. These spirits, which embody wisdom, intelligence, will, emotions, and other qualities of "humanity," traverse the cosmos incorporating these qualities into physical existence. They educate and urge the faithful to evolve toward the perfection of the Eternal Father. No person was created in the Supreme Consciousness; yet it is to this Consciousness that all shall return. This teaching echoes the beliefs of the ancient Gnostics of Alexandria, the Bogomils and the Cathars of southern France.

Matter

An eternal substance exists, known as the etheric, the generator of transformation and movement, basic and fundamental. It is preexistent, thus it is uncreated, not produced by God. Umbanda teaching is unable to provide a real explanation for this, other than to postulate the etheric as a substance not from God, yet somehow extracted from the All. The priesthood maintains that this mystery is unexplainable to the uninitiated. This substance, always mobile, transforms itself into basic subunits, or elements, which then build the universe. This substance is called "universal fluid" and it is always exploding, imploding, and changing form. This, in fact, is chaos, the eternally changing.

The divine power operating through this substance provides its direction, altering and coordinating its action to produce atoms. Thus the worlds of matter are generated. Matter is unintelligent, it is chaotic, but the intelligence of the Pai guides it.

We, however, are intelligent and are not of this matter but of another substance. We reside in this matter but are not of it. Therefore, there are two types of karma which affect us: the causal and constituted. Causal karma is that which motivates and mobilizes us within the chaotic, changing world of matter. Constituted karma is determined by the intelligence of God in us and is our plan to fulfill.

. . . and Cosmic Space

There exists a neutral vacuum, infinite and undefined. It is not comprehensible by the human mind. It interpenetrates all substances.

Mind, however, works through this space, stimulating it. This vacuum is of the same nature as God, uncreated; its reason for being there is known only to the Supreme Being. This is the biblical "house of the Father" proclaimed by Jesus. This space is divided into two aspects: the neutral vacuum which is pure emptiness, not penetrated by matter, and inhabited by spiritual ideals and awareness; and the world of phenomena, creation, and permanent chaos, the visible world. This includes the astral world as well.

40

. . . and Causal Karma and the Spiritual Cosmos

We are from the higher world and must return to it. This is the higher, original life of all beings from which we descended. We are given free will and also the law of causal karma, which we must use correctly to ascend back to the world of Spirit, which is pure, virginal, and undisturbed, somewhat similar, to certain degrees, to the Buddhist Nirvana.

. . . and the Sex of Spirits

Spiritual beings have tendencies—vibratory levels—which imprint upon substance and consolidate themselves as male and female. There exist eternal archetypes of one or the other which dominate each spiritual being. These energies objectify as sexual tendencies of one or another nature. Sex determination has no origin in matter, only in spiritual energies. Here, there is a disagreement in doctrine: some authorities state that a spirit is eternally differentiated as either male or female; others claim that one incarnates once as male and another as female. As in all religious dogma, there is always disagreement.

There are always traumas and exceptions, such as male and female homosexuality. These are transitory situations that in future incarnations are rebalanced.

The human organism is a product of spirit imprinting its pattern upon matter through the genetic coding in protoplasm. There are four basic elements: air, fire, water, and earth, which combine and produce the physical makeup of each person. Human protoplasm is different from animal protoplasm. There are also four root races which contribute to the physical differences of human bodies and psyches.

. . . and Breaking the Causal

There was an original Purpose from which we separated, an original Cause from which we deviated. For this reason the Father created the astral world which provides us with a return to wholeness. We live in a spiritual world subject to causal karma (cause and effect) with the direct use of our free will. Spiritual beings don't have etheric vehicles, nor are they related to the four elements, and can't create bodies for themselves. They have different states of consciousness, vibrating in pure spaces, which are permanent. These beings constantly imprint substances producing male and female creatures.

This dualistic identification is the original sin which intervenes in our relationship with original karma (purpose). We become slaves of matter and remain in its bondage through ignorance. Through constant disobedience to the law, we suffer within the confines of our limited physical world. Because of this, God created innumerable worlds and imbued them with part of his energy so that we could learn to return.

There are two ways to evolve through the universe—suffering and learning, and wisdom. Wisdom is imparted through the world of evolved spirits, also referred to as our guardian angels. Some few spirits also reincarnate as saviors to teach the return to the spiritual world.

The secret doctrine of Umbanda, properly speaking, is the wisdom imparted by the higher beings, which is the leaven that guides the devotees back to God, the Source.

The finality of Umbanda is not the curing of physical illness or the counsel given by the spirits in the tendas, but the ultimate return to the "world of light," freedom from the causal world—imprinted with duality and suffering—a return to the virginal state of spiritual emptiness.

How many devotees of the religion understand this as its goal? Mai Neusa told me that very few, if any, come to Umbanda for that; more often they come to petition the spirits for help, protection, or cure. I have observed that even among those sufficiently evolved to enter the priesthood, there are but few who perceive the true goal. And judging by the attitudes of some spirits, I would question whether even they are aware of the goal of liberation.

In general, then, the Umbanda system appears to be somewhat Gnostic; through direct experience, engendered by its rites and often passionate practices, a way may be glimpsed that leads the individual back to the knowledge of the All. The concept of a distant God, Olorum, and the nearer powers, the orixas, the necessity of initiatic knowledge and experience, all may indicate that indeed the Umbanda, or Aumband, is in fact the ancient gnosis via Africa to Brazil.

Influences on Modern Umbanda

UMBANDA is an Afro-Brazilian syncretist religion which combines elements of many religions, cultures, and philosophies.

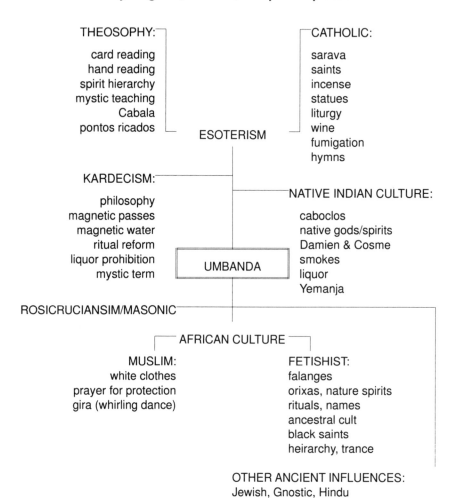

THEOSOPHY:
card reading
hand reading
spirit hierarchy
mystic teaching
Cabala
pontos ricados

ESOTERISM

CATHOLIC:
sarava
saints
incense
statues
liturgy
wine
fumigation
hymns

KARDECISM:
philosophy
magnetic passes
magnetic water
ritual reform
liquor prohibition
mystic term

NATIVE INDIAN CULTURE:
caboclos
native gods/spirits
Damien & Cosme
smokes
liquor
Yemanja

UMBANDA

ROSICRUCIANSIM/MASONIC

AFRICAN CULTURE

MUSLIM:
white clothes
prayer for protection
gira (whirling dance)

FETISHIST:
falanges
orixas, nature spirits
rituals, names
ancestral cult
black saints
heirarchy, trance

OTHER ANCIENT INFLUENCES:
Jewish, Gnostic, Hindu

Waldemar Valente, *Sincretismo Religioso Afro-Brasilero* (São Paulo: Companhia Editora Nacional, 1977).

Syncretistic Practices in Umbanda

Practice	Source
Enchantments	Amerindian
Saints	Roman Catholic
Orixas	African (Nagos)
Dress: diadem, bracelets	African
Arrows, Bows	Amerindian
Saudacao (greeting), sarava	Roman Catholic
Terreiros (chapels)	African/Roman Catholic
Chants and evocations	Muslim/Catholic
Dances	African/Muslim
Drums	African
Words of unknown origin	Native tradition
Pontos riscados (protective shields)	Theosophy/Mason/Esoterism
Charut, cigars	Amerindian
Liquor	Catholic/amerindian
Defumacao (incense)	Catholic
Ancestral cult	African
falanges	African
Orixas	African (Nagos)
Higher/lower spirits	African/Esoterism
Order of ritual	African/Catholic
Saints	Catholic
Dances (gira)	Muslim (Sufi)/African/Indian
Quiromancy	Esoterism
Cartomancy	Esoterism
Doctrine	Kardecism
Reformed terreiros	Kardecism
Mediumistic vocabulary	Kardecism
White dress	Muslim
White turban	Muslim

Notes

1. Olorum, also pronounced Ololun: Supreme deity of Umbanda and Candomble. Also known by other names.
2. Orixas are sometimes considered archangels, avatars, personalized gods, or characteristics of the divine.
3. Falange: A hierarchy which transmits power from God to the orixas to the devotees.

Chapter VI
São Jorge's Birthday

One day, while visiting the Federation, a newly-made friend of mine whispered to me so as not to be overheard, "This Saturday is an important Umbanda holy day."

He spoke so conspiratorially, as if to suggest that a holy day was criminal. It seemed that my friend was not only a Kardecist, but secretly, an Umbandista as well.

Dr. Julia assured me that Umbanda was a stepping stone from the Candomble to the Spiritist doctrine. It worked both ways. I met many Candomble priests who started their careers as Spiritist mediums. My friend continued, whispering in my ear, "This Saturday, there will be hundreds gathered in the municipal auditorium for Saint George's Day."

Saint George, made famous because of the number of Spanish Moors he killed during the conquest, is celebrated according to the Roman Catholic calendar on April 23. While millions of Roman Catholics go to church to honor him in other countries, millions of devotees of Umbanda and Candomble don their white clothes and crowd into Catholic Mass in the morning and then to Umbanda ceremonies immediately after mass is over. One priest told me that over half of his "Catholic" congregation wasn't Catholic at all, but if he prohibited all of his Candomble and Umbanda parishioners from attending, the church would be empty.

São Jorge in the Umbanda (and Candomble) is not exactly the same as the Roman George. One Pai told me that there is no relationship at all between the two saints. In Umbanda, Ogun—his divine name—is the energy of the spiritual warrior who fights his internal battles against great odds, like the Tao and Zen warrior. São Jorge gives us the power to go on in life, to live it well, and to be victorious in the end.

"When we were slaves of the Portuguese Catholics and couldn't openly practice our religion, it was necessary to mask our beliefs under those of the church, to identify our saints with theirs, and to bury our relics under the floors of the churches. Now, however, we are free to worship our own religion, and we should openly declare that our orixas are not their saints!"

Before the celebration of Saint George's Day, I visited the Museum of Sacred Art, located in an old monastery in one of the original villages of São Paulo. I had heard that it contained some worthy reproductions of the Catholic saints. As I passed through the rooms, I saw several statues of São Jorge, mounted on his steed, lance in one hand and shield in another. As I stared at him (and he at me) I thought, *How different he has become in his journey from Spain to Portugal to Brazil.* Little did he know that one day he would be venerated as a sacred orixa.

Saturday finally arrived, and decked out in my best white clothes, I began to trudge up the main highway to the municipal auditorium. As I arrived, the buses carrying delegations of some of the larger Umbanda congregations lined the streets. There was a fireman's band all decked out and a Boy Scout troop outfitted with the flags of São Paulo, Brazil, and the colors of Umbanda.

As I entered the building, I was surprised at the small turnout, but it was still quite early. I was ushered into one of the bleachers, where I sat conspicuously alone. Other people were talking, eating, and smoking, the environment more that of a carnival than of a religious ceremony. The various Umbanda congregations walked in, in full regalia, and the ceremony began—late, as befits most Brazilian functions. The auditorium was only half full, but the people were enjoying themselves.

After the presentation, at least one hundred representatives of Umbanda congregations from other Latin countries walked in. The president of the United Umbanda Federation, a Brazilian of Arab, perhaps Lebanese, descent, came in with an escort. Following the president, a local fire company marched in, playing the national anthem. Everyone rose from their seats and sang along.

As the singing died down, in walked the Boy Scouts and the Police Force sounding trumpets. The cacophonous sounds of the horns was a signal to various choirs, who sang the hymn to São Jorge.

By now, the auditorium was almost full; I could feel a certain tension in the air. At this point, carried upon the shoulders of several honored volunteers, in came São Jorge himself, sitting on his horse, ready to fight any Saracens present. It was nearly a humorous sight, and I laughed to myself, thinking how ironic that the only Moor present was none other than the president himself of the Umbanda Federation!

By now the people were going wild, chanting, throwing rice, flowers, and other objects of reverence at the statue. Some fought to kiss the feet of the saint. Other people were crying. I allowed part of me to get caught up in the enthusiasm of idolatry. Another part reminded, "There are space ships traveling to the moon. These people are participating in an old idol religion. They are worshipping like the ancients, thousands of years ago."

No problem. The pagan part of my personality rejoiced with them.

Finally the deity was ensconced upon an altar surrounded by flowers. People came forth to bow before it and pay homage. After this ritual, there were lectures, and I noted that many of the speakers used the same techniques as Western television evangelists, emoting to the listeners and motivating them to be better Umbandistas. All in all, that part was quite boring to the public. Most paid little or no attention. They were busy eating, socializing, and looking around. This was especially true of the youth in the auditorium, who were on the lookout for potential Umbanda girlfriends and boyfriends.

Then came the part of the ceremony that I was waiting for. All the mediums present entered within a fenced-in area at the front of the auditorium. As special prayers and chants were uttered, they began to go into trance. First one here, another there, then ten, then fifty, and more. In the span of only half and hour, about one hundred mediums were in trance and channeling São Jorge. Each was surrounded by members of their various tendas, to protect them and also receive axe (the blessing, the grace). When I realized what was going on, I decided to get up and walk around the ring and spy on the different mediums to observe what they were doing. Some were ecstatically leaping into the air, while others gave advice. Still others puffed away on cigarettes or walked around as though drunk (these, I was told were incomplete incarnations).

The scene reminded me of a Tibetan Buddhist ceremony that I had seen several years earlier, the incarnation of the Bodhisattva

Avalokitesvara in the ceremony of the Black Crown. The Tibetans, from my point of view, were more decorous, the Umbanda, wilder. However, I noted that the purpose was the same, the transmission of grace to the faithful.

The festival continued for several hours. I watched and listened and began to grow tired. Then, to my delight, I happened upon a young woman who spoke English and was more than willing to share her knowledge of the Umbanda ceremony with me. She introduced me to her father, who was himself a Pai do Santo *and* a photographer. He was taking movies of the proceedings.

Through him, I was introduced to a more commercial side of the ceremony which made me skeptical. He maintained that whenever he pointed his camera at one of the mediums, the medium suddenly went into a deeper trance. The medium performed for the camera. The photographer told me later, "Whenever there is a ceremony like this, the mediums vie with one another to see who is the best medium, best meaning more dramatic."

As I looked more closely at the people gathered around the mediums, I felt that there was something quite humorous about the participants. Many were elderly and otherwise staid grandfolks, in their conservative suits and sneakers, but participated in the proceedings with great fervor. I had observed the same type of behavior from the same type of people in Methodist women's circles, Baptist Missionary societies, the Holy Name and Altar societies of the Catholic church. All were as devoted to their respective gods, whether mounted on a cross or on a horse. While the scene was amusing, it was equally compelling, for I relearned something that I had seen at many other times and places around the world—faith is faith, wherever it is applied.

Around five o'clock, I remembered that I had an appointment with my friend Cleobe Brandao in another extreme part of the city. I had not eaten all day, and the noise and energies of the festival were becoming too much for me. Wobbly, I rose from my chair and found my way to the door. I must have been terribly confused, because I lost my way home and took at least twice as long to get back to my apartment. I changed my clothes and left, late, to get on the subway to where Cleobe and family were awaiting me.

Chapter VII

Who Incorporates

The humans can find so many distractions. At this time there's the problem of the humans trying to amuse themselves by concerning themselves with our business. They distract themselves from their own work. They may know about us—the spiritual counseling system—and that we are available to them. But it is dangerous for the humans to think that their duty to the Earth can be avoided by pretending to have some important career in the spirit world. . . . The spirit world takes care of its affairs. What remains is for the humans to get to work with their own business.

—Joseph (5)

Who comes through during a spirit incorporation may be more interesting than a philosophic discussion of what might come through. It is certainly a loaded question. People have responded to that question, at least in my presence, on a very emotional rather than philosophical level. Their culture, their religion, and their past training tend to answer this question for them.

I remember years ago, when I first began to consider the question of spirit mediumship, I reacted immediately with the idea that it just couldn't exist. Later, I investigated the matter more closely, because a member of my family was a fledgling medium, and I ridiculed it. After visiting some U.S. mediums, I reacted with an emotion very near to vehement foolishness. I was adamant about it—this "spirit stuff" could be, emotionally, very dangerous. Other people reacted even more strongly to it, becoming either immediately convinced of its validity (after their first contact with it) or quite fervently against it.

Fundamentalist and evangelical Christians are very quick to brand all spirit communications as satanic, and claim that if Satan himself does not appear in such communiques, then some other devil, witch, or evil spirit does.

I was not surprised that Evangelicals and Fundamentalists should act in this fashion. Nor was I surprised that persons on the Buddhist and Hindu spiritual paths should classify spirit-contact as illusory. I had been told by my own spiritual masters that such phenomena are real, but that getting too involved could cause the student to deviate from the goal of spiritual liberation. What did surprise me, however, was that several of the esoteric churches in Brazil were also against spirit communication, condemning all mediumistic activity as dangerous. One person, a friend's father, began to question my motives for studying mediumistic traditions in his country, for in Brazil, there are few people who don't believe in spirit phenomena. The fear of many is that these spirits, adored by so many, may be angels of darkness.

But there is one question which most people have, one that arises sooner or later in just about anyone; just who or what is coming through?

Ask any initiate of any mediumistic sect this same question; the answer becomes significantly more complicated. It depends upon the day of the week in some cases, on the spiritual lineage in others. In still other cases, it depends upon which spirit is on call. When I visited the different tendas, there were usually two sessions per week. On Tuesday night sessions, the preto velhos would be channeled, and on Thursday, the caboclos.

Though this is certainly a question of considerable theological import, I do not propose to answer it here. I do intend to present how the mediumistic religions approach this quandary and how certain mediums with whom I discussed it were able to illuminate me.

It is appropriate to cite a quotation of the investigator, Dr. Ranier, as it sums up the view of many spiritualists in Brazil:

A medium is an open door to the invisible world. What comes through the door depends to a large extent upon the personality of the medium . . . There are plenty of evil spirits around others who seem to have nothing better to do than fool about and amuse themselves at our expense. (6)

The medium De Padua stated that the type of spirit which comes through depends upon the quality of the medium:

A person who is uneducated, but is a medium will carry his cultural structure into his visions . . . In the spiritual world, therefore, he is attracting levels which correspond to him even more structured. Some mediums therefore are stratified, very wishy-washy, molded and confined and will attract simple minded spirits of like-mind who will feed them on "earthly" views of the spiritual world. The medium learns nothing, the spirit knows nothing to teach and the listeners learn nothing either. (7)

Pai Guillerme, himself a spirit, warns:

. . . the inhabitants of astral planes are often millions of times worse than earth beings . . . we have about thirty billion inhabitants in the astral plane . . . half of them need urgent help in morals and the benefits of other enlightened beings . . . more than half are in low consciousness. (7)

Another medium tells of some of the spirits who come through her:

I work one day a week with the spirits. Usually there are one or two . . . some work very slow, these spirits in precarious conditions ask me not to speak and to lower the light. (7)

This is why mediumistic literature warns the practitioner to develop the highest morals possible to channel through spirits of noble qualities. During one session, I asked the spirit Zoroaster what moral character meant. He answered:

Morality is the process of growth which ends in true love . . . there doesn't exist a fixed definition, it goes in accordance to the individual consciousness. . . . The spirits are attracted through rapport . . . (7)

Apparently, then, the more "spiritual" the medium, the more balanced, loving, and good the instrument, the more "moral," benevolent, and wise the attracted spirit.

The various mediumistic schools promote cosmologies that explain the type of spirits that exist who may channel through the mediums. The Candomble medium works with highly evolved beings, which he calls the orixas. Difficulties appear in the understanding of these delightful beings, especially in their own religious circles. Having spoken with different Pais, I divided the information into two basic theories that explain the origin of the orixas. Interestingly, I observed a striking similarity between the orixa theories and those of the Oriental Buddha in Northern and Southern schools.

Some Pais believe that the orixas were born as ordinary men, who, through their efforts, merited divinity. Thus, through great deeds and actions, they became gods. The other school of thought maintains that the orixas are cosmic beings who reflect, in specialized degrees, the light of the Father God, Olorum. On one hand, the orixas are similar to the ancient Greek gods, alive and well on Olympus, frolicking and having the best time intervening in the affairs of humankind. They compare easily with the Norse gods, assigned certain functions in the divine running of the universe.

One of the orixas, Exu, is quite mischievous, like Loki, a god who enters easily and intervenes in the affairs between other orixas and humankind. He is a combination of Prometheus, Mercury, and the Devil, all rolled into one.

Other Pais do Santo told me that the orixas were not originally gods, but superhumans who, through great feats of both physical and spiritual nature evolved into the highly developed beings that they presently are. Mai Vera told me, "The orixas are too deep to understand . . . they lived on earth at one time. They incarnated. . . . " (7)

They maintain themselves, like the Bodhisattvas of Buddhism, at the level of all humankind, to help when they can. However, unlike the Hindu avatars, the orixas do not incarnate but incorporate in specially prepared mediums to make their will known.

On a more esoteric level, these orixas are like the Gnostic Aeons, archetypal energies of the great archetype Olorum, God Itself. They are the luminous beings which surround the innermost secret. It is of note, however, that the majority of the people believe the orixas to be spiritual entities of the highest order. God is so far away that He cannot be contacted except through the intermediary activity of these orixas. They are above all the other spirits. Hence, the worshipper, by making contact with them through a medium/priest, has access to great wisdom and power. Be they what they may, the orixas are incorporated during Candomble trance sessions.

Pai Roberto Caldiera, a fifth generation Candomble priest, spoke to me of the special grace of these orixas. Pai Roberto had officiated at or attended many seances. When the orixas came through and spoke, the room invariably filled with a very powerful energy to which he could find nothing to compare.

I asked Pai Nivardo why there was a difference in the understanding of orixas from other aspects of Candomble cosmology. He said:

> The reason why there is so much confusion regarding the orixas is because, as a rule, it is difficult to find an educated babalorixa. It can be said that the orixas are characteristics of the one God. (7)

It is usually said that the orixas are seven in number, though I know that with all of their different appearances and cultural differences, there are many more. Some are women, others men, one is neither and one changes sex every six months. Their names vary from the north to the south and from one African culture to another. The orixas are sometimes called *vodoons*. They have both African and Catholic signatures and their celebrations are fixed by the Roman Catholic calendar, to the great dismay of the Church. It is said that in Salvador, on certain Catholic feast days, there will be more white-clad worshippers of Candomble than authentic Catholic present at mass.

The orixas are listed as follows with some of their attributes and corresponding Catholic saint's name:

Exu: Male, corresponding to the Christian devil. Messenger between gods and mankind, the originator of processes, He-who-stands at the limits. He is honored first at Candomble and Umbanda ceremonies.

Ogun: Male, Saint George, war-like, the spiritual fighter, the opener of paths and ways.

Oxossi: Male, Saint Sebastian, representing individuality and freedom, related to wild animals and their protector.

Oxum: Female, the mother of sweet, drinkable water and of the life within it. Saint Rita, she appreciates all that is beautiful, pleasurable, and sensual in life.

Iansa: Female, Saint Barbara, governs emotions, provokes experiences which could lead to learning. The power of wind and storms, joy, and happiness.

Xango: Male, Saint Jeronemo, the lord of justice, uses lightning to remind the world of his power. He is protector of rocks and stones.

Yemanja: Female, the Virgin Mother, corresponding to the Virgin Mary, goddess of salt water and the unconscious. She is usually placed under the altar, surrounded by water, mother of the orixas.

Nana Buruku: Female, Saint Ann, also a water goddess, server, protector of the realm of the dead, whom she collects and protects.

Obaluaie: Asexual, Saint Lazarus, a fearful orixa, he punishes and has control over plagues, illness, and skin pain. He inflicts collective punishment.

Ossaim: Male, Saint Benedict, protector of all that grows in the forest, especially the god of healing herbs. He is invoked when herbal treatments are given.

Oxumare: Alternates six months male, six months female. God of transformation, in charge of opposites and other dualities. Has no Catholic correspondence.

Oxala: Male, Jesus, father of the gods, fecundity. He was given the work from God, to fashion all of the other creatures.

Traditions change from culture to culture, and Africa, the homeland of the orixas, has many cultures. Generally speaking, these are the orixas most recognized and venerated by the Candomble in Brazil. While this information was given to me by several Pais, verified and cross-referenced from authoritative books, there are divergences with other sources.

Umbanda, also called Aumbanda, which is the most eclectic and Brazilian of the mediumistic religions, works with a larger number of spirit-beings. Umbanda recognizes a spirit world inhabited by higher and lower spirit entities. It allows for the incorporation of any spirit, but, for the sake of its ritual labors, utilizes mostly two classes of evolved spirits: the Black saints and the native Indian saints. Brazil was a slave state, and while at first the imported Africans were the main stock of slavery, they soon discovered that there were native Indians who could also be used for labor. Both groups were treated miserably and according to Umbandan theology, through their sufferings certain individuals grew spiritually. The preto velhos were Black slaves and the caboclos were the Indian slaves. Most tendas or Umbanda chapels have one or several that serve as the patron saints and who incorporate during seances.

Some of the more New Age temples, such as that of Antonio de Padua in Sorocaba, even incorporate American Indians. Another temple claims to incorporate Saint Germain and other of the "ascended" masters. Usually people from the higher economic classes frequent these centers.

Pai Roberto informed me that lower entities—spirits in evolution, and not very nice ones at that—were often allowed to incorporate, especially in the black magic rituals of the Quimbanda. While most Pais didn't want to talk about it, several admitted that the Quimbas also have a mission in the universe. Quimbanda, the so-called practice of black magic, is a persecuted faith. Most Pais who see it and call upon Quimbanda spirits will almost never inform the public, nor even other Umbandistas. An authoritative newswriter, Theresa Correa, told me that the activities of Quimbanda are still being persecuted in many circles and are often under observation by the police.

I am personally fascinated by the Quimbas, the so-called lower spirits-in-evolution. These spirits are headed by exu, the orixa who stands at the limits of things and is also the messenger of the gods and mankind. Exu is a controversial figure. Though identified with the Christian Satan he is not intrinsically evil. One psychologists, Dr. F. Luiza, in his book, *Umbanda and Psychoanalysis*, called exu the "creative, dynamic, chaotic and upsetting force which is latent in all living things." (8) It appears to be similar to the life force, a nonintelligent energy that is directed by higher intelligences in order to fill the universe with life.

Exu directs an army of elebaras (male demons) and pombagiras (female demons). These beings entice living persons to act in strange ways, to do strange acts, and to break their normal, programmed limits. While mostly feared in the Umbanda religion, probably because of its more Christian orientation, they are involved in healing work and aiding their devotees in times of need.

Pai Alfredo Jorge, the head of an Umbanda Temple in São Paulo, in an article in the *Planeta* magazine, said:

The exu is not fundamentally evil in himself. He teaches those who wish to do evil, how to do it. He is an instrument of punishment to those who deserve it as well as an instrument of redemption for those who overcome the difficulties of their existence and can reach a higher level of spirituality. (9)

However, Maria Miranda, a Mai do Santo of another Umbanda temple, says that it is not exu who is evil, but the Quimbas or lower spirits under him.

Olga Cacciatore, an investigator of Afro-Brazilian religions and the writer of the *Dictionary of Afro-Brazilian Cults*, says:

. . . they are obsessors, that is they possess humans, they bind them to themselves, giving them pains, evil, thoughts of suicide, etc. They are mystifiers, sometimes passing as higher light beings . . . they are controlled by the exu. (10)

However, exu has a benevolent side according to Pai Sebastian. He states that the exus have the capacity to take away pain and sickness for those who have faith in them. Many seek the sanctuaries of the Quimbanda when all else fails. In the *Planeta* interview, there were several people who sought out their help and received healings of illnesses that had not responded to medical treatment.

The worship of the exu, as practiced in the temples of the Quimbanda, is often chaotic and disorganized. Entering one such temple, though unaware that it was a Quimbanda temple, I could feel a special coldness. I asked the priest about that. He told me that the coldness was to drive away those who are weak at heart. Similar to the dharma monsters, those terrible looking entities who stand at the gates of Buddhist temples in the East, the terrible Quimbas protect their sanctuaries from those who would scoff at them. Pai Nildo, of Itaparica, told me that as they incorporate these lower beings, mediums will, as often as not, act as if to seduce the worshippers, and many of the cult practices end in sexual activity.

One evening, Pai Roberto drew the relation of the hierarchy of beings. His diagram is presented here:

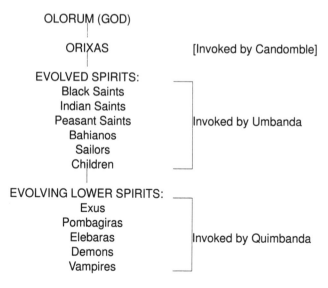

OLORUM (GOD)

ORIXAS   [Invoked by Candomble]

EVOLVED SPIRITS:
  Black Saints
  Indian Saints
  Peasant Saints   Invoked by Umbanda
  Bahianos
  Sailors
  Children

EVOLVING LOWER SPIRITS:
  Exus
  Pombagiras
  Elebaras   Invoked by Quimbanda
  Demons
  Vampires

There are many subdivisions of spirits incorporated by Umbanda mediums, too many to list here. Some exist to assist in specialized situations, such as illness or marital problems.

Spiritism doesn't credit a hierarchy of spirits. According to the moral condition of the mediums, one attracts the spirits which desire to incorporate. Spirit incorporations are not limited to national, religious, or linguistic barriers, though most spirits I observed in Spiritist seances tended to be from higher social classes than those invoked in Umbanda. They were, they said, in past lives, doctors, lawyers, and priests. Most were middle-class individuals and spoke in an educated manner. According to lore, one reason for the founding of the first Umbanda tenda was that evolved spirits from among the Black and Indian population wished to communicate and offer their services, but the Spiritists were too elitist to incorporate them.

It is interesting to note that Spiritists do not believe in demons. They prefer more highly evangelized spirits, with Jesus at the helm, to less illumined ones. They do not believe in lost souls; all will, in time, see the light and return to the Father. Therefore, at Spiritist seances only "moral" spirits are invited to make appearances, and many mediums will incorporate a slew of them.

At spirit-painting sessions, Rembrandt, Van Gogh, Matisse, Klee, and Picasso, or some little known but worthy artist might incorporate in the same hour. I witnessed a constant array of artists at one São Paulo seance.

In the case of Luis Gasparetto, professionals were called to identify techniques demonstrated in channeled paintings with their namesakes, all with surprisingly favorable results. Many studies were done on Chico Xavier, Brazil's most loved medium, who has incorporated thousands of entities. In literary seances, the writing style demonstrated in channeled manuscripts was typically found by graphologists and family members to bear uncanny resemblance to the writing of the spirit while incarnate.

In summary, the beings being incorporated during trance state might be conditioned according to the group's social class and religious tradition, but often are free and unexpected souls who tend to appear at random, phenomena discussed by the psychic investigator H. Andrade in his book, *Reincarnation in Brazil*.

According to this interesting account, during a Spiritist session in a private home, a young military officer, Ruytemburg Rocha, dead some thirty years, began to communicate with the medium. This same spirit was reportedly quite surprised to learn that he had been dead for some time. A detailed investigation, which included review of past army records and interviews with living relatives, proved that Rocha actually existed (11). It appears then, that any angel or devil might decide to show up at seances at the communicating end.

There is one question which is hardly brought up in spiritualist circles in Brazil, as is suggested by Jon Klimo in his excellent study of mediumship in the United States, *Channeling*. Klimo asks the question: might not the "spirits" which appear through channels be personalized impressions of the "higher mind?" This higher mind, also called the transpersonal self, is that part of the universe which is within us, the "all-knowledge, all-power, all-being" of metaphysical schools of thought. Klimo quotes Plotinus, the mystical philosopher, saying

There is in all of us a higher man . . . a man more entirely of the celestial rank, almost a god, reproduced into God. When the soul begins to mount, it comes not to something alien, but its very self. The self thus lifted, we are in the likeness of the Supreme. (12)

Founders of transpersonal psychology, such as Fadiman and Assagioli, speak of a "higher organization of self," a self which stands supreme within us, organizing our life. Kenneth Wilber, anthropologist and psychologist, believes that there is not only a higher self within us, but that we receive intimations of this self. (13)

Buddhism speaks of a Buddha-nature within each person; Hinduism proposes an original Atman, which pervades all things and is located in the center of each individual. Such modern metaphysical schools as Christian Science, Unity, and Religious Science speak of a "God within," the source of all good. All of these groups teach that the goal of life is the realization, recognition, and integration of this Source with individual life and living.

As the individual catches a glimpse of this transpersonal self, his being appears to receive more energy, information, and joy. It is at this point, should the person be previously programmed in some religious study, that personal interpretation may exhibit this contact as one with some separate entity. Or for cultural or spiritual reasons, one might identify this energy as some personalized spirit instead of recognizing it as the higher self. Referring to *the* spirit as *a* spirit, or God as a personalized being, the individual medium might make the experience more palatable, especially to his own nervous system.

I decided to ask some of the mediums if individual spirits might, in fact, be a reflection of a Higher Self, God, or the Universal Mind.

Sheyla Avellar, a youthful Spiritist medium, also involved in transpersonal psychology in São Paulo, told me in an interview:

> . . . at the beginning I believed my contact to be a spirit. It had a name and a history. But now, more and more, I am beginning to believe that it is really my own higher information source. (7)

Cleobe Brandao told me that she could interpret her spirit experiences as "accessing a higher level of awareness." Pai Nivardo, though not formally educated in psychology, is a student of some psychological theories. He stated that it "is possible that the spirits are all reflections of the mind." (7)

While psychiatrists, psychologists, and members of the Spiritist-Medical association told me that in some cases this could be the case, most affirmed that there were spirits, separate intelligences, who were influencing their patients. Dr. Carlos Tinoco, author and one-time Spiritist, now a student of Oriental religion, told me that previously he interpreted all phenomena as spirit initiated; however, now he might consider them to be functions of a Higher Mind.

On the other hand, Mai Neusa, Mai Zelinda, and many others objected to this idea. They believed in a Higher Mind-God, but they were absolutely convinced that these activities and phenomena could not be other than what they said were—spirits. In most cases, however, it was eventually admitted that neither Spiritist, medical doctors, psychologists, or even the spirits themselves had the last word.

Dr. Andrija Puharich investigated the healings of Arigo, who claimed that it was a spirit, a Dr. Fritz, who healed through him. He sums up his opinion:

> We have Arigo's thesis and claim that everything he did was programmed by a guide, a voice, a spirit entity. This is one of the greatest problems challenging us. I cannot discount this thesis because I cannot disprove it and because, certainly, the weight of evidence, particularly in the area of medical diagnosis, leads me to believe that Arigo was working with

intelligence far beyond that which he possessed in every other situation, and beyond that of the great medical diagnosticians whom I have known in my lifetime. One of the problems before us is to try to determine whether this is indeed an aspect of mind as related to the individual brain, or whether this is mind unrelated to a specific brain, in the true sense in which Spiritists, for example, teach and believe. (2)

Chapter VIII
Important Differences between Spiritist Faiths

I feel it important to deviate from the adventure for a moment and to explain some terms which are not always properly understood by those who stand outside of the Brazilian experience. I have used the terms "spiritistic" and "spiritist" throughout previous chapters. Spiritist religions are those who believe in the existence of spirits *and* practice communication with them.

Correctly speaking, all religion is spiritistic because there was usually some type of intermediary or revelatory experience at the founding. Islam was founded upon a revelation of Allah through the angel Gabriel. Jesus was influenced through the Holy Spirit. The Hebrew patriarchs were visited by angelic beings. All religions that believe in the existence of spirits and continue to practice mediumship are spiritistic. However, in the Brazilian context, Spiritistic religion includes the Kardecism, the Candomble, and the Umbanda, as well as other smaller movements, such as the Valley of the Dawn and off-shoot Spiritist groups. These groups admit the existence of a spirit world *and* actively practice spirit communication.

A Spiritist is a person who accepts the existence of the spirit world, practices mediumship, *and* accepts the Codification of Allan Kardec. His religion is Spiritism, Kardecism, or Espiritismo. All of the Sspiritistic religions have mediumism as their common factor.

When I was investigating the different mediumistic religions of Brazil from the outside, before making more extensive research, I fell into the same mistake as most people who have a superficial understanding of mediumship in general and of those religions which participate in them. There is no one type of mediumistic practice. Also it is unworthy to group all mediumistic activity under the same label.

In the United States, for example, we are living in a moment of popularity and an upswing of interest in mediumship. Most people, however, group all mediums together. My own investigations reveal differences among the Spiritualist mediums who pioneered the movement in the middle 1800s and the modern "channelers" of today's popular New Age movement.

Brazil, as I have pointed out in the previous chapters, has three principal schools of mediumship religion, which, due to vociferous attacks by its enemies, are generally classified under the name of *macumba*. Macumba is a rather derogatory name used by the enemies of Spiritism and all of its various forms. It implies that the practitioners of such arts are allied with satanism, witchcraft, and/or the black arts and are usually people of the lower and peasant classes. Evidence to the contrary is true. There is little macumba in Brazil. Mediumship has long since become fashionable and sophisticated. The Spiritists tend to be educated and members of the professional classes, as are many of the clergy of the Candomble and Umbanda. It is true that the three schools are cousins through mediumship, but a closer look reveals that they are, at best, second cousins.

The origins of the three religions are different: the Spiritist faith stems from the investigations of Allan Kardec and can be called an imported European religion. The Candomble is also an imported religion, from Africa rather than Europe. Of the big three, the only mediumistic religion with indigenous roots is the Umbanda.

In the public's eye, Umbanda is considered to be an offshoot or sect of the Candomble. Many Candomble Pais refer to it as such, usually with a derogatory expression on their face, as if to imply that Umbanda is a degeneration of the true faith. The Umbanda and Candomble often share mutual federations and are both classified as Afro-Brazilian religions. Yet there are Umbanda centers that purposely exhibit very little of their African roots.

All three religions share a belief in a Supreme Being, though they may each refer to Him by a different name. All groups agree on the existence of a spirit world and the use of mediumship to access and connect with the inhabitants of this world. They affirm that beings in the spirit world do interact with beings in this world.

All three religions have produced mediums who can enact psychical and mediumistic phenomena. There is no evidence that any one of these groups practices "better" mediumship than any other. The Kardecist (Spiritist) brand of mediumship may be more sedate and refined—however, not essentially superior to that of Umbanda and Candomble.

Among their various doctrines, all three groups believe in karma, reincarnation, and the need for positive social works.

As I associated with the three schools, I began to notice differences among them. The Spiritist does not hold ritualistic services, while the Umbanda and Candomble hold many different types. The Kardecists hold that rituals are superfluous to the practice of mediumship, while the Afro-Brazilians believe them to be necessary. The Candomble especially is rich in rituals, having adapted many of the Roman Catholic rites to their own needs.

The Afro-Brazilian faiths have priesthoods with vestments, sacerdotal rights, orders, and privileges—songs, statues, gods, sacrifices, and symbology. All of this is lacking within the Spiritist system. Spiritism, on the other hand, is well organized and has a canonized and codified doctrine which serves as a catechism for the unification of their followers and the teaching of others. This is obviously lacking among the Candomble, which teaches through ritual and passes on its knowledge through initiatory rites and grades, and the Umbanda, which, despite an extensive amount of literature, is insufficiently organized to provide a study plan.

Were I to choose one of the three faiths to be my own, it would be difficult indeed. I like the intellectual and almost stately scientific attitudes of the Spiritists, but I also enjoy the emotional energies present in the practices of the Candomble. I admire the freedom of belief in the eclectic Umbanda as well as the cosmology of the Candomble. Umbanda contains some teachings which parallel Buddhism, especially the lineage of enlightened beings who serve humankind, but their terms and practices are often confusing. The pure African rhythms of the Candomble stir up many primordial longings buried deep within me and have considerable psychotherapeutic value.

I suppose that I would be similar to the millions of Brazilians who might be members of the Kardecist religion—frequent Umbanda services and attend an occasional Candomble ritual. The Brazilians that I have met tend to be quite eclectic, selecting one religion for its artistic value and another for its logic. In any case, Brazil's religious arms are open to all.

Chapter IX

Cleobe Brandao, Spirit Painter

I met Cleobe at a Spiritist function standing some feet away staring at me. Within a few minutes she approached me, and we began to converse about Spiritism, painting, and about her own work. She was delighted to find out that I spoke Spanish, which she enjoys speaking. We were thus able to communicate quite well with each other. We made an appointment for the Sunday evening following our meeting, and an invitation to dine with her family followed. Cleobe Brandao is one of the many spirit painters in the country who serves without wishing anything for herself. I must admit I wasn't really interested in her until I saw one of her small portraits. What caught my attention was the iris of the eye of a little girl which she channeled. It was so detailed, with such minute strokes, I decided that if Cleobe wasn't really channeling this portrait from the spirit world, at least she was a darn good painter.

As a practicing iridologist myself, I was concerned about the iris signs. What I saw in an iris, which was little larger than a dot, was amazing. I would have problems painting the dot. Here she had painted a dot with so many different lines in it, all significant of body strengths and weaknesses, in iridology language.

I had spent the day attending the celebration of São Jorge's Day in the municipal auditorium. I left the building in a state of confusion and got lost on my way home, a route which I knew quite well. When I finally got to my apartment, I called Cleobe to tell her what train I would be on.

Riding the train to her house was a lesson in surrealistic living. I couldn't understand the stops when the conductor called them out. Then I couldn't remember where I was half of the time. I kept on staring at the train route and then at the other people in the car. It was if I had just arrived from another planet and had never seen earthlings before. At certain moments I would break out in laughter. It appeared that the afternoon's festivities were too much for my nervous system. My first large Umbanda gathering, and I became unbalanced and ready for the asylum.

When I arrived at the station, I began to worry that they would not pick me up, leaving me stranded. I was sure that everyone was looking at me and thinking to themselves that I didn't belong in Brazil. By the time Cleobe arrived I had convinced myself that my investigations would be a disaster and that I had better get a ticket home.

Of course, my fears were unfounded because I was only two kilometers from Cleobe's house. When she looked at me, she asked me where I had been. I told her about the celebration, and she said, "It seems that you have blown your *chakras*." She assured me that when I calmed down a little, I would recuperate just fine. We bought a bottle of wine to help with the process, and after a cup or two, I was balancing myself off very nicely, laughing at my fears.

After all my years of study and investigation, I think that that night I realized for the first time how the mass can influence its parts, how my nervous system was affected by spending eight hours in the auditorium. It is not that there was any intentional tampering. The event was so far out of my cultural milieu that I was not ready to endure it. My mind and body knew it, even if I did not, and as the days went by I became stronger. I was now using parts of my mental system which had been dormant and therefore weak.

While Cleobe's family prepared the meal, she and I had the opportunity to discuss some of her life. Her family was Roman Catholic, and she had intended entering religious life. At an early age, however, she decided that the monastic way was not hers and began searching for a way to serve God and humanity.

She began to attend a Spiritist center. One day a medium suggested that she train for mediumship, as she displayed a tendency in that direction. Cleobe also is a speech therapist, working with deaf children, a job which she adores. She told me that that type of work allowed her to develop levels of consciousness and sensibilities which contribute to her mediumship.

We spent a good hour sharing our thoughts and exploring a little bit of each other's spirituality. Because of a common language, I was free to ask many of the questions I wanted to ask of so many others. "Cleobe," I asked, "what is a medium and why would anyone want to become one?"

"We are mediums because we have the capacity to enter into contact with energies beyond the normal. Also we have the desire to help others. Finally, you do not choose to be a medium, it is chosen for you."

"How did you grow into mediumship? Was there anything in your life which stimulated you in this direction?"

"I felt an emptiness in life, regarding everything. I wanted to feel love for people and also feel loved in return. I suffered terribly over this, and then I sought help. I received it from a Spiritist woman who counseled and taught me. I soon began to feel an enfoldment in something, to experience a spirit presence. At this point I decided to attend and study in a Spiritist center.

"Also since I was a child, I saw my mother practice mediumship. She never was a Spiritist and doesn't believe in it, even today. I studied to become a nun but soon arrived at doubts about this path. I left the convent and returned to work. Then I began to learn about mediumship and things related to life. I studied for five years in the Federation. Helping others, I felt the *presence* of a child."

"How did you experience your initial contact?" I asked, fascinated.

"I was driving in a car and very briefly, it was as if someone else was there. Then I developed the capacity to hear. Then the spirit was seen. Finally my body began to move, especially my hand. The child began to explain things to me . . . I felt very good. My mind continued to observe the presence. I feel the hands activate, and I know that the spirit wants to paint. Then I go pretty much unconscious. I turn my hands over to it voluntarily . . . but I won't allow myself to go completely unconscious. Trance is, for the first few moments, difficult, but as it continues, I find it easy. At the end of trance I feel that I am far away and have some difficulty in speaking for some minutes. Later I experience mental clarity . . . The child works through psychomotor mediumship. Later I began to attract others . . . I soon learned that this child was my own in another lifetime."

"Do you have any technique to prepare yourself to receive a spirit?"

"First I have to clear my mind, think of something positive, read the Gospels, ask help from God, Jesus, and Mary. Mary governs my work. I personally don't believe she was a virgin, but had a normal conception."

I began to throw many questions at her now. "Can you invoke spirits at any time?"

"I can't. I feel when they want to paint. I have one day to work each week . . . I feel a voice telling me that they want to work. I feel some heaviness, usually in my chest, shoulders, and arm. I usually feel cooler. My hands get very cold. I have heart pains . . . When I feel these signs, then it is the best moment for their intervention. I tranquilize myself and ask God for help. I work with my eyes open, there is not need to close them, yet I work in low light, and I don't see what I am painting. Sometimes I paint in the darkness. Some works are produced quickly, some aren't."

"Do you experience any special emotions, either yours or the spirit's?"

"I feel all emotions. If the spirit doesn't like the work materials, I also feel his distaste. I feel all of his emotions. One spirit arrived with strong emotions, especially Gauguin. He worked with strong color tones and powerful strokes. I worked with chalk and he kept on breaking the materials. He didn't like the materials and became very angry. I told him that I didn't have any other materials. He calmed down and we began to work . . . I enjoy working with Van Gogh. He is very calm."

"With how many spirits do you work and how often?"

"I work one day a week with the spirits. Usually there are one or two . . . some work very slow, those spirits in precarious conditions often ask me not to speak and to lower the light. Sometimes there are seven to eight spirits in one and a half hours. Speed isn't important, understanding is."

"Have you experienced any personal transformations or changes through your mediumship?"

"I have felt worried. I am getting old and I feel rushed to work. I may not finish what is projected for me. The spirits told me that if I don't finish, they would finish with another medium. I feel more peace, tranquility, more assured of my personal life."

"Why do the spirits paint?" my inner voice asked me. A good reply was coming.

"Through art, man may work on his feelings so that the world evolves better. We know, as the age closes, a change is coming. We all feel the need to change. The mediumship of art gives us the opportunity to see things better. . . . The spirits treasure the simple things of life, like flowers. Through spirit music and culture, the mentality will change. Art helps open the emotions of people. Now we suffer, and the spirits bring us the art and music needed to evolve."

"Why does Brazil have so many mediums?" This has been an important question asked by many people.

"Spiritism says that Brazil will be the 'brain of the world.' We should work harder with the Gospel of Jesus to feel love . . . in other countries the mediums charge for their services. We give everything in love. The Gospels aren't taken to the people by force. They are presented so that the person may experience that love and consciousness of the truth. We don't have to preach! This is what we call Evangelism, teaching by love and not mental or physical force."

At this point we were called into the simple dining room to enjoy some Brazilian food. The family knew that I am a vegetarian, and since the Spiritist religion recommends this diet, they had no problem with finding some meatless pizza. They later drove me to the subway station, and I took the last train back to the center of the city, arriving home just a few minutes before one in the morning. There I found my roommate studying for his university classes, and I recounted the day's experience to him.

I set up a table in the corner of the living room, which was quickly filling up with literature, gifts from the various spirits, including anointing oil, chalk, dried up flowers, and letters. He laughed at the end of my narrative and said that I knew more about the inner pulse of Brazil than did most Brazilians he knew.

Chapter X
An Architect and Medium

Sheila is a fine example of the new breed of Spiritist mediums: talented, well educated, traveled, and creative. Also, while she takes her mediumship seriously, she also has activities apart from her service. When I met Sheila the first time, she was running around the hall of the Spiritist Federation making a video for her own movie on creativity. It was then that I confronted her and asked about the possibility of purchasing a copy of the film for my own use. She later arranged for a copy of excerpts from the Jose Medrado demonstration to be given to me.

About a week later, we met for an interview. I discovered that Sheila had been functioning for ten years as a medium and donated time each week at a Spiritist center as a counselor and assistant. She also participated in personal therapies, as she was concerned with her own transformation.

She told me one afternoon: "As I practice mediumship, I find many personal traumas coming to the fore. If I am to be a clear medium, I must work on them. Also mediumship is no guarantee that personal growth takes place!"

She is also involved with transpersonal psychology, which helps her with creativity. She applies Jungian therapy, exercises, and diets along with her mediumistic practices and is extremely open in questioning her own Spiritism.

"What made you gravitate towards mediumship?" I asked her as we sat in her living room one Saturday morning, drinking herbal tea.

"I was a photographer and I began to 'see' the real images of the people I was filming. My body began to intuitively catch a feeling of the characteristics of that person . . . not the image that they would like to

71

project, but what they were hiding . . . I also began to feel the person behind the mask. I could feel and also project myself into the person.

" . . . I began to feel the falseness of many people; often it felt like scratchiness in my body, or nausea when I felt others. . . . I would feel foolish, dizzy, and disoriented whenever I came into contact with a lower-energy person."

"All of this must have been very uncomfortable for you. How did you begin to develop your gift?"

"These senses began to develop when I was very little—about five years old. I perceived and felt these sensations. But no one in my family was Spiritist-oriented. In 1978, I began to work with Jungian therapy. The psychologist was also a Spiritist, and she detected that I had mediumship capacity. She administered some tests: electroencephalograms, also a test to see if I am a genius, because I learned everything very quickly. Her therapy helped me enter into a more spiritual lifestyle. She worked on my 'dis-obsession,' which means she worked on those spirits around me."

"Why would she work on the spirits around you? Can you explain this statement?"

"The spirits are related to me. I was Catholic, but I had Spiritist ideas. I received a cleansing. Then I developed the visual sight of the aura. I could give energy and help to spirits who were suffering on other levels. I wanted to liberate everything and feel myself liberated as well. I began a long journey through regression therapy. I went back into the womb to clear out my problems. I experienced my own regression and catharsis in my birth experiences. This was very good. My equilibrium is because of my mediumship development plus my regression work . . . from here I began to study for mediumship. It was very slow until I had my first incorporation. I began to attract some spirits. . . . "

"Explain how you enter into mediumship trance."

"I work semiconsciously . . . I enter into alpha, and the spirit takes control of my arm, creating spontaneous movements. I feel my person getting less substantiality. I feel a person who is not part of my person . . . I used to be worried about this—what if a negative spirit came? But one day I received, intuitively, a message: Don't worry, let the process flow. I began to have strange happenings. I was guided from books to books, each one connecting with others. All were answering my questions and teaching me, explaining my process . . . now I can incorporate very quickly. I can talk with a spirit without any problem.

"I kept incorporating until I made contact, rapport with my guides, with whom I am now synchronized. My spirit guides include an Egyptian temple priest. He manages my hands during automatic writing. I have another who teaches. Another is a Hindu who practices Tantra. These spirits are fulfilling a plan to help me. I have a Chinese and a Japanese spirit also. I feel very close to Oriental things. I have a relationship with these spirits."

"What do you feel in this relationship?"

"I feel 'will' in my mediumship—a guiding will . . . so these spirits couldn't be genetic memories . . . I have some doubts. These could be unconscious universal mind functions. . . . "

"How do you initiate the mediumship process?"

"I can enter mediumship at any moment . . . first relaxation and I say a prayer or affirmation . . . the prayer is like a mantra and internalizes . . . I repeat it one time . . . then an incorporation takes place."

"You say that you have spirits of other nations. In what languages do they communicate with you?"

"My spirits talk in Portuguese. Sometimes they use words in their own languages. My Chinese spirit talks in Chinese—I don't know if it is, but I believe it to be Chinese—the spirit, should it incorporate in a Brazilian medium, should naturally speak Portuguese so that the medium could understand."

"How do you communicate with your spirits? Do you talk with them?"

"Others speak with spirits. I can't speak with them because I am semiconscious. My mind is controlled by the entity. I can't think anything . . . my ego observes. I see suffering spirits, many painful ones, . . . at the end of the session I feel light, I feel connected, peaceful, in a good place, balanced and very well."

"Have you experienced any special problems related to your work?"

"I don't have any problems when I don't practice mediumship . . . my work for others is heavy . . . a person may have very negative characteristics—depression, nervousness, terrible energies—all of which may be caused by negative spirits. These spirits are around them. They upset the mind, the person becomes crazy, talks strangely, has strange emotions and feelings . . . these persons seek out a medium. I

73

enter into trance, the spirits incorporate into the other mediums present—we work in a group.

"In a past life the spirits who had persecuted a personality return to continue the persecution of the same entity in this life. Once these spirits are indoctrinated, they see the truth and want to evolve on to higher levels. The medium is an educator of the spirits so that they will liberate themselves."

"What about protection from evil spirits? This is a question U.S. New Agers always ask me."

"If you have a good life and a good vibration, you will not attract bad spirits . . . a clairvoyant could see your guardian spirits but could not incorporate them. They could communicate but not incorporate.

" . . . This doesn't mean that you don't have problems, but can manage problems. There are many unbalanced spirits . . . a person must be balanced physically, mentally, and spiritually. I feel very protected from the things that occur. They are fine for me. They don't annoy me, because I feel that all things are lessons. I feel peace. . . . Spiritism has helped me a lot. It awoke me to a lot of theory. It really helped me to feel good with myself."

It was interesting to speak with Sheila. She had a different point of view than other mediums. She attributes this to working with Oriental spirits, who are influenced by Taoist and Buddhist doctrine. Her attitudes of flowing with the mediumship experience, of not worrying about protecting herself, of not judging the experiences as good or bad are very Zenlike. Also, her own inner spiritual work apart from mediumship and her involvement in therapies all contribute to make her a well-balanced medium. I have encountered fanatics among mediums and persons who, despite tremendous gifts, have undeveloped personalities. Dr. Julia told me once that the Federation encourages psychological therapies along with mediumship development. Sheila appeared to be very peaceful inside and therefore attracted creative entities, which helped her be a creative filmmaker and architect, as well as a fine counselor and medium.

Chapter XI
Wandering the Federation Halls

By now I was spending most of my days at the Federation when not interviewing other mediums on the outside. The activities of the São Paulo Federation include classes, service projects, and treatments. I asked one day about the treatment aspects of the Spiritists and was invited to visit some of the sessions on the lower floor of the building, called the "Transitional House." This evidently means that people who are in transition or in need of temporary help visit this floor to be worked on by the spirit mediums. If they need more permanent assistance, they are recommended to other institutions.

As a patient enters the Transitional House, he or she is given a paper to fill out with details of their problem. They are presumed to have sought help previously with medical doctors, psychologists, or others, but to no avail. As a final resort, they seek out the help of Spiritist mediums. After a waiting period, they are invited into one of the side rooms, where they may sit and have their aura cleansed by one of the presiding mediums. Then there is an interview in which it is decided whether the sickness is caused by an obsession or not.

Spirit obsession means that some personality is attached to you, causing some ill affects upon your personality. The treatment may be exorcism, education, or the development of mediumship. Several psychologists told me that many problems are caused within people who don't know that they are mediums and unconsciously sensitive.

If what the patient needs is "energy," he is directed to the appropriate room for treatment. Should the person be obsessed, he enters a different room, where there is, already in a trance, a medium who diagnoses the situation by communicating with the attached spirit. Then there are prayers, readings from the Spiritist books, and exhortations to go on to higher planes. Should the person be in need of healing for physical illness, there is another room, where mediums work in a group. They lay their hands upon the patient for about five minutes while they are in trance state.

All the federations that I visited were filled with people seeking help. Should they need more extensive assistance, they are sent to the hospitals, clinics, or economic agencies, where they receive treatments and practical help.

On the top floor of the Federation is a small library, which contains many old books concerning Spiritism and related mediumship religions, such as Umbanda. The library is often used by others, and the president of the Federation granted me permission to transcend some of the rules of the place. I would often spend several hours reviewing old magazines and tomes from the early days of the Spiritist movement.

Then there were the many discussions held with individual students in the cafeteria. I was informed that Sunday was vegetarian day at the Federation. Several vegetarian members would cook there in order to offer alternatives. Also Esperanto, a universal artificial language was taught there and in all of Brazil, an interesting fact. While this language has lost quite a lot of popularity in the United States and Europe, it is moving along quite well in Brazil. I met several Esperantists in the street and wished to renew my own use of the language.

Chapter XII
An Orixa Incorporates

Santa Cruz, São Paulo

One day I found myself sitting comfortably in the office of a German lady who lived in São Paulo most of her life. She spoke English as well as Portuguese, and I was gratified to have finally found someone who could communicate in my mother tongue. She ran a nonprofit vegetarian organization, which was valiantly striving to show people an alternative way of living. Their library and conference rooms are the finest I have ever seen; the volunteer workers were dedicated to its ideals. The lady in question wanted to meet me, and during the conversation the subject turned to religion and to mediumship, as could be expected in Brazil.

Everyone there is interested in religion. I had never seen so many churches as in Brazil. Each day, as I left my apartment I would pass the traditional Roman Catholic churches, then Methodist, Baptist, and Presbyterian. Then I would see Mahi-kari, Sokka Gakki, and World Messianity. The Greek cathedral, the Assemblies of God, four churches of the Kingdom of God, and more sects than I can remember made my daily walk interesting. It seemed that everyone belonged to something, at least one church each week. Most people went back and forth or created their own belief system, borrowing from the vast diversity that is religion in Brazil.

As our discussion turned to Umbanda, the lady said that a good friend of hers, in fact, a next-door neighbor, had an Umbanda tenda. Should I like to meet her, it could be arranged.

"Of course," I rejoined. "When?"

77

A phone call and a half hour later, an elderly, very dignified Italian-Brazilian woman dressed in black entered the office and greeted her friend and me. We discussed her work in Umbanda and her ideas of the religion. After another half hour, she invited me to come on Wednesday night to visit her congregation.

Mai Zelinda is another typical Euro-Brazilian Umbanda priestess. Fair of skin, she is descended from the Roman Catholic Italians who settled in the southern part of the country and converted to the Umbanda religion. She was trained as a Mai do Santo in the Candomble tradition but finally opted for Umbanda because she resented the animal sacrifices so popular in the African faith. She did not mix very much with other Umbanda priests and objected to those who charged for their services.

Mai Zelinda owned a small restaurant, which maintained her family and her work. The restaurant is situated at the entrance of the terreiro, her house and a very simple Umbanda chapel and auxiliary buildings in the back. It was the poorest center that I had thus far seen, though I was sure that there were others even poorer.

Mai Zelinda wasn't interested in having a large congregation, satisfied in training her twenty or so novices for the Umbanda priesthood. Among her novitiates were university students and young professionals.

Her students ranged in age from eighteen-year-olds to people of advanced years. Two of them were almost through with their religious training and ready to be ordained as Pais, who would go off and found their own chapels. All were from the white middle class.

One disciple, for example, was a public accountant, socially correct and very successful by day. However, few of his clients knew that the man who labored over their books was an Umbanda priest in the evening!

One of the younger participants told me his own very interesting story. Deeply involved in drug abuse, he had seen the error that was his life and began seeking a spiritual path. Raised as a Catholic, he found no solace. He then investigated the Protestant groups and some esoteric societies, but finally encountered the path to his fulfillment in the Umbanda.

I asked him how a "white" teenager could fulfill his needs in the Umbanda. He said, "In the world of spirits there are no Blacks and

Whites." A refreshing comment, for it sounded like a modern-day Guru Nanak declaring, "Before God there are no Muslims or Hindus!"

One Saturday night I was invited to Mai Zelinda's Umbanda center to anticipate and also to film the incorporation service of Orixa Ogun, who, as we previously learned, is called in the Roman Catholic church by the name of Saint George. It was near his feast day and a special observance was scheduled, with only a few people invited other than the novitiates.

It should be made clear that an orixa is not an ordinary spirit, but rather a universal characteristic, an archetype and aeon, one of the archangels. In the Candomble and Umbanda theology, an orixa is the closest that one can get to God, Olorum. It was a special energy which was to be incorporated that evening.

Mai Zelinda's tenda was decorated quite differently from that of Mai Neusa's. The sanctuary was prepared with candles, flowers, and an abundance of statues of the saints. This one tended to express its African Candomble influence, perhaps because Mai Zelinda was trained in the Afro-Brazilian tradition.

The altar stood at the very center, in the front of the *gira* area, separated from the rest of the chapel by a white drape and a wooden barrier.[1] The altar itself was made up of three levels, with Jesus on the topmost peak, then a mixture of orixas, with caboclos and preto velhos on the main level. On either side of the altar were other statues, including one of an old Negro man dressed in street clothes who was the spirit patron of this congregation. Finally, under the altar sat the mysterious Yemanja, the Goddess Mother of all, surrounded by salt water and enveloped in darkness, a single candle in front of her.

Mai Zelinda typically incorporates several spirits, but this night she would dedicate herself only to Ogun, becoming his *cavalho* ("horse"). This meant that she would serve as the human instrument which the energy would mount and by which he would express himself. She entered the room, enveloped in a traditional Bahian dress, her head wrapped in a white scarf, and performed the fumacao (smoking the chapel), so as to seal it from any interloping spirits.

All along, there were drums and singing. I recalled that there were no drums in Mai Neusa's chapel. Finally the dancing began. One visitor, invited from the northern Candomble, was visibly moved, and within a few moments she entered into trance state. The dancing quickened and Mai Zelinda herself fell to the floor and was unconscious.

Something had come through. Mai Zelinda rose from the floor; her physical stance was completely changed. Her gait was more decisive and masculine. Her body began to shake, and soon she was whirling around, apparently without direction. She whirled faster and soon began to make noises, the shriek of the orixa as it broke through into consciousness!

She was touching the other novitiates, imparting axe, giving them energy. Two began to enter into trance; one of them was the accountant.

Suddenly I was smiling to myself. Imagine an accountant going into trance. It seemed so ridiculous. I thought of some of my friends who are accountants in New York. I had to keep myself from laughing out loud as I mentally projected them onto the floor of the chapel, shrieking and whirling around. I hope that I am not offending any accountants, but, hey, it was funny.

This one, however, was quite involved in the gira. Later on I spoke with his wife about his double life. She shared my mirth.

"All day he sits behind his desk, attending to his clients. Then at night he takes off his suit and is suddenly transported into the land of the spirits. It doesn't hurt his business though."

Mai Zelinda was now walking around the chapel, ordering everyone around. She was quite bossy, commanding her assistants to carry out her orders. As she looked at me, I noticed that her eyes were unfocused, she seemed to be using trance vision. As I looked back, I had the feeling that I was looking at someone else.

Finally it was time to pay homage to Ogun, who was working through Mai Zelinda. We lined up waiting to be touched by the sword she carried. The sword is one of the mystical instruments used by the orixa to convey *axe* to those who approach him.[2] She stood there, warriorlike and regal.

As I approached her to pay homage to the incorporated divinity, she first touched my shoulders with the sword. Though the touch was very light and symbolic, I felt a powerful electrical charge run through my body. Then, to my surprise, she embraced me, lifting me up off the floor!

I had the distinct feeling that I was, in fact, in the arms of a very powerful warrior, not an elderly grandmother. The charge, it seems, left me somewhat pliable, though not weak—perhaps a little bit shocked. Perhaps that was why she could lift me up so easily. I had been hugged by a Mai before, in a friendly way, but tonight it was like a wrestler's hug, and she did not seem to notice that I hugged her back.

When she put me down, I looked up into her eyes, and her face appeared angular. She continued her ministrations, moving around like an athlete does, on the balls of her feet.

After homage, Mai's entire character changed. Mai became like a four-year-old, running around the chapel, fight with the children, and babbling like any normal child of that age. In fact, at the same moment, the other two mediums changed as well. The voices of the three of them became high-pitched, like those of children. They became *crianzas* (child-spirits).

It is difficult to understand the concept behind the crianza. This is not unknown in the Orient where the belief is that God, in order to satisfy his creation's longings for love, appears in many forms. In the Mahabarata, he appears to women as a child so that they can love him as such; in the Bhagavad-Gita, he appears as a warrior or teacher. The same may be said for the orixa. Some people can love him as pure spirit, but very few. Therefore he may manifest at times like a mysterious neutral spirit, at others like a little child, and at others according to his traditional roles, in this case as a warrior. Thus he may associate with his worshippers as they understand him best and love him even more.

As a crianza, Mai Zelinda was wild, running around, touching everything and squealing with delight, so convincingly that she was often difficult to be around. The worshippers hugged her and gave her candy, which she would stuff in her mouth or give to the other children. The little children especially liked her as a crianza and laughed with her. Soon she was running on the chairs, rolling on the floor, and acting like a spoiled brat. There was one moment when I wanted to swat her. Of course, I didn't. She was, after all, really an eternal being, and I would take no chances with my salvation.

I was amazed at this large, heavy woman running around the room. Beset by physical problems due to her age, she seemed to forget all about them. She would throw herself onto the ground, roll around, and do things which no seventy-year-old I know would do. When she fell down, she didn't even try to protect herself. I feared that she would get hurt, but I was told by her husband that she is never injured in these sessions.

At one point, my cameraman, who was German and spoke English, yelled something to me. The crianza immediately stopped short and squealed at her friends, "What did he say, I don't understand." The people tried to explain to her that we were speaking in English, a language which she had never heard. She asked us to say something else and then broke into the cutest laughter when we spoke. When they explained to her that it was "a different tongue." She wanted to see our tongues to see how different they were from hers.

The crianza did not want to disincorporate when the time came. She acted as a petulant child would when her parents tell her to go to bed. She had to be coaxed back into the spirit world. As the novices sang the traditional farewell song, the crianza disappeared and Mai Zelinda began to shake. She was caught by her assistants and laid down upon the floor. In a few moments, she was up again, but this time she was only Mai Zelinda.

The service then concluded with the litany of thanks to the spirits, to Jesus, and to God for his protection. Then the curtain was closed as the final hymn was being chanted, and Mai passed out the altar flowers to those of us who had the privilege of being present.

When the medium Zelinda came out of trance, she was quite rested and energetic. She asked to see the video when it was ready. She couldn't believe that she romped around the room so, a woman in her seventies. She laughed and thought that the entire service was quite comical.

Notes

1. gira: Sacred ceremonial dance
2. axe: Grace, power, energy

Chapter XIII
Mediumship: Definitions, Classifications, and Paradigms

"But what," one asks, "is so interesting and important about materializations, rapport and psychoenergetic phenomena?" . . . In the light of present scientific knowledge, such phenomena cannot exist. They violate what science knows about the material universe. (2)

By now my wanderings had taken me around the city of São Paulo, the stronghold of Spiritism and one of the largest centers of Umbanda. This was the final week of my stay before I would travel north and eastward to encounter the Candomble and other forms of mediumship religion.

Due to discussions with my new friends, Cleobe, Sheila, and Julia, mediums at the Federation, and Mais Neusa and Zelinda, I was finally beginning to understand what mediumship was about. Still, I wasn't completely satisfied with my information. I had only scratched the surface and decided to consult with some of the authorities in the field who were investigators.

One day I made an appointment to visit with Dr. Marlene Nobre, the psychiatrist daughter of one of the great lights of Spiritism in the center being used by the Spiritist-Medical Association of Brazil. The Spirita-Medica, as it is known, was created for scientific investigation of mediumship and spirit phenomena. Its members meet several times a year locally, and once a year nationally, to present information on holistic medicine, transpersonal psychology, and reports by reliable investigators on items under study. The association is open to doctors of all kinds, as well as therapists and others with a scientific foundation interested in delving deeper into this field.

Dr. Nobre, who, besides being the mother of a family and counselor and volunteer at several Spiritist clinics, is the president of the Spirita-Medica Association. I wanted to get some orientation from her. It was hard to get an interview with her, but Dr. Nezo pleaded and begged on my behalf, and an hour's time was granted.

Dr. Nobre was very tired, but gave the time as promised. She was a very spiritual person and discussed with me her own venture into mediumship and the peace that it gave her. Over the hour, which ran too quickly, she related her experiences into a web of soul-enriching stories, but finally our time was up. Before I left, she advised me to read all the relevant research reported in the journal of the association.

I was later introduced to the famous Dr. Hernani Andrade, considered to be the foremost investigator of Spiritism and psychic phenomena in Brazil. Dr. Andrade's ancient and cluttered office is located in an old building in Santa Cruz, a downtown sector of São Paulo. After phoning him, we were invited to visit him the following day.

Upon our arrival we were treated to Brazilian tea and chocolates. He told us that all of his American guests loved the chocolates that his country produces, and so he always kept a box on hand. Filled with tea and stuffed with chocolate, I sat back like a satisfied young son to listen to this man of dedication and wisdom.

Dr. Andrade first showed me the famous scientists, psychologists, and others who visited him. He mentioned names, which were household names among the psychic and paranormal community, like Krippner, Carl Rogers, Plutarich, and others. They visited him from everywhere: New York, California, Kansas, and North Carolina.

Dr. Andrade had arranged for Madame Elsie Dubras, a Scotswoman who was born and raised in Brazil and spoke several languages, to be present. She was instrumental in introducing me to one of São Paulo's greatest mediums, Antonio Gerardo de Padua.

Dr. Andrade has written several very serious books, one entitled *Ten Cases of Reincarnation in Brazil*; the other, *Biological Organizing Model*. Along with these two and many others, we were finally packed off with our treasures, not only grateful for the wisdom, but for the chocolates we took back with us.

Brazilian Spiritistic culture has many outstanding authorities who have profoundly studied mediumship and offer us some definitions based upon research and observation of dozens of cases. One of the most serious and respected investigators is psychiatrist and author Dr.

Eliezer C. Mendes. Dr. Mendes arrived at his understanding of the concepts of mediumship through long years of clinical investigation, which he calls "clinical parapsychology." In this book, *Intrusive Personalities*, he defines mediumship:

> Mediumship is a condition of a living soul when it enters into contact with the vibrations which come from other souls, either found on this physical plane or those who have passed on to the plane of disincarnate spirits. (14)

It is quite interesting to note that his definition includes the capacity to access souls who are not yet dead. Telepathic communication, for example, between two living persons is within the scope of his definition. He states elsewhere that all people have the gift of mediumship and that animals have it as well. Thus mediumship appears to be an invisible network of communication between all human and animal entities.

While living in São Paulo and studying at the Spiritist Federation, I read investigations and articles about supposed cases of animal mediumship. However, it is not to be assumed that all Spiritualists support these theoretical ideas.

While universal mediumship is generally accepted as doctrine by Spiritists, many Candomble and Umbanda mediums deny this. Mai Neusa and many others answered that although mediumship is a growing phenomenon it was not, as yet, the common gift of all humanity, but the special attribute of certain conditioned souls. Many people reported mediumship; however, what they were experiencing was not a spiritual linkup, but the latent powers of their own minds. Mediumship, defined by these people, is a working, conscious relationship between the spirits and the mediums. In fact, not all people "influenced" by spirits were mediums either!

The founder of Spiritism affirmed that mediumship, though underdeveloped in most human beings, is a natural gift. Back in the late 1800s, Kardec explained:

> . . . certain persons gifted with a special power or faculty who are called mediums, that is to say, go betweens or intermediaries between spirits and men. The conditions which give this power depend on causes, physical and moral, that are as yet but imperfectly understood, for mediums of all ages, of both sexes, and of every degree of intellectual

development. The faculty of mediumship, moreover, is developed by exercise. (15)

Mediumship in the United States is generally limited to what is called "channeling," or the phenomenon of bringing forth the ideas of the invisible spirits to the level of human communication. Mediumship in Brazil, however, because of its different orientation, helps us learn about the soul and therefore has a much broader range of manifestation. According to famous spirit-surgeon Edivaldo Oliviera Silva, "Mediumship shows what the soul can do."

Dr. Rafael Ranieri, Brazilian psychic investigation, lawyer, and one-time police commissioner, for the state of São Paulo, defines a medium as "an open door to the invisible world."

Professor Newton Boechat, a Brazilian psychic investigator, reminds us that mediumship is much more than mere phenomena. He offers, "It [mediumship] shows that you cannot overlook the moral factor in psychical research."

Brazilian mediumship is interconnected with spiritual factors as well as phenomenological manifestations. It is classified under several categories, among them: incorporation, clairvoyance, physical feats, and materializations. Let us briefly review the definitions of some of them.

Psychographics: Spirit writing. Dr. Carlos Augosto Perandrea, a physician and investigator, wrote a book investigating the phenomenon of spirit-writing, which was channeled through the famous medium Chico Xavier. In his book, *Spirit Writing: Proofs Revealed Through Graphology,* Dr. Perandrea quotes the definition of spirit writing (psychographics) according to Allan Kardec:

> Spirit writing is the transmission of the spirit's thought through writing using the hand of a medium. The medium-writer is the hand and the instrument, but the soul or incarnate spirit is the intermediary or interpreter of the foreign spirit who desires to communicate. (16)

Xavier was a practitioner of this type of mediumship for more than forty years. Dr. Perandrea compared the style of writing channeled from persons on the other side of the veil to the script extant during their earthly lives. He utilizes graphology for this process and, in hundreds of cases, found an uncanny resemblance between the channeled script of the presumably dead and that of letters they left behind when they died.

Incorporation: According to Edgar Armond in his book, *Mediumship,* incorporation entails a direct encounter with spirits, similar to meeting a friend in the street. In this encounter, spirit entities act, speak and live for a period of time through the medium's body. Mr. Armond describes incorporation as one of the most interesting forms of mediumship:

> . . . it helps us to have direct and personal understanding with the spirits. It facilitates the possibility of learning from them and teaching unconscious spirits who are immersed in mental obscurity, the good as well as the evil ones, helping them to realize acts of spiritual charity . . . (17)

Intuitive: Intuitive mediumship is probably more common than any other form. According to Spiritists, great ideas are impinged upon the minds of most people through the intervention of disincarnate entities. These might be considered original revelations, illuminations, or ideas, but are really influences of higher spirit beings.

Curative: Curative mediumship is a form related to the healing ministry. Channeled through the mediums Francisco Xavier and Waldo Viera, M.D., in their book, *Mediumship Mechanisms,* spirit Andre Luis explains that techniques such as magnetic passes, prayer, fixing of the mind upon the patient, the will of the patient, and the education of that will are all part of curative mediumship. He further instructs that in order to activate all the favorable life-agents, the medium calls upon these spirits to aid and assist him in his healing work. (18)

Transport mediumship is the movement of objects from another place to the presence of the medium. The transported item may be an object or even the medium himself. Key to his form is the medium's capacity to transport his own consciousness to other places, including the spiritual world. To this extent, transport mediumship may be comparable to out-of-body-experiences. It has been rumored that there are mediums who transport their bodies as well, though I have no first-hand knowledge of this phenomenon.

Materialization consists of the manipulation of energies to produce things that are apparently real. According to the spirit Emmanuel, as channeled through the medium Chico Xavier and recorded in his spirit-dictated book *Words from Emmanuel:*

Materialization is simply a matter of condensation or reconverting fluidic values and making visible the subtle and intangible. After all, the world itself is one vast long-term materialization phenomena, much of it having previously existed only in men's minds! (18)

In an interview during his incorporation, a spirit known as the "Dutch physician" explained to me that he materialized his medicine through the intervention of ectoplasmic substance; however, he was not able to explain just how this was done. Sai Baba of India is reputed to materialize objects from the air, but the mediums of Brazil affirm that that is done through spirit intervention and not by mental processes.

What all of these types of mediumship have in common is the coparticipation of host mediums with guest spirits. Therefore, while the phenomena manifested during a session might be categorized as "psychic" from a materialistic paradigm, Brazilian mediums, investigators, and spirits would classify them as spirit interventions. Dr. Andrade told me personally that he has never found "psychic phenomena without the presence of an entity."

Taking these various forms of mediumship into consideration, we might arrive at some common ground to explain them. Materialization, writing, healing, etcetera, can all be reduced to some form of information transference; that is, the information is passed by the spirit to the medium's unconscious, as the means by which such phenomenon may occur. Whether the spirit "resides within" the medium, as the Afro-Brazilian religions believe, or are in contact through influence, as the Spiritists teach, at some point the spirit's will is transformed through the agencies of the medium's body and mind to enact this information.

Therefore I offer the following definition:

Mediumship is defined as the art and practice of accessing information and energies, which reside in the more subtle and spiritual worlds, for their manifestation in our human world. Mediumship religions would define these energies and information in a personal way as spirit entities.

This definition is applicable to the cultural and religious models of the mediumistic traditions of Brazil. As we shall see later, they may not be applicable to the models developed in the Soviet Union or the United States.

Mediumship has long existed in the forms of European witchcraft, Semitic-Hamitic religions, Chaldean practices, and animalistic shamans since the dawn of thinking man. As a result of the table-rapping of the Fox sisters in early nineteenth century Rochester, New York, the Spiritualist movement was born. It purports to prove the existence of a spiritual world and a life after death and uses such spirit phenomena as ectoplasm, writing, materializations, and messages as the means of substantiating these claims. The movement quickly spread to Europe and South America, where it is much stronger today than in its homelands.

Scientific investigation began by the study of the phenomenology of mediumship. This gave birth to the discipline of parapsychology, a field of study that was greatly influenced by the philosophical necessities of the culture that the investigators served.

The first model of phenomenology was developed in what was then the Soviet Union, where a purely dialectic materialist model was approved by the state. Investigators were almost totally state-funded, and their investigations ran under the official control of the Academy of Sciences. Due to political pressures applied upon the new science, it was assumed that the findings would substantiate the psychic quality of the human brain rather than the spiritual aspect of related phenomena. The Soviet model, as a result, totally excluded the problem of the existence and survival of the soul.

The United States and Western Europe originally adhered to a Spiritualistic model, which accepted the survival of the soul and the possibility of spirit phenomena. The Society for Psychical Research in both England and the United States seriously studied spirit mediumship and spirit phenomena as realities. In the 1930s a shift occurred, principally caused by the Rhines at Duke University. This shift was directed away from spirit phenomena and toward the powers inherent in man. Presently, however, there is a resurgence of serious interest in the transpersonal notions of man, survival after death, and the mediumship phenomena and their possible relationship to spirit entities. This is the emergence of the current neoSpiritualist model.

Brazil represents yet a third model. The Spiritist model fully accepts such paranormal phenomena as mediumship manifestation as proof of another spiritual world, postmortem survival, and communication with spirit entities. Spiritism, codified by Kardec and brought to Brazil at the beginning of this century, has three aspects: the religious, the philosophic, and the scientific. This third aspect resulted in scientific investigations leading to the establishment of proofs that appeared to verify Spiritist parameters.

The defining characteristics of the Spiritist model are that it proposes a spiritual element within human beings, which permits the interaction of energy fields between physical and spiritual materials. This model, then, incorporates its scientific studies into religion and philosophy. Perhaps this could occur only in Brazil, whose religious soil was saturated by Roman Catholicism and African tradition. Both systems prepared the soil of belief with a preference for saints, miracles, and spiritual beings.

In an opposite way, the Soviet Union officially tried to eliminate such beliefs in order to confirm the established dialectic materialism of the Communist state, and so its scientific explanation had to work within the materialist framework. Brazil was already imbued with both native and imported mysteries and perhaps conducted its exploration so that its results verified psychologically self-fulfilling channels of thought. Prof. Hernani G. Andrade, engineer and Brazil's most famous psychic investigator seems to think so. He states:

> The Brazilian face establishes a close connection of the scientific aspects of Spiritism with the Parapsychology, principally with the ancient metaphysics brought to Brazil at the beginnings of this century. (19)

In summary, then, we have three models for mediumistic phenomena: the dialectic materialist model, the neoSpiritualist model, and the Spiritist model. It is through this third model that we now proceed to understand mediumship and the incorporation process.

A final thought. I learned that the spirit Miramez stated repeatedly in his communication, "The Fullness of Mediumship," that the final purpose of the mediumistic process is the moral regeneration of the human race. (6) This regenerative process was to be fulfilled through a close association with the spirit world. Thus, mediumship was no less than a moral obligation by which incarnates would cooperate with the invisible world for the reform and transformation of our own. A mighty task indeed!

Chapter XIV
Intense Talks with a Medium and His Spirit Guide

Two days after my interview with Dr. Andrade, I was invited to the office of Mrs. Elsie Dubras. She is a long-term reporter for the *O Planeta* magazine, which is dedicated to the dissemination of articles on psychic, spiritual, and Spiritualistic phenomena. The *Planeta* had a wide circulation throughout Brazil. Its interviews are often helpful in ascertaining the possibilities and whereabouts of who's who in the spirit world.

Mrs. Dubras told me of her experiences and the many mediums in Brazil and also mentioned that many years ago she was the "discoverer" of the famous medium-painter, Luis Gasparetto. Mr. Gasparetto is well known in the United States due to the publicity accorded him by Shirley Mclaine.

After about an hour together, I requested a list of those mediums whom she felt worthy to visit in Brazil. She immediately mentioned two of them: Antonio Gerardo de Padua of Sorocaba, a city about one hour's distance from São Paulo, and Mai Santinha of Bahia. I noted their names, then questioned Mrs. Dubras on how to contact Pai Antonio.

She said that this was not the easiest thing to do. She would have to call him indirectly through a series of intermediaries, one of whom would then contact him directly. Also, it seemed that Pai Antonio was not too fond of publicity, being much overworked. She did not hold out much hope of getting an appointment in less than a week. By then, I informed her, I would be finishing up my research in São Paulo and would be traveling northward to Bahia for investigations of the Candomble.

As we sat there thinking of what we could do about this situation, the telephone rang. When Mrs. Dubras answered it, she began to look at me quite mischievously, as if making a joke out of me. Then she covered the mouthpiece and told me that it was Pai Antonio Gerardo, who was calling her "on a whim," that she "might just have something important to suggest to him." She formally introduced me to him, which must have piqued his interest, for he instructed her to invite me to visit his church on the coming Wednesday. There we would meet and discuss certain themes of mutual interest.

Of course I would accept his invitation to visit, and the appointment was confirmed. Since today was Monday, I had to make plans to get out there within a day. Elsie told me how "lucky" his telephone call was and how lucky I was to be invited personally by Pai Antonio, as he is quite shy in these things. On the way out, Elsie loaded me down with magazine articles concerning the Umbanda and Candomble religions plus articles that she wrote concerning several of the mediums whom she had encountered.

One of her stories interested me a lot. She had made a trip to Bahia to visit the seer Mai Santinha, who creates honey out of roses. I will include my own episode with her later on, but the interesting thing here is that after observing the medium in deep trance, Elsie asked the Mai if she could transfer this gift to others. Mai Santinha, who was still in trance then put her hand on Elsie's shoulder and gave her a rose. Elsie was then able to change the rose into honey as well! At the conclusion of the interview, Elsie opened her desk door and showed me the small vial of honey which she produced. I was very impressed and vowed to visit this Mai Santinha, no matter where she lived.

Wednesday came quickly. I invited a friend to accompany me, as he spoke Portuguese and Spanish and could therefore serve as translator. We met at the Sorocaba bus terminal and traveled by city bus to the temple where Pai Antonio performed his Wednesday night activities.

We arrived early and stopped to buy new batteries for our tape recorder. One hour before the service began, people began to line up in front of the church to get seats. By the time the doors opened, there were several hundred people present, coming for purification and healing of disease. I learned that people from all over the continent came to attend service at this temple. The word was out that this was a very special healer.

I was getting somewhat anxious because the service would begin at seven-thirty: it was already six-thirty, leaving only an hour for an interview.

At that moment the medium arrived. I sent in my introduction note. To my surprise, an assistant told me that the Pai would attend me as soon as possible but that he had to sweep up the temple and wash the pews first!

By seven o'clock I was almost hysterical, thinking that there would be no interview at all. Then the door opened and a messenger asked me to enter, Pai Antonio would be glad to attend to me now.

Antonio Gerardo de Padua was a young man of thirty years, quite presentable and soft spoken. Very enthusiastic in his work, he presided over a Spiritist group called the Universalist Temple of Jesus Christ. His use of the term, "universalist," he explained, was to indicate the he is neither bound nor indebted to any of the mediumship religions and is free from their organizations. In his services, he used elements from Candomble, Umbanda, Kardecism, and what he calls the "New Age."

This was reflected in his temple. He was especially enthusiastic in telling me that under the floor of the temple, there is a bottle of water from the Ganges River. He also had crystals and other esoteric items. The church building itself appeared to be a Christian temple, with a small steeple on the roof. Inside, instead of a cross, was a sacred vase of the Candomble which was illuminated at night. This is his "power vase" which contained objects sacred to the Candomble religion.

Upon entering the church, one was confronted by a long rectangular sanctuary with a life-sized statue of Jesus with children standing against the front wall. One might think he was in a Christian church but for the statues of the principal orixas of the Umbanda and Candomble above the door. To make matters more confusing, there are representations of caboclos, preto velhos, a painting of an American Indian guide, and other objects representing different religions. No wonder his temple is called "Universalist!"

Pai Antonio is one of the few mediums with whom I enjoyed talking. He lacked the pretentiousness so often found in so many mediums. The people call him Pai Antonio—an infraction in Spiritist circles, where Afro-Brazilian words should not be used. But then, Antonio is a functioning eclectic.

Antonio de Padua channels several spirits, including a Native North American. His most recent and famous spirit incorporations centered around Pai Guillerme, who in spirit form granted me an interview, which I taped. That was my first long interview with a channeled spirit, and the spirit was as enthusiastic about it as I was.

Antonio told me that Pai Guillerme was very intelligent and cultured in his last life and enjoyed speaking with his equals. He often got tired of the seances and their proceedings, with people constantly beseeching favors, and was looking forward to a nice chat with me.

"Why not," my own spirit smirked at me. "What's so unusual about sitting down with a disembodied being and chatting for an hour?"

Pai Antonio had an even more famous spirit who worked through him, Dr. Clayton, a Dutch surgeon. They performed outside the temple on Friday nights. Dr. Clayton did not like to work inside the temple, being a nonbeliever in organized religion, and felt better working under the open sky.

Elsie Dubras showed me photos that she took of Antonio as he channeled Dr. Clayton. In several of the photos, a string of luminous pearls stood close to the medium. In others there was a flash of light around him as he worked. This was Dr. Clayton. I was quite impressed with the photos and am sure that Mrs. Dubras had not touched them up. There was nothing for her to gain as her investigations are honest and upright.

As I looked around the sanctuary, I noticed that among the several hundred people who come for his ministrations, there were many Europeans who flew in to consult with him. By now his novices were filing in, most of whom were under thirty years old. It was the youngest group of students I had seen in a tenda.

There was one elderly woman, a Candomble Mai, among them. Then there were several teenagers of about fifteen to sixteen years old. In all there were forty novitiates, quite a large group to work with. This group, however, had all the idealism and enthusiasm of youth. They were playful and at the same time interested in the work that they were doing. They were the ones, Antonio's followers, who built this temple.

I was ushered up to the front of the temple to a seat off the gira floor, which was separated from the pews by a barrier. The uninitiated are not allowed to come forward except by invitation. Upon the floor was a tile, beneath which were deposited many of his power objects: stones from different parts of the world, crystals, holy water, etcetera.

The drums were on the left side of the gira floor, and there was also an electric organ for hymns.

Services at the temple differed from one to the next. Sometimes they were strictly Spiritist, then Umbanda, often eclectic to suit the needs of the visiting spirit. Dr. Clayton, I was told, being a Dutch Protestant abhorred the rituals while Pai Guillerme, a Brazilian Catholic, was quite comfortable with them.

When Pai Guillerme incorporates in the medium, the medium is dressed in a robe and has a paper crown on his head. His voice becomes deeper, and he speaks with a Portuguese accent from earlier times. I received psychic passes from the Pai but cannot affirm to have experienced anything. Others, however, cried, some trembled, and still others fell out on the floor.

I received some special attention from Pai Guillerme and asked him questions, most of which were recorded. I was informed that the Pai was a Brazilian physician who practiced abortion and other surgical matters for the rich. He is now trying to undo his karma by giving his time to those who need it.

It is often confusing to comprehend the philosophy of the various spirits. They teach reincarnation as a doctrine of the faith and yet feel that they must return through a medium rather than reincarnate. Most spirits seem to be quite doctrinal in their beliefs, accepting by faith these ideas.

It was now seven-thirty, and I was feeling quite conspicuous. I asked Antonio if perhaps he should start the service. He told me that the interview was too important and interesting to allow two hundred people to interfere. He then laughed and we continued talking.

"Please begin," I asked Antonio, "to talk about your mediumship history."

"I had two major periods of mediumship. First my incorporations were unconscious. Now I leave from my body. I project myself outside of this world into the spirit world and participate in work there as well as here. . . . Many times I go away from here. I project myself outside. Then another entity works with my body. Each day I work with another spirit. I must work with each in a different way. . . . "

"As I travel around the world I notice that among the many healers, not all of those seeking cures are actually cured. What about here in your temple?

"About fifty percent of the people get cured. The spirits don't cure anyone. They carry the possibility of the cure. They don't pretend to cure. About three of every six persons cure here . . . the people seek my help after they are already advanced. They come after they have used up the avenues of medical treatment. . . . Also they have usually spent all of their resources. When the people come at the last minute, they are very complex, and it is very difficult to help them. The spirits do their job, but that doesn't mean that the patient will respond. . . . The spirits work slowly and organize the material which is disorganized. Personal will, dedication, karma, unfoldment are important to cure the body. . . .

"There is a law, very clear in the spiritual world, that the spirits, from the moment they enter into the spirit world, continue living and doing things the way they were accustomed to on earth. Scientists, for example, continue to be scientists. Upon leaving behind the human baggage there is no guarantee that they advance mentally or otherwise. In Brazil there are many spirits who work with scalpels. They did this because they don't know another procedure, such as dismaterialization. They use traditional methods with spiritual understanding. . . .

"A medium exists as a modulator that maintains and registers various frequencies, depending upon how he manages lowering and raising the frequencies . . . a person who is uneducated, but is a medium, will carry his cultural structure into his visions . . . he will create dogmas. He creates layers of belief. In the spiritual world, therefore, he is attracting levels which correspond to him . . . some mediums therefore are stratified, very wishy-washy, molded, and confined, and will attract simple-minded spirits of like mind, who will feed them on *earthly* views of the spiritual world. The medium learns nothing, the spirit knows nothing to teach and the listeners learn nothing either. But some people believe their nonsense to be the truth." The Pai Antonio dumped a barrage of information on me.

"Do you mean that a spirit who worked in a limited way as a human being would continue to work the same way? For example, a medical surgeon would continue to be dedicated to his techniques?"

"Yes," he answered. "Many spirits don't learn anything new in the other life. They cling to their earth memories and studies and don't let go. These they communicate to mediums on earth."

"Antonio, what do you learn from your mediumship?"

"Some water falls from heaven into a hole and goes nowhere, some water is absorbed into a sponge. I learn something every day from the spirits, but other mediums learn nothing. They teach me each day. I have learned a lot about people, about human activity and nature . . . it is important for us to realize that we are on the planet to develop consciousness, not just to breathe, visit, eat, etcetera. The spirits give me the opportunity for analysis for self-evaluation to develop my self-understanding. . . .

"Each day I have to live with people who are in problems. We have national karmas, family and individual karmas, all of which are often desperate. The spirits help me to understand my presence on earth. Once understood, the student appears. As says Andres Luis, a spirit of Chico Xavier, once the servant is willing, the service can be given. We are prepared to serve. We are on earth to serve."

"Why, in Brazil, are the spirits so important? They are often worshipped instead of God."

" . . . it is true, we must remember that all the spirits are incarnated and each will respond in his own way. We can go directly to God, so that He may do the work. The spirits are not exactly intermediaries. They are cooperators. We live in the same city, but we divide people into groups—i.e., spirits and people. That is the problem. Spirits, through their incorporations, aren't intermediaries but cooperating beings as if they were here on earth . . . spirit friends are here to help. Some people see them as saints to be worshipped. But they are here to serve and help us, as if they were on earth. . . . "

"What about the teachers from the other religions?"

"Many illumined beings have come to earth; Jesus and Buddha among them. Jesus gave us the bases of the superior spiritual world. Buddha is more connected to Oriental philosophy; the practices and modes of living are ingrained over millennia and are part of the culture. . . . We don't have many foreign cults nor contacts with many Oriental cultures. So we are limited."

"You have said several times that this temple is universalist. Can you explain this better?"

"The spirits at this temple are freer than in others. They don't follow prestructured systems. We try to avoid being identified with other medium systems. We are universalists . . . The people come for spiritual operations . . . unfortunately, the majority don't seek wisdom . . . people seem to resist change . . . perhaps for each thousand who come, there is one who understands, and for that one we wait and serve. I don't get discouraged."

"Why are there so many rituals? Are they really necessary?"

"Some spirits use no rituals. One of mine, who is Dutch, uses no rituals at all. We go to another place, since he won't work in a temple, like this. Other spirits want all the rituals. Are rituals needed? No, they are not. Nothing is needed for the spirits. The rites are support services. The people need them. The people, if they don't see things, they won't believe. Like the placebo of medicine. They help the person psychologically . . . but these things, the people can't understand. The spirits understand this. But the people don't want to comprehend. We could eliminate all of this today, and the people will still receive help. But the public expects the rites, and complains and loses faith if they don't have them. The spirits do their part, the people do theirs.

"The spirits work in deobsession on the patient while the patient should be working on selfobsession. To do this they use support aids. The Catholic loves rituals; the Brazilian loves rituals. Spiritual communion has become materialized. But it is not needed to be so. No, no rituals are necessary. Dr. Clayton is from a Protestant country, and he hates rituals . . . one hundred ninety-three spirits incorporate here and in the astral plane to help out at our temple. . . . "

By this time it was eight o'clock and our interview was ending. Pai Antonio told me to stay and have a direct interview with Pai Guillerme during the service. He introduced me to his wife, who was told to explain to the spirit why I was here and to introduce us formally. He then went to dress for the occasion.

The service began with an introduction, a few prayers, and then the drums and sacred dances. The young novices danced with enthusiasm and, little by little, entered into states of dizziness, rather than trance. This was later affirmed by the spirit guide as true. Quite a few of the young men appeared to be in trance and were vivaciously embracing the prettier female mediums. I was somewhat suspicious of their motives but found it entertaining to watch.

Two lines of mediums were formed, and the several hundred visitors were invited to pass among them to receive exorcism. I was invited to join the line and found myself being touched by the mediums. First, you must understand, the singing was continuous and quite attractive. Then you came into contact with the first mediums, who jumped in the air, screamed, and made passes over you. Then you continued up the line, where others did the same. Finally you entered the presence of Pai Guillerme/Antonio, who casts out the obsessive entities.

All around me were people crying, falling on the floor. I observed, oddly, that during all this, nothing was happening to me or to my friend, Marvin. We came with no expectations and so learned that the emotional energies around us were obviously not contagious.

When I got to Pai, I was told to stand beside him, as he would like to talk with me. He said that I could ask him anything that I wanted and he would explain, within his limited understanding, whatever he could.

Ah, here, I thought, *is an unpretentious spirit.* Pai Guillerme was not one of those know-it-alls, like I had met in other places. In fact, it turned out that the spirit had as many questions as I did!

I found Pai Guillerme's stare and carriage to be aristocratic, that of a well-born person. He was also quite direct as he spoke with me and was willing to converse on all subjects. I had little problem understanding his accent. My first question was direct and to the point. "Where are you now in relationship to the medium?"

Every group had given me the official line about the medium/spirit relationship. Perhaps now I would learn something.

" . . . this medium has the faculty of astral projection. The dominant spirit is at his side, united with him . . . I am inside his body. I am fused with him . . . the cerebral cortex and the pineal gland are the major mediumistic centers . . . I feel somewhat uncomfortable entering into the medium's limits. I feel the anomalies of the person, which are unfamiliar to me . . . We see the physical body as well as the emanations, the chakras, plexus, aura. We detect the sicknesses in the aura. . . . "

"When not incorporated in the medium, where do you live?"

"I don't as yet live in the higher spiritual worlds. I still live near the earth strata, which has many incorporated spirits with earthly desires and aspirations, These spirits are very materiallike, yet still have forms, feel heat and cold as if they were incarnated. . . . "

"How do the spirits evolve?"

"We evolve by serving others. We can also serve in the astral world in the temples, in healing . . . the inhabitants of astral planes are often millions of times worse than earth beings . . . we have about thirty billion inhabitants in the astral plane . . . half of them need urgent help in morals and the benefit of other enlightened beings . . . more than half are in low consciousness."

"The spirits often talk about Jesus. Why do they not mention the other teachers?"

"The name of Jesus is an example. Here in Brazil we speak of Jesus because he is well-known. When we speak in the Orient, we use other examples. We refer to a spirit who is better known to the people, because they may lack information about Jesus. There are differences between Jesus and Buddha. However, we us them as examples. . . . "

"What part of the medium's brain do you use during contact?"

"If the medium projects himself into the astral, we don't have to touch the content of his brain. The majority of the mediums present have their spirits at their side, connected through the pineal gland . . . they are in semiconscious trance."

We talked about many things and I found the spirit to be quite congenial. I would have liked to invite him out for pizza and continue our discussion, but I supposed that was not within spiritistic protocol.

Our time drew to a close. Pai Guillermo gave me a hug, which was exceptionally warm, and our paths parted. He encouraged me to continue with my research and told me that I was being guided. As I was about to leave, the spirit touched me and added, "Doctor Dennis, your work will be surrounded by success because your country isn't free yet from dogma, superstition, fanatical religiosity; *Your people still do not understand respect for transcendence.* Be assured that your work will be very well accepted, since you work seriously and are not given to banalities and superficialities. For this reason your work is progressing perfectly and will be very well accepted."

Transcendence, to me, means that condition of "suchness" of which the Buddhists speak. It is the "beyondness" of life—beyond doctrine and dogma, beyond the practice and the vehicle. It implies freedom from being stuck in any one form, of being liberated and free. It means the purity of oneness and the uniting of the part with the whole. I remember a talk I once gave at a Spiritualist church, where I spoke of "oneness." One listener said, "Not that again. Tell us about the spirits who participated in the sessions."

When I lived in Virginia Beach, a town flooded by mediums of every type and sort, I found it very rare indeed to meet a person who had a direct relationship with the universe, with God. Instead, people seemed to cling to the intermediaries, divided over the personalities and teachings of their mediums, grasping at the branches, wholly unconscious of the *root*. I was reminded of the Tower of Babel, where people ran aimlessly about, each yelling in his own tongue something that no one could understand. But then, everyone was so wrapped up in his own opinion that none could take the time to listen to another. Perhaps this is the lack of respect for transcendence of which the spirit told me.

An important final communication of the spirit Pai Guillerme was for me to seek guidance from another medium, Dr. Valdo Viera, in another city. Pai Guillerme asked for a piece of paper, laid his hand on it and gave it to me. He said that the paper was impregnated with a message and that the medium could read it.

When, at last, I met Dr. Viera, he knew from whom the message came and what its content was. This was my first example of psychic mail.

I hadn't time to discuss Pai Guillerme's final message to me. To this day I am still attempting to learn what was imparted in it.

Chapter XV
How the Spirit Gets Inside

Two will rest on the bed: the one will die, and the other will live.
                                    —Gospel of Thomas (20)

We now traveled north to a third major city of Brazil, Belo Horizonte, armed with letters of introduction to the Federation in that locale. I planned to stay only one week in that city, and the Federation was helpful. My purpose was to visit the Spiritist Psychiatric Hospital. The Federation secretary telephoned the head of the hospital, Dr. Roberto Lucio, and a meeting for the next day was immediately arranged.

The hospital is quite a large affair, with several hundred patients. It is the oldest in the nation, named after Andres Luis, a medical doctor and Spiritist who pioneered work with the mentally disturbed. He is now believed to be an enlightened spirit, aiding research from the other side.

The doctors and others who work there are mainly Spiritists who donate their time as volunteers for a minimum wage. The doctors, especially, give several hours of dedicated time each day and then work in their own clinics. If Spiritism needed no other proof than this, that it could motivate medical doctors to donate half of their day to volunteer work, it would be enough to convert me. I was continually amazed at the level of service which I found among the Spiritists. It was quite inspiring to me. If our own mediums could see this, it would create a revolution in the New Age.

At the front door we presented ourselves at reception, and Dr. Lucio soon came to receive us. A young man, he gave the impression of being as equally dedicated to his spiritual work as to his psychiatric responsibilities. After showing us around the hospital and discussing his therapeutic philosophy, he called a meeting, attended by some twenty administrators and doctors. We discussed the differences between mediumistic states and mystical awareness, pathology, and the root of spirit intervention. Of all the themes, we spoke the most of the spirit/medium relationship. In some religions, this is commonly called "riding the medium," as a person rides a horse. In proper terms, this is called spirit "incorporation," a word of Latin origin meaning "inside the body"; in Brazil, the term *incorporacao* is referred to in all of the Spiritist literature as such.

Incorporation is the intimate relationship derived from the intermingling of an invisible spirit with the medium's nervous apparatus. The entity dominates the functions of certain communication systems within the instrument (medium) for the purpose of making itself known to incarnates. Other parts of the body may be left entirely free to function, especially the vital processes. The nervous system may thus be managed by two entities: the medium's normal persona, operating the vital functions and the entity, exercising a type of selective repression of those parts not valuable to its expression and using those that are.

During the incorporation of one Dr. Arikson, the medium Vespacio exhibited REM state. Dr. Arikson conducted several hours of surgery while incorporated. Vespacio's eyes and vision were not needed by the entity to enable him to see. He had transvision; he could perceive by using psychic abilities. Vespacio's physical eyesight was repressed by the spirit, and his eyes meandered back and forth in his head as though in dream state.

The same was observed in the case of Mai Neusa, wherein the incorporated entity had no need of her eyes which remained transfixed and unmoving in any direction—the fixed stare of a blind person.

But what of the brain of the medium? Studies are presently being made to develop a model, but none seem to explain the mechanics of why or how the incorporated entity manipulates brain functions. They only attempt to theorize what parts of the brain might be utilized.

One such neurological model of brain function during incorporation presented in 1987 by Dr. Paulo Bearzoti, a neuropathologist. According to his model, incorporation occurs through the occipital parts of the encephalon. Other important functions of the brain in this study include the domination of the reticular formation because of its relation to wakefulness. This same reticular formation has an inhibitory function and an excitatory effect on other nervous structures as well.

Dr. Bearzoti reviews the various parts of the brain and explains how they might be used by the incorporated spirit. (23) But are they, in fact, used, or is a more subtle linkage at work?

Dr. Hernani G. Andrade, a famous Brazilian parapsychologist and engineer, suggests an entirely different hypothesis, one which he had developed over many years of psychic and mediumistic investigations. Andrade is a man of no small stature and is known to such North American investigators as Carl Rogers, G. Meeks, the inventor of Spiritcom, and I. Stevenson, investigator of reincarnation. Andrade's model is called the BOM, or the Biological Organizing Model. Dr. C. Tinoco, the head of the department of mathematics at the University of Manaos, Amazonia, and writer of the book dealing with Dr. Andrade's model, *Biological Organizing Model,* explained the salient features of the concept.

We live in a universe of no dimensional limitations although we experience ourselves as limited beings inhabiting a three-dimensional consciousness world. There are, however other dimensions, as suggested by the new physics and oriental religions. Several worlds might be superimposed upon our own, forming a more complex world of four or more dimensions. The BOM's are composed of four-dimensional atoms formed throughout time by the interaction of particles from these various dimensions, or the psi world, and the molecules of organic compounds that form living matter here as we know it. While living matter is formed and destroyed, the Model connected with it continues and contributes to the formation of a new being. The BOM contains all of the information necessary for new creation. It contains not only the genetic code, but also the entire spiritual and reincarnational experience of the race and the individual. The Model interacts upon three dimensional man constantly. The paranormal phenomena such as telepathy, clairvoyance, psychokinesis as well as poltergeists, reincarnation and psychic surgery exist only in part in our dimension. They originate in a fourth dimension. They interact with ours on certain occasions. The point of interaction is through our brain, specifically the Perispirit, which in Spiritist terms, is the intermediary between the body and the mind. The human brain is made of matter, whereas the invisible world is made of psi-matter. There must be something which makes this interaction possible. This is called by Dr. Andrade the Bio-Magnetic Field, a "preexistent structure connected to the normal biological process but located outside of our familiar physical space." When the Model connects with matter then life can exist. (25)

Dr. Tinoco further explained, as if the above weren't enough, that it is through the model that entities may come to influence us. Not only are past lives recorded in the model, but also in the possibility of spirit contact through the "perispirit." The model maintains the physical body as it replaces the informational aspect of the medium's consciousness with that of the spirit's model. The spirit is a model, though without a physical body. On its own plane, the model forms an adequate envelope for its expression there. During incorporation, the spirit's envelope, or perispirit, also envelopes the living medium's model and, through it, takes over the functions of the body, mind, and brain.

Professor Ney Prieto Peres, the director-founder of the Brazilian Institute of Psychobiophysic Research and codirector of the Department of Investigation for the Medical-Spiritist Association of São Paulo, an engineer by profession, contributes to the understanding of Dr. Andrade's model.

> . . . there is a "dome" or registration zone which is responsible for the integration of the psychological, intellectual and mental experience. The constituent aspects [the spirit and perispirit] polarize within tri-dimensional space, interrelating themselves on the molecular level with all of the cellular groups of the complex human organism. (25) The dome of the spirit interconnects with the body of a medium. The dome of the medium is freed temporarily from its informational continuation with his body and brain.

Most Brazilian psychic investigators are also medical doctors, with some exceptions. Most of them are also psychiatrists, and so there is a tendency to explain the incorporation connection in reductionist and materialist terms. Most doctors cite glands as the points of spirit control, while nonphysicians often cite meridian systems and chakras as the portals. However, one point was often cited by all, the hypothalamus gland.

The hypothalamus is situated in the center of the brain and is often mentioned in esoteric studies as the seat of the soul. It is believed in many cases that the incorporating spirit somehow inhabits, touches, or influences this space, thus controlling the body and the awareness of the medium.

One spirit, however, disagrees. He told me in an interview that it is the pineal gland. "The trance is psychic, affected through the pineal. We work through the medium's mind so he can feel our thoughts and move his body."

Another says, " . . . the cerebral cortex and the pineal are the major mediumistic centers." (22)

Another theme discussed at the hospital was that of voluntary and involuntary incorporation. Many of the pathologies in modern psychology are in fact (if the Spiritist psychiatrists of Brazil are to believed) nothing more than unconscious mediumship and intrusive spirits. Often Spiritist therapies succeed where traditional psychiatry fails.

Incorporation may be voluntary or intrusive. When a medium opens himself up as a channel he is practicing voluntary mediumship. Voluntary incorporation is used to obtain information. There is an act of will in which the medium submits to the force of the spirit that has invited him to commune.

When a spirit clings to, intrudes upon, and forces communion with or through a medium, this is intrusive incorporation. This is also called obsession. The term "intrusive personality" was first used by Dr. Eliezer Mendes, psychiatrist, to describe those symptoms of mind and personal action that might be attributed to a spirit that has attached itself to a person, thus creating mental aberrations, strange to the normal psychological actuation of the individual. These may manifest strange behavior: verbal profanity, licentious acts, unaccustomed cruelty, and psychosis among other characteristics. Such involuntary possession, according to Spiritist doctrine, may be the cause of eighty percent of mental and physical problems.

Investigations among psychiatrists, psychologists, and medical doctors (Praater & Denizard, 1985; Ferreira & Luce, 1984) who are Spiritists, and mediums are being conducted to differentiate symptoms caused by intrusive spirits from those of other causes. Many such psychiatrists are developing guidelines to adequately treat patients who are ill through spirit-induced causes and through pathological deficiency. Wilson Ferreira, M.D., points out the importance of studying obsession in order not to distort the diagnosis, which might ultimately hurt the patient. Should the symptomology be of spirit obsession, then

106

the standard treatment must be spiritual. If the diagnosis indicates organic or psychopathic causes, then traditional therapies should be administered. Since Spiritists control more than sixty percent of the psychiatric hospitals in Brazil, they may very well know what they are talking about.

Doctors at the Psychiatric Hospital Andres Luis told me how normal procedures are combined with voluntary spiritual therapy to assist patients. Dr. Lucio and others felt that there was an overwhelming amount of evidence to the effect that possession was the cause of many "psychiatric" problems.

This is not an isolated opinion. Scores of doctors and psychiatrists proclaim, without fear of ridicule from the their colleagues, that the cause of many illnesses could be spiritual in origin. In many clinics and hospitals, the doctrines of Spiritism are being tested. When a patient doesn't respond to normal psychiatric procedure but then responds miraculously to spiritual therapy, doctors understandably begin to question if there may be something to all of this.

Dr. Alberto Lyra, a psychiatrist, lists mental perturbations in three classes, according to decades of his clinical experience. First are mental illnesses with traditional causes—neurosis, psychosis, organic, and psychogenic. Second are illnesses caused by pure spiritual obsession which have resisted traditional psychiatric intervention. Usually these types of illnesses respond to Spiritistic treatments. The final group, he claims, is caused by a type of possession that is associated with episodes of neurotic, psychotic, or psychopathic behavior. These also seem to respond to spiritual treatment. (23)

These doctors go so far as to say that medical treatment simply may not be sufficient in the treatment of such disease. Dr. A. Sech, a psychiatrist and director of a mental institution, recommends that all hospitals should include, in addition to medical care, psychologists and social workers, a staff of people solely dedicated to spiritual healing. The function of such a department would be to help individuals afflicted with mental ills caused by spiritual possession. (22)

Another group of medical doctors, all Spiritists, suggested that spiritual treatment works and that sensitives should be included among the auxiliary workers of a hospital. These sensitives could diagnose the origins of spiritual disease and facilitate the cure. (23)

This is not so strange. As early as 1981, the U.S. Health Department in Santa Fe, New Mexico, renowned Spiritualist, founded a licensing program by which sensitives, called "spiritual healers," could visit hospitals and other healing places and apply magnetic passes and other techniques to ailing patients.

Dr. Hannah Krueger is famous today for training over seventy-five thousand American nurses in a program in which they spend some time each day in the strategic application of light pressure to their patients. Called the "Healing Touch" program, studies maintain that this technique improves patient response to standard medical programs by activating internal healing capabilities.

Dr. Modesto Gil, a psychiatrist and Spiritist reminds us:

> Human beings live in two worlds. On one side he is under constant stress caused by visible conditions; also he suffers constant bombardment of mental and spiritual vibrations from incarnate and non-incarnate beings. (23)

It may sound strange to hear such talk from a psychiatrist, but the spirit world is a reality to many people on this planet. If modern medicine speaks about the mental causes of stress, factors which are for the most part invisible, is Dr. Gil's idea any different?

The intrusive personality has been the object of fear and terror for centuries. The Roman Catholic church often classifies such personalities as "demonically possessed," using exorcism as the appropriate therapy. A look at the Gospels portrays Jesus as "casting out" spirits from mentally deranged individuals. He felt it important enough to teach this gift to his disciples and dispatch them throughout Judea, teaching and exorcising.

In Costa Rica, a Catholic priest of my acquaintance, Reverend Howell, told me that he spends one day per week doing exorcisms on many of his parishioners who went the psychology route unsuccessfully. He sees a fine line between demonic possession and "mental illness." While he questions the reality of these entities, he does not question the fact that his parishioners believe them to exist.

Candomble and Umbanda practitioners believe these intrusive spirits to be spirits seeking revenge against the human race. Spiritism claims that these spirits are misguided and morally uneducated. They are stuck and lonely and wish to be recognized. However, Dr. Lucio told me that these spirits do not always respond to spiritual therapy, and electroshock is often utilized in his hospital to dislodge them from their victims.

In the movie, *The Exorcist* (1973), a highly dangerous intrusive personality is portrayed. Most cases, I was informed, of such intrusion that present themselves in Spiritist hospitals are not so dramatic as that; however, I did see changes in the physical presentation of the body during incorporation.

I saw mediums walk as cripples, hunched over, with aberrations in vocal tone and meter, and with skewed or otherwise different facial expressions. Much of this, admittedly, could be acted, but much of the acting could come from deep unconscious aspects of the personality. Is it not possible then, that many patients in mental hospitals have, quite simply, unconsciously ceded their mental space to some intrusive spirit, who then appears as a personality deviation of the human host? Certainly, my medical hosts believed this to be the case in many of their clients.

Chapter XVI
A Case of Spiritistic Mail Delivery

The spirit Pai Guillerme in Sorocaba had given me a letter of introduction to Waldo Viera, a medical doctor and famed medium in Rio de Janeiro. However, my friend and I were not interested in visiting that city at that time because of the high crime rate and the high costs of living there. Instead we traveled to Belo Horizonte.

On my first day at the Spiritist Federation, I spent some time browsing around the bookstore, where I came across some books coauthored by Chico Xavier, Brazil's most loved and saintly medium, and Dr. Viera when he was a young medium. I was told that one particular book was coauthored simultaneously by the two mediums, though each was in a different town. One section was dictated to Mr. Xavier while another was dictated to Dr. Viera. When the two sections came together, there was enough continuity in the material to produce one entire book.

While I was musing over these books, I said out loud that I wish that I could find Dr. Viera and meet him. A student standing next to me, intervened in my wishful thinking and said that he would be in town within a day or two to present a talk. I followed up on this information and was told that in five days he would be in Belo Horizonte, giving a talk at the cultural center.

Returning to my hotel, I asked my traveling companion if we could change our plans to stay here a week. Tomorrow we would visit the psychiatric hospital and then spend three days in the hills of Ouro Prehto, where gemstones and crystals were mined. And off to those hills we went, enjoying our days in the historical and natural beauty of that place.

Finally, the night of the conference arrived, and I presented myself in the doorway an hour before time, hoping that the medium might come early. I was disappointed in this. About ten minutes before the conference, Dr. Viera, dressed in white and looking like a venerable Oriental master, entered the building with his entourage. He had a long white beard and jolly dancing eyes, somewhat mischievous for my taste. I told one of his assistants that I had a letter of introduction for him, but I didn't tell him from whom or where. Of course, the letter was a blank piece of paper, supposedly with a message impregnated by Pai Guillerme. Dr. Viera held it between his palms and said, "Ah yes, a letter from Pai Guillerme, entrusting you to me. You must be a potential medium. The only other person who Pai sent was Gerardo Antonio de Padua. Take my telephone number and call me in Rio. Then we will make plans to meet." He then wiggled his nose, like we think that witches do, and I felt tickling on my face. I mentioned this, and he said, "Good, you are very sensitive." Then he did something else and said, "Good, very good. You must come and see me."

As things worked out, we never got a chance to meet in Rio, but then one never knows the future, does one?

Chapter XVII

The Secret Tradition of Candomble

After two months in the south of Brazil, I was ready and excited to journey northward. We had already stopped in the last industrial city of the south, and our plans were to go directly to Brasilia, the national capital. However, try as we may, it was impossible to get a seat on the two bus lines which traveled direct. We stayed over a day or two more, trying to get a reservation, but everyone was booked, since there was a rumor spreading that national transportation would go on strike. Finally we decided that we were meant to make alternate plans.

When we left São Paulo, we had the option of traveling six hours on a pleasant highway to Rio de Janeiro. But after much discussion, both of us felt that we did not want to stop there just yet. So when we couldn't go directly north, we decided that it was our destiny to go to Rio. We traveled to Rio the next day from Belo Horizonte.

The trip was long, but passing through the mountain villages that surround Rio made the trip worth it. We arrived in Rio as the sun was going down. Again we had the feeling—flee from Rio—and so, sensing that the feeling was mutual, we decided to bus out to Espiritu Santo, a small and pleasant state just north of Rio. The bus ride was longer than we imagined it to be, and we found ourselves, at two o'clock in the morning, sitting in an abandoned bus terminal. After an hour or so spent in locating a hotel, we slept till midmorning, then ventured out to the beaches. We spent two lovely days in that area, and not having any contacts to seek out, we rested. Then we decided to continue our travels on to Bahia dos Santos, the state of Bahia.

The state of Bahia was the first imperial capital of the empire of Brazil. It was to Bahia that the court of Portugal, in fear for its life from Spain, fled and established the royal house. Then they moved down to

Rio, where they lived in style for years. I had heard of Bahia many years ago when I was studying the Baha'i faith. In fact, I noticed that by interchanging the last two letters I had the word Bahia. The master of the Baha'is, Abdu'l Baha, had even mentioned Bahia, Brazil, where he said that the breezes of divine favor had blown. I had always wanted to see what was so special about this state.

Bahia dos Santos ("Bay of the Saints") is commonly believed to refer to the "saints" of the Catholic church; we now know better, for Bahia is the world capital of the religion known as the Candomble, and the saints are none other than the holy orixas.

"Candomble" originally meant the place where the secret rituals were practiced. Today it refers to a religion that is practiced by some thirty million Brazilians. Candomble is often referred to as the Afro-Brazilian cult, because It was brought over to Brazil by the black slaves who served the Portuguese dons. These slaves were utilized to plant and harvest sugar cane; in the day they did so, while in the night they practiced their native rituals. When the masters were in good humor, the slaves were often grouped on the patio area in front of the main house, the area now known as the *terreiro,* where they were counted and then allowed to dance and sing. Unbeknownst to their masters, in this way they practiced their native cult.

Also unknown to the Portuguese dons, some of these slaves were priests and their jumping around was not normal jumping, but holy mediumship, incorporating the sacred vodoon or orixas.

In order for their native Yoruba religion to flourish in its new soil, it became necessary for the ancient gods to go underground and reappear in a new form, a phenomena not uncommon in Roman Catholic countries. In Spain, thousands of Jews went underground, practicing a superficial form of devout Catholicism, yet on the *Shabbat,* shutting themselves up in their homes to pray as they wished.

I discovered a similar situation among the indigenous tribes of South America. I witnessed, in the small rural towns of Ecuador and Guatemala, how the native population would first throw a corn offering into the fire pit at the entrance of the Catholic church before entering the mass. That was to remind the ancestral gods, and maybe the Roman priests, who it was really being worshipped inside of the temple. The African population also went underground and attended to Catholic obligations. What's more, in their minds they created a syncretism

113

which continues to this day. Candomble is therefore a mixture of the magic rites of the African peoples, mainly Yoruba, and some of the traditions of the Catholic church.

The stories and legends that surround the lives of Mary, Jesus, and the Catholic saints are of great importance to the Candomble because they help to delineate the personalities of the saints, making it easier to identify them with the appropriate African deities. Despite this mixture, Candomble's roots are deeply buried in the soil of Africa.

The descendants of those Africans and other Brazilian devotees still identify their orixas as Roman saints, worshipping them with great ceremony on their saints' days. One high priestess of the Candomble told me personally that the followers of that religion have the best of creeds, for they can appeal to the power of the Roman saints as well as to the power of the African orixas.

Although the Africans were successful in hiding the orixas under the guise of Catholic saints, it did not take long for the Portuguese to realize what they were doing. Candomble consists of an intricate system of rituals and ceremonies of a distinct magical nature, much of which the slaves conducted in the woods. Others were held in the patios of the plantation houses, and still others in the Church itself! This resulted in persecution which forced the slaves to cloak their religion in secrecy. All the rituals, especially the initiations, were conducted under the stringent vows of secrecy still observed by practitioners of the faith today. That is why, in modern Brazil, it is hard for an outsider to gain authentic information.

I spoke to several Pais who told me that some European investigators had offered them money to reveal the "secret" of the faith. Some less morally bound Pais have sold "secrets," for the most part invented from their imagination for commercial ends, and have found their way into books.

Candomble is a nature religion, a magicoreligious system that has its roots in natural forces. Each orixa is identified with a force of nature and with a human interest. One orixa, for example, Xango, wields the forces of fire, lightning, and thunder and also controls enemies and general difficulties as well as raw power. He also symbolizes unfettered virility and male sensuality. Yemanja is identified with the salt waters. She is the symbol of motherhood and protector of women. The supreme force of all is Olorum, the transcendent god.

Candomble and Umbanda hold similar beliefs. Thus, many of the Umbanda priests and priestesses were formerly Candomble Pais and Mais do Santo. Candomble, however, has continued to hold to African traditions. According to these traditions, the powerful orixas, who will be discussed in a later section, are the proper object of devotion.

The priesthood of Candomble is held in the greatest reverence and fear. Candomble Pais do Santo are paid for their services and very rarely are crossed. In popular circles, they are persons who are not to be fought with nor perturbed. They wield tremendous power. Their rituals are African, and their songs and drum rhythms are very enticing.

According to the Candomble priests, the principal difference between them and Umbanda is that the Candomble holds the aforementioned secret, one which is never revealed outside the craft. This secret ("segredo") gives power to the priests, a power which is supposedly not contained in Umbanda. For the record, while Umbanda is viewed by some Candomble Pais as an important sect of the mother religion, they often share the same federations. There are, however, moves to form separate organizations, and in São Paulo, there are already separate movements.

The world is created by *axe* (pronounced ash-ey), or divine power, grace. Everything is formed through it, and every possibility arises though its possession. The orixas are the supreme vehicles of Olorum's axe. All invocations, propitiations, spells, and rituals are conducted to acquire this power from the orixas. With axe, all problems can be resolved, all enemies subdued, and normal functioning restored.

The propitious rituals are the ways of invoking the orixas to intervene in our problems, to give us some of their power. These rites are presided over by a Pai do Santo. Preceding his elevation to the priesthood, each Pai was an initiate, or a *Filho* ("son") do Santo. He takes on the name of the saint into whose mysteries he has been initiated. When he is finally ordained, he can initiate others as Filhos and Pais. At this point the priest becomes a *babalorixa* or *ialorixa* ("archpriest" or "archpriestess").

The Pais are the direct link between man and nature that is accepted as God. The fundamental work of the Pai is to reestablish harmony between the parts and the whole.

The Candomble has no missionary effort; it is not interested. Its millions of members are initiated after they attend several of the rituals

115

and experience the positive effects of the orixas. Some of them are motivated to receive an initiate name and become a Filho do Santo. As the candidates grow through the various levels of initiation under the severe patronage of a Pai or Mai, they may apply for the priesthood and become a Pai themselves. This will take many years, and the candidates must dedicate a lot of time to their training.

I was invited to attend some of the lower initiate ceremonies for the Sons, one of which took place in a forest terreiro. The singing, dancing, and trance activities were as fearsome as they were sensual. The primal emotions evoked at an authentic Candomble are astounding.

Unfortunately, especially in Rio and in Salvador, unsuspecting tourists are taken to attend dramatic representations of Candomble. These presentations are staged solely for the benefit of foreigners and are "cleaned up" rituals, which are kept within the proper limits of decency and do not evoke the primal images that I enjoyed on these occasions. The Candomble cannot be learned by books, and everything written about it can only approximate the emotions involved. The secret national religion of Brazil remains a secret to those who have not taken the time to enter into its sacred nature, where the orixas still have undivided power.

Chapter XVIII
Settling into Salvador

The trip from Espiritu Santo to Bahia was quite long. Therefore, we decided to travel three quarters of the distance and spend a day or two at the beaches of Porto Seguro, where we were soon stranded due to the predicted transportation strike. Instead of staying for a night or two, we stayed for a week in a comfortable hotel. The food was wonderful, the company interesting, and my companion was occupied with the local women day and night.

I used my own time to hunt down spirits and Candombles. There were several in the area, but the time was not right for them to reveal themselves to me. A true Candomble doesn't just pop up. One must first be introduced to the Pai, then await an invitation. Talks with the hotel owner assured me that there were Spiritists and others around, as he himself was a believer. We spent a whole night once, talking about spirits, one in particular, who seemed to be residing in the hotel. Both of us had felt its strange presence.

Finally the transit strike was over and my companion and I boarded a bus to Bahia.

After an all-night ride, our bus pulled into Bahia at the crack of dawn. The bus terminal is located in the back of the city, in a relatively new part, filled with shopping centers and other modern conveniences. It wasn't the Bahia we expected. Still, my spirits were high, and I was excited to be in the "holy city." We called a friend from the station, who appeared about an hour later to take us to a hotel.

The hotel sat in the very oldest part of the city. This was the once fashionable Terreiro do Jesus, where the richest of the Portuguese once lived. Being Sunday, the area was quiet; the churches were filled with white-clad Candomble worshippers. Our room was directly in front of

117

the Franciscan church and looked out at a stone wall carved in a most enjoyable fashion. I wish that I could say the same for the hotel; it was extremely inexpensive and smelled like it, but it was home for a few nights.

We bathed, then decided to walk around the area. Four buildings away from the hotel was the Spiritist Federation, situated in an old, historic building. It would soon be transferred to its new, modern building in another section of the town. I was delighted to be so close and made plans to present my introductions there on the following day. As we walked around the city, we were delighted to find out that we were living in a historical gold mine. The area was not kept up; some people would even call it dirty. But I preferred to call it uninhibited. It was obviously a dangerous area to walk in after dark, but in the first rays of morning, it was magnificent, graced with many churches and a view of the bay. This was the upper city, of which I had read much.

We soon came to a sidewalk cafe looking out over the bay. The bay was beautifully blue, with large boats, tugs, and pleasure crafts floating by. The warm air lulled us into a peaceful reverie, especially comforting after the long bus ride.

Sitting in the bay is an island, Itaparica, which we decided to explore. My friend and I thought that it would be adventurous to find a house on the island and boat back and forth to the city. We asked directions to the ferryboat docks and set out immediately for the island to try to find a house.

The ride to the island was very relaxing, the wind blowing over the bay, the sunlight above. By the time we arrived at the island port, I felt renewed and very positive about being there.

On the island, we somehow found ourselves walking on a side road, which appeared to follow the beach. The road soon became a dirt path, and even that soon seemed to disappear. The midday sun was hot, despite the breezes coming in from the ocean. I soon decided that it was time for my daily siesta. We hadn't slept for over twenty-four hours and so, sought out a shady area under the trees to rest.

By the time I opened my eyes, we had rested for two hours or so. As I stretched and remarked how great I felt, I saw a small trail leading up the hill and into the bush. We trudged along the trail for about twenty minutes and then found ourselves looking out on the ocean. A tract of property separated us from the beach. Just ahead of us was a house which reminded me of a pagoda. A man about my own age stood out in front. I stepped forward and said in my worst Portuguese, "I hope that I am not trespassing, but could we cross your land?"

"Of course," came the reply. "But tell me where you are from."

I filled him in on a few details and told him that we were looking for a house to live in on the island.

"I have a house that you could live in," he rejoined.

"But we are vegetarians and would like to have our own place."

"I also am vegetarian," our unknown friend answered.

"We also need a quiet place to practice meditation."

"I also meditate, so that would not be a problem."

Soon we were sitting in his outdoor kitchen, awaiting what turned out to be a fine dinner. When we finished, he said, "Of course, you will move in immediately."

Ever the practical one, I said we would not until we discussed the rent. My friend frowned at me, instinctively knowing that money matters shouldn't be discussed at the dinner table.

Our new friend, Lalado, said, "There will be no rent." Pointing at Marvin, he said, "You will set up an organic garden and Dennis will teach me about massage. It will be an even trade." Taking our leave, we promised to return the next day with our answer.

Tomorrow came, and we soon moved into Lalado's house. Unfortunately for me, the hill upon which it sat was too steep for me to walk up and down without help. I moved into a smaller house about a quarter of a mile away, while Marvin lived on the hill. I needed some space to be alone and write my notes, so it worked out quite fine.

Chapter XIX

The Candomble Priestess

Several people told me to see Mai Vera. "She is a very powerful priestess and has a lot of information about Candomble."

Mai Vera is a successful accountant. I called her at her office, but she was not readily accessible. She was reluctant to talk to me and gave me several excuses for not meeting, but my persistence won out, and Mai Vera finally invited me to join her at her apartment one Sunday morning.

I expected a typical Mai do Santo: uneducated, rather rustic, old, even fat. Instead I found a youthful white woman, married with children, a professional, and certainly not cast from the mold which produced the average Candomble priestess.

I was transparent. She obviously surmised my surprise and smiled at me. "I am not what you imagined?"

"No" I smiled back.

"One of the problems we have is the Candomble image. People still think of our faith as a black religion. We are African in roots but universal in thought. We express the ancient universal truth which is embodied in the 'secret,' but is found in all the ancient paths. The 'secret' is available to anyone who will dedicate time and energy to strive for it."

"Tell me, Mai, what is Candomble in its essence?"

"Candomble is a university: apprenticeship, student, son, professor, and priest. There is no set time for learning. Probably about fourteen years to learn. We are like scientists seeking the form and ways of mediumship. Candomble is our laboratory . . . We have a problem with mediumship because there is not a scientific approach to it. With the magic of Candomble, we make contact with the spirits.

" . . . Candomble is more of a group. It is an old African religion. The public has a poor idea of a Pai do Santo: old, black, ugly, and uneducated. This is not true. We have many priests who are well educated and intellectual. Candomble is a study of the spirit and is very deep knowledge . . . I don't have to use candles or rituals in the house. I enter into trance with magnetic currents. In my sanctuary, you note that it is a Candomble center with all the decorations. It has a social room as well as a sanctuary. The spirits don't need rituals to work. The spirits vary in what they want in terms of rituals. Those of good karma require very little . . . The rituals are according to the sect. Candomble has its own procedure for working."

"How is it that a white Portuguese from a well-to-do family becomes a Candomble priestess?" I asked her.

"I am from a strict, very Catholic family much against the Candomble. I was the opposite of a Mai. I was not too interested in becoming one. I became sick, empty, and I went to the hospital. I continued to be ill, very ill. An orixa one night incorporated in me. He told me that if I accepted my work, he would grant me health and joy. I recovered very rapidly, and I was spiritually mobilized.

"A Pombagira came to me. She was very pretty. I felt her energy and received her blessing . . . I don't live off of Candomble. I have another work. I accept offerings for the maintenance of the center . . . but Candomble is my service to others.

"Often the Pais make a business out of Candomble . . . my entities come to me at moments of need. I don't need to call on them. When I was a 'daughter,' I still called them. They don't serve us. They come when we serve others."

"Mai, can you explain something of the different spirits who serve the Candomble?"

"These are not individual spirits. They are parts of one whole, one unit, though they appear as separate. All entities have different names, but ultimately they are the expressions of the one Spirit.

"Some spirits, obsessors, enter and play with us. The are *eguns*. They aren't intrinsically evil, but are often very old and confused. Sometimes a young person or even an infant is obsessed by one of them, and so they act strangely. The egun causes problems. These are not psychological tendencies but real entities . . . We call upon the orixas to eliminate the eguns.

"In Candomble you have to prepare yourself to experiment in a spirit laboratory . . . Some Candombles come from very religious families. The priests study the nature of the orixas, eguns and the exus. I didn't study from a book, but by direct experience with incorporated entities. Our school consists of entities that teach the students. Candomble is very deep, deeper than a university . . .

"Candomble has a bad name because many 'fathers' shouldn't be admitted. There are also many homosexuals who are priests. Candomble can do this. Were they really practicing, they could have stopped. Many priests are so one-sided that they have no other life . . . Many of the homosexuals find acceptance at the hands of the spirits. The spirits don't condemn or distinguish. They feel bad and seek help from the spirits . . . My center receives all types of people—drug addicts, problems—and we help them cure the problems."

"Please tell me about the orixas."

"The orixas are too deep to understand . . . they lived on earth at one time. They incarnated. The eguns are placeless, bodyless. When you touch a medium possessed by an orixa, he feels warm and alive . . . with an egun, cold and dead. He will jump when you touch him. He is freezing. . . . Orixas are patron saints, respected. The exu is considered evil, but he does the work of the orixas. We don't mix with the egun. He will complete but is not a good energy . . . orixas are messengers of God. They give messages, protect the medium. Some were alive like us, but evolved through purification to become one with God. Exus and eguns are lower: Olorum (God), orixas, caboclos, exus, and eguns . . . Exu is an entity that came to earth without physical desires and needs. He incorporates and acquires characteristics. . . .

"All spirits are divided into levels. There are exus who are very high. Elebaras are exus and pombagiras are also incarnations of exus who live on other levels. The understanding depends upon your own criteria . . . If an exu wants to incorporate, that's fine. But not in my house. When an exu incorporates, it is sometimes a violent takeover, a war. The egun is worse. He can send you to the hospital. The exu is a force, he contains both negative and positive force. The exu amplifies and expands the energy that you have. If you are negative, your negativity will expand. If you have a positive magnetic energy, he will expand it also. What you are he reveals more of."

"I have met many types of mediums. They practice conscious or unconscious mediumship. What do you do and experience?"

"I practice unconscious mediumship. I feel when I am going to incorporate a spirit. I see the spirit when it touches me. I see it through the form that it wants to manifest, like seeing television. . . . There are many types of mediumship: you can see, smell, hear, taste, and incorporate. I can perceive the entities as persons . . .

"Foreign spirits from other sects can appear in Candomble if they feel a need and experience rapport with those present . . . It can be that all of these spirits are one spirit. I said that before . . . Culture influences the perception of the spirits . . . any spirit that comes down from heaven to earth is welcome. The spirits are perceived as African, but they are not. They are only spirits . . . The medium of the United States probably lacks information. That's why their mediumship is different. Some people are more spiritual, they are born so . . . spirituality attracts the spirit . . . the forces of God."

"I hear a lot of people telling me that Quimbanda is practiced by many Candomble priests and that Candomble has a dark side to it. Is this true?"

"Quimbanda is different from Candomble. Candomble has a black magic side. It is not important where its powers come from. You must have access to different tools both black and white . . . There are spiritual sicknesses that have nothing to do with the body. If a person has cancer, but his cause is spiritual, it may be that he must die to learn his lesson. Karma governs everything. Many people learn nothing. They want a cure but resist learning. I believe that Candomble should help a person learn about his life and karma."

Chapter XX
A Spiritist Healing Clinic

It was, by now, a rarity to encounter people who didn't believe in spirits, reincarnation, karma, etcetera. How different it was from other countries where I had lived; I continually had to explain my ideas to people. Here, it was assumed that any intelligent person believed in these concepts.

My reputation had apparently preceded me, for when I finally made contact with the Spiritist Federation, they knew all about me. I presented my credentials to the leaders of the Spiritist Federation. They opened their doors to me and arranged a visit with Mr. Sousa. Mr. Sousa is a very old Spiritist and highly erudite person. He told me that the Spiritists of Bahia were less rigid than those of the other states because of the close associations with the African Candomble. Many of their Federation members also studied with the powerful Bahian Pais who conducted the rituals here. Any time that I had a problem or needed help in reaching other groups, this man was on hand to assist me. It was through him that I heard about and met the medium Vespacio (who allows the spirit Dr. Arickson to work through him), Mai Santinha, and the Dutch physician.

After my first visit to the Federation, I received a telephone call from Joseval Carneiro, a second generation Spiritist. Mr. Carneiro is a very educated man and achieved high positions in the state and federal governments. After introducing himself, he offered to drive me to the Nazaret Spiritist Center in order to meet some of the finest mediums of Bahia. First, however, we dined at his home and I met his wife, also a committed Spiritist.

There were only about twelve participants at this phenomenal meeting, where I was to see an extraordinary demonstration of paranormal surgery that involved materialization. The general public was not invited. The medium, not wishing to be identified, was called the Dutch physician because he channels a Dutch medical doctor who participated in World War One. The spirit's technique was to insert syringes into the patient, supine upon a table, and materialize medicine from dry cotton which would fall upon the patient.

The medium had been an ardent Spiritist for most of his life, but had been a working medium for only about a year or so. Despite his short time of mediumship, he was the current president of one of the largest centers in Bahia. He was never very interested in becoming an active medium, saying that it "just happened."

As is Spiritist practice, all present repeated the Lord's Prayer, and the medium, in an instant, incorporated his spirit guide. I experienced this spirit as jovial and very loving. He spoke softly and with care to those around him, never shouting or ordering anyone as did other spirits I had witnessed.

His work tonight consisted of directing the activities of five assistant mediums and the materialization of "medicine." The mediums first prayed, synchronized with each other. The Dutch physician asked them all to concentrate upon him, to give him more energy.

The spirit/physician was handed a large piece of hospital cotton. It was ordinary white cotton from a package which was just opened in my presence. I was very impressed over what soon occurred. He began to squeeze the cotton in his right hand. In a few moments, the ordinary white hospital cotton began to turn from its normal color to bright orange, like that used by the Hindu Sannyasins. It appeared to have been dipped in Mercurochrome. The liquid began to drip and flow from the cotton in enormous amounts and fall upon the patient.

The spirit must have assessed my amazement. He turned to me and gave me the cotton to hold. Surprisingly, it was dry. He questioned me on that point, and I said that it was definitely dry. He then took the cotton back and squeezed it again; about a cup of liquid flowed from it.

He then pulled off a piece of the cotton and awarded it to me for my collection.

Meanwhile, the young patient on the operating table experienced some pain, yet no one was even looking at her. She reported a burning sensation within her body, as well as the feeling of penetration and incision during a cutting process.

The medium was unconscious through all of this and looked around, apparently without using his eyes, which were fixed and unmoving. Under normal conditions the medium had a slight curve to his back, but during trance he was rigid.

A second medium was working with a glass in his hands, which the physician instructed him to hand to me. At his instruction, I drank the liquid in the glass and found it to be plain, ordinary water. I also smelled the glass; there was nothing unusual about it.

The medium was staring out into space. He began to agitate the water with his finger. The water soon became cloudy and more dense. Some of this new liquid was given to the patient to drink and some to me. I tasted it and found it now to be quite sugary.

The medium sometimes became conscious and then went unconscious again, practicing both types of mediumship. When incorporating, his body assumed a somewhat different pose, rigid, but coming out he relaxed.

The Dutch physician was playful during the session, observing me and doing things that might shock my intellect. Many times he said to me, "How do you explain this," and then materialized something. The other mediums were moving around, acting as extensions of the physician, as fingers on a hand.

At the end of his work, the principal medium disincorporated first, with a nod of his head and a slight shaking of his body as if coming awake from a deep sleep. Then his assistants also awakened. Not one of them remembered any of the previous session.

Such a demonstration in the United States would create quite a sensation, but in Brazil, these are easily accepted phenomena.

Chapter XXI
Psychic Surgery with Dr. Arikson

Salvador, Bahia

I was soon to learn two things: Salvador, Bahia, was the home of a great many excellent mediums, and there were more than one type of spirit medicine. I remembered what Pai Guillerme told me: healers in the spirit world were often limited by techniques that they learned while incarnate on earth. After death, an earthly surgeon would continue as he was trained until he learned more subtle techniques.

According to Pai Guillerme, some of the most dramatic healing techniques exemplified by modern day Spiritists from Brazil and the Philippines are unnecessary. A simple touch or a healing idea are all that are really necessary. But the earthbound spirit falls easily into his incarnate habits and tends not to progress swiftly enough.

Joseval Carneiro called me again and invited me to another meeting at the Centro Espirita Andre Luis, the healing center in Nazaret, where some days before we had seen the work of the Dutch physician. This time, however we would see a spirit enact a different type of spirit medicine.

Brazil is a poor country in need of medical services. Therefore, according to some of the spirits, there is a host of European spirit doctors working there. Tonight we would view one of them, Brother Arikson, channeled by the Brazilian medium Venacio.

I spoke with the medium before his incorporation. I studied his physical characteristics, especially his particular way of walking and speaking, both of which change noticeably during trance work. As a person, Venacio tended toward some feminine characteristics. As an incarnate spirit, he expressed himself as decidedly more masculine. Dr. Arikson gestured a lot, holding his hands in front of his chest. His Portuguese took on a different accent, like that of a foreigner who speaks it as a second language. His gait differed as well; Venacio lost his Latin swing.

Dr. Arikson was a Nazi, a medical doctor during the Second World War. He especially hated Blacks and thought them dirty and ignorant. He was killed before the war ended and didn't want to speak very much about his past. During his incorporation, he said that he was ashamed of what he did before, and had therefore been indebted to work in Brazil, where a majority of his patients are Black. This would "balance out" his karma, as he explained it to me.

Dr. Arikson worked rapidly, operating on each patient for thirty seconds. He told me that he operates together with an invisible spirit group, which cares for anesthesia, clotting, vital signs, etcetera. He diagnoses and decides if he should operate, make a home visit, or offer nonsurgical advice. He is very frank with his patients, often yelling, very dominating. He told me that the people act like children, and so he responds as a stern father.

It was hard for me to keep up with his fast pace, literally moving from table to table for an hour without stopping. I accompanied him as he attended to about two hundred people in a two-hour period. I was amazed at the rapidity of his work.

He separated all people with eye problems into a smaller room. Then he began to attack (I know no better word) these people, pulling up their eyelids and inserting his forefinger into the socket. I had the feeling I was going to faint. It didn't seem to affect the patients. He would squirt some water into the eye and forcefully rub the eyeball with his finger. Apparently needing only moments with each person, he worked through the room of about twenty people in less than five minutes, then ran back into the main operating room. Most of the patients later reported little inconvenience and no pain.

Two surgeries stood out in my mind. These were two women with cancer. The spirit took a large hair-cutting scissors and literally shoved them into the breast of one patient, making a large incision. The patient hardly reacted, but did feel some pain. The scissors penetrated about one and a half inches inside the patient's body. The incision bled, but the blood coagulated almost immediately, within about three seconds.

I watched the blood become especially thick and then dry up. The medium wiped it away and the incision would bleed again. The surgery included cutting and scraping out the tumor. A medical observer assured me that the tumor was very real. He operated this way only two times out of two hundred.

The other surgeries consisted of passing a plastic pen over the afflicted body part. Several of the men had prostrate problems and the medium would insert a finger into the anus. The men usually screamed for a moment, though the spirit assured me that he hardly touched the body. I doubted that this was true, but discovered much later through personal experience that it was indeed so.

Other people needed more delicate surgery. These would be treated in their homes and were sent away with the "operating time." They were given a written list of preoperation procedures. Dr. Arikson informed me that he would visit them in his invisible form at the appointed time.

The spirit remained calm most of the time, but occasionally lost his patience with some of the children, whom he called spoiled. He also criticized the people, saying that they overate. For those with nose problems, he would probe the nasal openings with a plastic pen, pushing the pen into the nose an inch or so. For my benefit, the spirit wiped blood off on the sole of my shoe and then continued to use the same instrument in his operation, telling me that in psychic surgery, there is no danger of infection.

During the session the spirit asked me why I was on crutches. I replied that it was my karma. At the end of the session, he ordered me onto the table, passing his hands over me, mumbling that I had cancer. Having been cured of it years ago, I wasn't so sure that I was going to like this.

I had been experiencing pain for a few weeks in the area of my heart. Often this pain would become quite intense. Also I had some eye problems but didn't want him to stick his fingers into my socket. So when he asked me what my problems were I didn't tell him anything. However, the time that he passed his hand over me, he said that I had a serious problem with my heart.

"Since you do not need ritual to be healed, I will dispense with the pen and other things and work directly with you in the invisible." He merely touched me very lightly with one of his fingers; in fact, he hardly touched me at all. What I felt, however, was a searing hot pain shoot into my heart and caused, by what I experienced, as three knife incisions! I had never experienced such pain. Then I felt as if something was being sewn up. The pain was excruciating. I felt nausea, dizziness, and my body contracted. I screamed out in pain, and the people had to hold me down on the table.

It lasted only about four seconds, but when it ended, I could hardly walk. I was sweating, and there was still pain in my heart. The spirit counseled me to go home, eat lightly, and get a lot of rest; he said that I had just been through some serious heart surgery. I would feel pain for two or three days, then it would disappear. I followed his advice and was dropped off at the last ferry. Walking very slowly, I boarded the boat. Disembarking after the ride, I walked the half mile to my house. Every step was painful; my heart felt that it was stitched, and I didn't want to force myself much.

I stayed in bed for two days. As Dr. Arikson had said, the pain disappeared on the third day. My circulation improved; the coldness that often accompanied my sleep was no longer there. My face was pinker, and I had a better appetite. Best of all, the pains did not return for some time and then, only very briefly.

I must state again that I had never confided my heart condition to anyone, not even to my traveling companion. Dr. Arikson had diagnosed me correctly; following the psychic surgery, the pain subsided, never returning to afflict me again. Many people have told me that I looked younger than before, and it is true that I now have more energy and can work longer hours.

After treating me, Dr. Arikson walked into another room and, with a few people praying around him, disincorporated. Venacio, now in full control of his body, returned to the meeting room to answer any questions about his work. Despite all his work, the medium appeared to be full of energy and quite relaxed. He had no memory of the previous events. Venacio said that he always blanks out and goes somewhere else and does not participate at all in the healing work. He said that he is often approached on the street by people who thank him or kiss his hands in gratitude, but he cannot remember them. Venacio does not charge for his work. At one time he held down a job to support his work, until a person died and left him a small allowance. This, he said, allows him to dedicate himself full time to his healing ministry.

Interestingly, he related to me that his mediumship does not help his own spirit to evolve. He gains nothing from his practice. It is his service to others.

Chapter XXII
The Woman Who Makes Honey

I was now living in Salvador, Bahia for about three weeks, and my investigations were going full swing. This I attribute to the small group of friends I had made since my arrival. Through Lalado I had been introduced to a vegetarian restaurant in the Comericio district of Salvador. The owner of the restaurant is Socorro de Ceu, which can be translated as the "help of heaven." I had an uncanny experience when I met her, which contributed to all of the help that she gave me.

It was the second day after our arrival to Bahia. We had met Lalado and accepted the offer to situate ourselves in his house. We had made it a point to meet for lunch at a vegetarian restaurant. As I walked in, a woman came to welcome me there. She was very warm and ushered us to a table. After we were served, she came by and sat with us, presenting herself as the proprietress. After a pleasant visit, Lalo arrived and the three of us ate lunch. The food was so good that I decided to return there the following day.

On that day, Socorro sat with me again. This time, however, she was somewhat perturbed. She said she wanted to tell me something and asked me to suspend judgment until I had listened to her tale.

It seemed that Socorro had seen me before, that I had entered the restaurant, dressed the same, and even sat at the same table about fifteen days ago. That would make it about twelve days before I actually arrived in Salvador.

That night, Socorro told me, she had a dream concerning me, in which her "guide" asked her to help me all that she could. Socorro was, in her past, a Spiritist medium. She had her own center that served as guide for about one hundred people. She told me, "The people at the center depended on me for everything. They couldn't make any of their personal decisions without asking the spirits. I felt that there is something not right in this, so I walked away from the center and left them on their own."

After a series of personal illuminations, she decided not to practice active mediumship for others again.

I accepted Socorro's offer of assistance. I became a regular customer at the restaurant, and Socorro began to introduce me to individuals with whom I soon developed friendships. All of them were people interested in the spiritual life. Through several of them, I began to know others who were mediums or who could introduce me to mediums. Thus my "spy ring" came into being.

I met a man by the name of Joseval, who telephoned one day to invite me to go with a group of paranormal investigators, Spiritists, to see a very unusual medium—one who made honey from roses. I had originally heard of this medium in São Paulo from Elsie Dubras and accepted the invitation.

That Saturday, I went first to meet the other members of my group: Thelma Bastos, a medium, and Edivaldo Torres, an engineer and Spiritist. After spending a little bit of time getting our cameras ready, we went off to a florist stand to buy loads of red and white roses, the only type that the medium would work with. It would prove, I was sure, to be a powerful day!

We all got into the same car and drove one hour to a small house outside the city, bought for the medium by her followers. I was anxious to meet this famous medium who puzzled scientists from all over the world.

Hildete Andreade S., called Mai Santinha ("saintly mother") by her devoted followers, was an elderly woman of short structure and kind heart. From the northern Indian state, she was very proud of her native heritage. She spoke in a soft voice when she was not challenged, but when in an argument, raised her voice louder than anyone else. At first sight, Mai Santinha gave the impression of being a native medicine woman, a woman of wisdom. She could very well play the role in any of Carlos Casteneda's books. She practices a type of universal mediumship philosophy claiming belief in Spiritism; however, should the ornaments of her prayer room be seen, she fell clearly within the eclectic lines of the Umbanda. During incorporation services she uses Catholic hymns as well as Umbanda chants. What makes her so very interesting and original is that while in trance, Mai Santinha is able to produce honey—without bees.

One very picky investigator told me that it wasn't real honey, but whatever one called it, she materialized a sweet thick syrup which was evaluated as a type of honey by several laboratories. But for me the important point here is not whether it is honey or not; the important point is that *she materializes!*

Mai Santinha is not the only medium in Brazil who materializes. Pai Antonio Gerardo, the Dutch physician and many others do the same. I often tell my Eastern seeking friends that if phenomena is the final proof of a spiritual master (which I know through personal experience is not) then Brazil is filled with high-ranking masters. There are phenomena galore in every province, every state, and even possibly every city of Brazil. You can't turn a street corner without running into a paranormal medium. That is why Brazil is often called the "India of the Americas."

Whenever she is in trance state, people offer her white or red roses, which she prefers. Unceremoniously, she crushes them in her hands and honey begins to flow. Three times she materialized honey in my presence. We arrived at her country home and spent about six hours in her presence. During the first three hours, we spoke with her about her history and how she became a medium. Then we asked her how she does it and why. What does she perceive?

Mai Santinha tried her best to stick to the questions, but her desire to share the overall experience often led her off on tangents. After about two hours she asked to be excused so that she could prepare lunch and dress for the afternoon. On this day, she would conduct a type of open house, where people could come and receive the honey she would make.

After a brisk lunch, I took a quick walk outside for some air. Suddenly I heard Thelma yelling for me, "Come quick, something is occurring."

Running as fast as I could on crutches, I arrived to find the medium squatting down on the floor. I thought she was sick, but that was not the case. She was—amazingly—materializing honey on the floor!

Mai Santinha appeared to be unconscious. Her eyes were closed, and she made strange sounds. I noticed that the floor, which was painted cement, was quite dirty. I wondered what poor fool was going to eat *that* honey. Suddenly, a voice, deep, bass, and definitely commanding, said, "Give this honey to him!" I looked at her, but she continued looking at the floor, materializing honey. Edivaldo extended his hands to receive the honey.

"No, not to him," the voice ordered, "To the bald one."

"Oh, God," my inner voice squelched out in my head. "Not that dirty honey. And she insults you as well in the process." I made no move.

"Eat!" came the voice of the medium. She rose from the floor, came over to me, and pushed a quantity of the stuff into my open mouth.

"Tell him," she said to an assistant, not deigning to speak to me directly, "tell him that it will spiritualize his system and that in the spirit world there are no germs."

I swallowed the stuff, imagining that the next day I would have a world worm conference in my intestines. However, that was not to be.

Mai Santinha began to shake, her arms raised over her head, her hands making circular movements, rotating. In a minute, she was out of trance.

Speechless, I went outside; I really needed air after viewing the materialization event. My brain was rattling around, trying to understand how this could possibly be. I had seen it, tasted of it, was so close to it. I could see that there were no tricks involved. I needed fresh air to think about it.

Suddenly there was Mai, in trance. "Up to no good, without doubt," said my inner voice. She was peeking at me from around the corner of the house. It was a strange way to be looked at. It was both seductive and innocent, like a child who is looking at a strange thing (me!). I began to experience this strange sensation, as if I was immersed in water or some fluid, warm and sticky, flowing around me. I noted that my body was quickening to the feeling.

Mai Santinha came up to me, stalking in circles counterclockwise around me, not looking at me. The energy building up was overwhelming; I felt quite faint. Finally, she made some hand movements, gestures, toward me as though dusting me off. I was reeling and had to grab onto the car in order not to fall down.

Despite the fact that it was lightly raining and a cool wind was blowing, the heat around me was incredible. She had erected some type of conical magnetic field around me. I was disoriented, dizzy, and faint. My head was throbbing. I stood there, unable to move, looking with amazement at Mai Santinha.

The amount of honey she could make apparently never depends upon the amount of roses. In fact . . .

The Mai approached Edivaldo, about ten feet away from me, and opened up her hands as if asking him for a rose. Edivaldo clearly said that he had no more roses to give her. Then, mindless of Edivaldo's response, response, she closed her hands together for a few moments.

When Mai Santinha opened her hands again, she held a white rose in them! Again closing her hands, she converted the rose to honey and gave it to him, Edivaldo, to eat.

The materialization of the rose stunned both of us. It was now Edivaldo's turn to be speechless for a while. I merely sobbed as my mind began to crack and fragment, then to dissolve, liquid mind-stuff, mind-dust. My world was beginning to collapse.

For the third time within my field of vision, Mai Santinha began to immediately materialize more honey as one of her devotees walked up to her with a rose and an empty bottle. This woman, educated and from the cultured class, told us that she had cancer and that through the honey treatments, she was greatly improved. This was verified by her doctor, who accompanied her. Mai Santinha filled her bottle and sent her on her way.

After this, I just wanted to go home. I begged my companions to take me home before they would have to have me committed. They merely laughed. I told them, "North Americans are too logical to see too much of this stuff in one day." It was too strong. My body was strung out, and I was psychically sick. I needed rest.

"No," they said, "There will be more."

I refused to see it. I ran into the house and sat with her son, who was watching television. To him all this was old hat. He could not believe that anyone in their right mind would spend all of that money to come from North America to see this stuff. All he wanted out of life was to go to the United States and buy a big car. None of this mediumship for him!

By now, Mai had grouped about fifteen people into a circle and was coming out of the trance. They were saying the Lord's Prayer and singing hymns, but I couldn't have cared less. Thelma came in to beg me to attend the service.

"No, not me," I said. "I've had enough for today." Thelma walked out of the room, laughing at me. In the ensuing hour, the Mai delivered a sermon, and then the day was over.

As the other guests were having refreshments and talking, Mai came into the house, as energetic as ever, and sat down with me at the table. I looked at her, wondering if she had something planned, something up her sleeve. She didn't.

We talked about her and my life when, suddenly, spontaneously, a deep voice came out of her—she was gone again. The voice said, "We know the work you have been doing for others, and we approve. Don't become downhearted. Your service is valuable. Continue."

Just as soon as she said it, she was the Mai again, talking as if nothing had happened. She was like a grandmother to me, holding my hand, patting me, and talking about things not related to her mediumship. This obviously powerful woman could also be gentle and compassionate. A wealth of characteristics, she had.

Mai Santinha is not an intuitive medium. She does not feel the spirits; she sees the "entities," as she prefers to call them, as rays of light. They take on human characteristics as they approach her. They are separate from her, not projections of herself. She usually sees these beings, she told me, but there are times when they are not near her. She speaks with the spirits but cannot explain how or by what means.

The Mai does not invoke the entities, which come to her when they want to. Subsequently, she finds herself going into trance whenever and wherever she may be at the time. I imagine she must trust them not to overwhelm her when it might be dangerous for her.

Mai Santinha has no power over honey-making. She is totally controlled by the entities and remembers nothing at all of her work.

She also works with past life readings and kundalini energy. She claims to be able to open up people's chakras as well. Mai Santinha educates lost spirits through "alphabetization," her word for spiritual education. When she sees a past life, it presents itself as though on a movie screen. The supplicant must fast before she can read his life energies. Santinha could not explain the techniques she uses to liberate a person's energies, She merely speaks with them, telling them what she sees. If necessary, she shocks them with what she calls "mediumistic energy." She couldn't explain exactly the nature of how this works, but it is similar to an electroshock experience, which serves to separate a person from the energies of his problem.

Mai Santinha also administers herbs and vegetarian diet as treatment. She never charges for her services; any income goes to charitable works. She is very sure of herself and her mission. I was impressed with Mai's bearing and her way of presenting herself. In private, she was very sweet and gracious. She lived very simply, satisfying her basic needs without ostentation.

The following excerpts are from my notes taken during her initial discourse with our group. I think that they will be of interest.

I was trained in the Uruba (native) traditions in the Amazon region . . . my mother was a medicine woman and medium. She sang the sacred songs, she healed and used her rituals to help all of the people. I watched her and learned many things from her. She gave me my initial training.

Then I met, later on in my life, a medium who told me that I had the capacity. She was a Mai, and I lived with her, learning all that I could . . . I began to attract some entities. I did several formal trainings with her over the years . . . we use massage, herbs, and breathing for healing . . . to use the energies latent in nature. We must respect nature. We must respect the energy.

The medium, one day, told me that if I held roses in my hands, I would attract great forces. That night I took roses in my hand and turned them into honey. My teacher told me that I must be very responsible with this power . . . at first, it wasn't easy, because some Christian ministers attacked me, saying that I was using satanic powers. They had no power, which is why they were against me.

People began coming to me for help I couldn't turn them away. I began to heal them with honey and herbs . . . I see the entities. I see lots of lights around people, sometimes it looks like smoke . . . I see with my eyes . . . The energy fuses with my own energy. I don't feel anything. The energy sometimes feels pleasurable. I remember nothing . . . I don't know where I go.

These energies are chemicals, and they enter into my body chemicals and produce power. I don't know where I go. I feel that I am studying at that moment . . . The energy is spiritual . . . we have several energies—some for surgery, integration, disintegration, vampire energies which suck us dry and leaves us weak, all of these are energetic processes. We have atomic, vital energy. All of them are for all humanity not just me and other mediums.

I see some of this energy as light and colors. I learned that each light is for a certain illness . . . each energy is from nature. I apply them to each person . . . They have various forms, sometimes they incorporate in me and I see them like, for example, a child. Several materialize as forms. When they are in form they can teach wisdom . . . I feel and identify them. I seem them coming from a distance. They get close to me and then they become one with me. I experience them as separate entities up until the moment that they incorporate and I go unconscious.

There was a lot more of which Mai spoke to me, but much of it was of a private nature and not suitable to record here. Soon my friends came to collect me. I stood and gave Mai Santinha a good-bye hug. It was truly a privilege to know her and to see her at work.

Chapter XXIII

Stepped-Up Energy Reactions

What was happening to me? Edivaldo took me home for some dinner before driving me to the ferry boat. I don't remember much of what he said, things were still too fuzzy in my brain. A new energy was being formed within me, shaking me to my roots. Two months among the Spiritist, adventuring among the Umbanda; now in a short time, I had met three incredible mediums, received psychic surgery, tasted a mystical honey, and received special graces. All this was tearing down my old paradigms. When Jesus said that you can't put new wine into an old winesack, he was quite right. I was hoping that a new sack was going to replace the old or else I was in trouble. I remember walking the half mile from the ferry to my little beach house and falling into bed.

I fell quite soundly asleep until I felt a rustling in my bed. I jumped out, thinking that it might be a snake, or worse. I turned on the light but found it was nothing. I was feverish and sweating profusely, my heart was beating heavily. I turned off the light and got back into bed. A ray of moonlight passed through the closed window, casting odd shapes and dim shadows throughout the room. I suddenly felt scared, scared to the roots of my being.

"Hold on," said my inner voice. "Calm down, observe."

Oh sure, I thought. But what else could I do? No telephone, my closest friend at Lalo's house up the hilltop. What else to do but wait?

My body began to shake, and I felt that I wanted to throw up. Was this poisoning from the food? Then I remembered the honey which Mai Santinha had pushed into my mouth. Was this the process of spiritualization which she mentioned?

For the next few nights I slept badly, turning over in bed, seeing imaginary lights, and hearing occasional sounds within my head. My face was haggard for lack of sleep. After a few days of this, Marvin decided to sleep in the house to take care of me. Soon, the manifestations (for lack of a better word) stopped and I noticed that I was somehow . . . different . . . but in what way?

I became more aware of the fragility of life, its impermanence, of how fast it was moving by. The desire for spiritual things became more extreme. It became important to stop criticizing and judging, and to flow through life seemed the most important goal I could attain. I related much of this to my circle of friends in Salvador one day, and they commented upon the changes. We had all become closer, and there was mutual love apparent among all of us. We began to feel spiritual family ties. People seemed kinder to me. Something positive was occurring.

Chapter XXIV
Spirit Writing with Thelma Bastos

One day while talking with my friends on the investigation committee, I was told that Thelma, who was part of the team, was an accomplished medium in her own right. Mr. Torres, another committee member, told me of his experiences with her and encouraged me to seek her out. Finally, she told me that she would like to give me a session but was so filled with work at the Spiritist Center that she wasn't sure she could fit me in.

After quizzing her on the type of work she does, I made an offer; if she could find some time for me, then I would do some of her work. We struck a deal, and a week later I was seated in front of her at the Spiritist Center waiting for her to incorporate her spirit guide.

Thelma was a responsible high school administrator, who also found time for spiritual investigation, training mediums, and exercising mediumship herself. I requested an interview with her and her spirit because she is known to be a high-level psychographologist, or spirit writer.

She writes in the script of the spirit who enacts through her while she in a semitrance. She channels half-consciously and observes much of what comes through her. She allows the spirit to control her writing arm and her voice but rarely allows full unconscious control. She believes that unconscious trance limits the possibility of personal education. I found Thelma to be very balanced and cultivated. Her views are advanced and she questions the information which manifests in her readings, not readily accepting it as truth.

Thelma explained the workings of her mediumship and then requested to work in low light; the brilliance of full light inhibited meditation. I turned down one light, turning on a distant one. She turned on a tape recorder and played soft music, said a prayer, and waited in silence. I noticed that her body began to tremble slightly and her eyes went into REM.

Suddenly, with no apparent provocation, she began to write on large sheets of white paper. When Thelma incorporates, her face changes, her lips push out like an elderly man, and she speaks with an accent. Though her eyes were closed and she wrote very rapidly, she never went off the sheet. Her spirit worked in a pattern, only five sentences occupying about one-fourth of the page, then proceeded to the next page. Of course, I watched for trickery, but despite her velocity, she never went off onto the table the way that an unsure person might do. In this fashion, she wrote ten deliberate pages without stopping and then signed the letter.

After writing, the spirit, called Zoroaster, initiated a verbal interview between us. Though he began the interview in Portuguese, he adapted himself and soon was speaking in Spanish, a language which may or may not have been spoken by Thelma. In our previous conversations, she never used Spanish with me, so I am assuming that it was not part of her knowledge.

At first I wondered if Zoroaster was supposed to be the ancient Iranian prophet. That indeed would have been a significant interview. Alas, he said that was only his spirit name. He was the head of a group of cooperative spirits who channeled through Thelma once a week. He told me that he was more like a composite personality. I told him I was not quite sure what that meant. He tried to help me understand:

Ultimately all things are expressions of the one Universal Spirit differentiated in many forms. We, participating in the awareness of separateness, only experience ourselves as differentiated. Spirits also see themselves as apart or part of the cosmic Unity. If they are lower spirits they are separate individuals. Some group together, feeling union among them. We do this and experience our one light reflected in several of us. That is a composite personality. I imagine as we progress we experience our groups as broadening until we are one with the Totality.

I realized that Zoroaster was a very evolved being compared to some other spirits, who still saw themselves as individual entities. It seemed as well that as spirits evolve, the earth work lessens and spirit phenomena are less dramatic. The higher they evolve, the less interest they have in our world and the more absorbed in the Oneness they become. As another spirit told me:

> As one becomes aware of the One, and union replaces separation, there is less need to do and more need to be: to be still, to flow, to experience. A spirit in this position knows that surgery and other paranormal work is on the fringe of reality and a waste of time from the cosmic viewpoint.

I was amazed to find the differences in awareness among the various spirits. Zoroaster conversed with me for one hour, during which the medium's stature changed and he tended to hunch forward. I had the distinct impression that he took on this posture for my benefit. At the end of the discussion, the spirit wished to give me his traditional blessing. Thelma, still in trance, got up and walked around the table with her eyes closed, bumped into nothing, walk up to me and placed her hands on my head in benediction. Then the medium returned to her seat. Not a full second later, without any indication, she and the spirit disincorporated.

The conversation consisted of questions centered around the nature and consciousness of life in other worlds, of Jesus and other teachers, diet, and some less philosophic concepts. I found Zoroaster somewhat general in answering my questions, straying from specifics as he told me:

> In these questions one must remain open-minded and not get dogmatic about them. Just because one is in the spirit world does not mean that he has access to all truth or is a person of wisdom. Death on your side does not guarantee illumination!

When the spirit left her, Thelma's face changed as did her stature and voice. She translated the spirit's message, which, in essence, praised me for my spiritual integrity, my willingness to seek in places where others feared to enter, and my scientific attitude. The spirit assured me of success in my endeavors and that the spirits stood willing to aid me in any way.

Hare some excerpts of my conversation with the spirit Zoroaster:

"Are you the same as the Persian prophet of that name?"

. . . I use the name "Zoroaster," but that is not my reality. A name is not important, the message is of importance and the work that we do . . . we are a group of entities which heal, teach. Our purpose is to help you self-realize your creativity and potential . . . My last incarnation was in the Second World War in Germany . . . mediumship is an open canal!

"I've asked this question before but I want your opinion. Why is there so much spirit work in Brazil?"

. . . there is so much spirit work in Brazil, yes. But it is in all parts of the world; people don't understand and open themselves up to it. The fact of mediumship is scientifically demonstrable, but it depends upon the receptivity which people have to it. Brazil suffers and depends upon our help . . . we all incarnate the potential. Here the people are more mystic.

"Without seeming too judgmental I would like to say that some spirits seem to be unbalanced and very egocentric. Many who speak in the United States make tremendous claims to their self-importance."

Morals and ethics go in accord with your own consciousness. Morality is the process of growth, which ends in true love . . . There doesn't exist a fixed definition; it goes in accordance to the individual consciousness . . . Some of us use our forces to rise up spiritually, others do nothing and pass from incarnation to incarnation.

We have many egotists here on our side. They don't impress us very much, but they attract like vibrations in their mediums and impress many on your side. Judge them by their fruits. Do they strive to make earth a better place?

"One medium told me that the same spirits wear different masks and adapt themselves to the different gatherings they attend. For example, a spirit who appears as a European teacher in a Spiritist meeting may appear as an African spirit in the Candomble or a crianza in the Umbanda. What is your feeling toward this idea?"

The spirit is attracted to the medium by the various feelings, ideas, vibrations, and words which the medium's environment uses. And so we go to all different gatherings. We synchronize ourselves to the forms and needs of diverse groups . . . our goal is to serve, to offer service . . . We are attracted by the motivation of people. That is what we see. The form is secondary.

"Can a spirit incorporate in a medium without trance?"

Incorporation can't exist unless trance exists. However, a transmission of ideas can exist without trance through the intuition . . . Spirits and mediums attract each other, little by little through the affinity of ideas, thoughts, until both think the same. Under these circumstances, there is a transmission through impulses and thought waves, without incorporation. These two souls draw together. Yes, there can be communication without incorporation.

"You are a discarnate spirit. The medium is an incarnate spirit who withdraws to create space for you. Can the medium's spirit incorporate in you in the same way that you incorporate in him?"

No, the medium can't incorporate in me . . . The medium can block incorporation by questioning and disbelief, but no, it can't incorporate in me . . . We work by cooperation. By disequilibrium and disrespect, the relation is broken. The desire to be a medium is decided before the soul's incarnation. It is not a decision made from one moment to the other. The entity incarnates and the moment arrives for the flowering of mediumship.

"What of Samadhi, of the Hindu masters? Is this not a higher state than incorporation?"

They practice a state of consciousness . . . they don't seek spirits . . . they believe that they are Spirit. They do healing from that state.

"What of Nirvana?"

It is total harmony of the body-mind-spirit. It is a state of total silence, deep, a very deep connection with the spiritual world. This is eternal, full vision, true connection, a complete detachment, this is not trance . . . If we dedicate ourselves to deep meditation, we can gain this. It is not trance but a spiritual conquest . . . I cannot speak of it because I am not there. Were I there, I could not speak of it.

"Is Nirvana total absorption?"

I believe so; that is true. The great ones attain this; they integrate their thoughts with the universe. But they don't lose their individuality. We are individual and in the world of individuality. Even when we expand into greater consciousness and identify with great cosmic beings we don't lose our individuality.

"From your point of view, what are the Buddhas?"

They expand and identify with the great cosmic forces. They become the forces and do the work of these great energies.

"Why do Spiritist mediums only mention Jesus?"

In Brazil the people speak of Jesus, in the Orient of other persons. That is a corporeal vision. We are all spirits. They come with specific work to help humanity. However because of the culture and religion, we identify with one or another. But with the integration of the East and West seeking out yoga and meditation, new Oriental therapies, there will be an intermingling and synthesis. The world passes through the transformation process and synthesis is very important. All paths which lead us to God are important. It does not matter if we are Catholic, Buddhist, Protestant . . . what is of value is that we grow into cosmic beings . . . many spirits have incorporated with the mission to bring us together. They see this world of wars, conflicts, and strife and came to help us. They help us grow, to illuminate, etcetera . . . they deny themselves to their work.

"What do you see as the final purpose of mediumship?

Mediumship is a process of necessity. Without need there could be no mediumship. Interchange is an aspect of evolution . . . we arrive at an evolved state when something has been understood. We are more conscious, more aware, more receptive, more intuitive . . . We are very far away from the medium. But the medium is very receptive and captures our thoughts . . .

"I am concerned about the levels of creativity in the mediums themselves."

147

The production seen in mediumship isn't from the mediums but from the spirits through them. The medium produces nothing. He is an instrument. His lack outside of trance depends on his process of interest, rapport, maybe he has no intent . . . If he wants to paint, he can; if he has enough interest, he could paint as well out of trance as during it. Some want to paint bad enough so they develop their capacity. There is no relation between what they do in and out of trance. It is all related to desire, rapport, and intention.

"What happens to the 'I'?"

The medium develops confidence in the spirit. But the person doesn't abandon the body. The "I" remains . . . there is no space to go to . . . space is construed by us. It is true, however, that the medium's spirit is not "present." The medium's trance doesn't require that the spirit leave the body. The trance is psychic, affected through the pineal. We work though the medium's mind so he can feel our thoughts and move his body. The medium feels the thoughts if he is conscious or unconscious. All communication depends upon the rapport of the spirit and the medium. The medium can leave his organism over to the spirit because he confides in him. But the medium's spirit doesn't fully abandon his body. This would be irresponsibility . . . the spirit isn't inside the body of the medium. There is a connection.

So ended the conversation between me and Zoroaster, apparently a spirit with much wisdom and honesty.

Chapter XXV
Quimbanda: The Dark Side of Umbanda

Friday nights are very special in Umbanda. Thousands of Umbanda priests enter private chapels, many of them located in the basements of, or behind, the principal sanctuaries. The public is not usually invited into these private shrines. They are usually kept dark, and special prayers and invocations are made. These are the sanctuaries where the Quimbas are invoked.

Quimbas are spirits which wander about the earth without having found their space. It is an entity utilized by the *feticieros* ("fetishists") for realizing malevolent spells.

Quimbanda is a derivative sect of the Umbanda, which makes use of black magic in order to satisfy the requests of its supplicants. The altars in Quimbanda temples are draped in black, blood red, yellow, and other colors of the infernal spirits. There are tridents with images of Satan upon them. This is the Umbanda interpretation of Quimbanda.

One night before an Umbanda service, I wandered about the grounds, sticking my nose into different places. I noticed a small sanctuary off to one side, rather out of the way, which had an iron gate closing it off. I peeked into the small room, actually a saint's house, the size of a sepulcher or mausoleum seen in expensive cemeteries.

The space was quite dark, except for a few red, black, and yellow candles burning in the pitch-dark, and infused with an incense I could not name. The room had a very special type of darkness to it and a silence which was quite heavy, almost tangible. It was clearly a very sacred place, and yet there was something different about it.

As my eyes adjusted, I was able to penetrate the darkness. I could see the outlines of statues on a simple, yet dignified altar. In the center

149

was a demonic image, not frightening, but quite similar to the Greek Pan; the legs and waist were animal and the chest and head were human. It had goat horns and a tail and held a pitchfork in its right hand. Clearly a replica of what most Christians would consider a devil to look like.

The statue was surrounded by what appeared to be sensual women, black and white, in seductive positions and obviously very attractive. These were his pombagiras and members of his falange. There were also male statues of minor devils who were the *elebaras*. There was a plate of food in front of the Devil and small tridents stuck into pails filled with sand. The entire panorama was fascinating but wasn't one to induce fright; on the contrary, I felt myself standing in front of an ancient god of fertility, liberation, and of the forests. A moment later I felt a hand on my shoulder. A voice told me that I shouldn't be in this room, that it was reserved only for special occasions.

I later asked Mai Neusa, the director of this tenda, about the room. She stated rather stiffly that it was a saint's house, but obviously didn't want to give me any more information. I found out later that I had entered into the house of the exu and his falange members—a chapel dedicated to Quimbanda.

A few months later I was invited to visit a country tenda on the island of Itaparica. We located the sanctuary, and before entering into the compound, we had to pass an altar. It was a round, metal dish, about half a yard wide. It was filled with sand. In the center of it stood a symbol of some type that I could not identify. It was a pronglike object with other pieces of steel leaning at different inclines.

Around it there were offerings of money, cigarettes, incense, etcetera. As I looked at it, I felt a cold hand run over my body, making me tremble somewhat. I could feel a very powerful wet coldness surround me, and my scalp prickled with the sensation. I wasn't sure of what it was, but I knew I didn't want to stand in front of it much longer and moved away. Later, speaking with the Pai, I asked what that altar was and to whom it was dedicated. He explained that it was the altar of the guardian of the sanctuary, an exu. He said that it emitted a coldness that prevented anyone wishing to disturb or to do harm from entering the sacred grounds. Another manifestation of Quimbanda.

According to the dictionary of Afro-Brazilian cults, Quimbanda is defined as an offshoot of Umbanda, which practices black magic. It is somewhat parallel to the practices and forms of Umbanda, but has its own lineage of transmission. It employs Catholic images and worship. The orixas are also worshipped, albeit with a different emphasis.

Quimbanda gives special preeminence to the exus, pombagiras, and lower astral spirits, employing songs, dances, and colors in the rites. Umbanda postulates Quimbanda as its opposite pole; Umbanda practices white magic and Quimbanda, black. Most of the rites of Quimbanda are performed at midnight.(12)

There is a lot of confusion regarding Quimbanda. Many years of poor understanding on the part of the public and among its representatives have produced a system that is, more often than not, used to satisfy the ego.

This, together with a poorly established syncretism between the Catholic archfiend and other concepts have produced a mixed-up vision, which even today is accepted as the exu, the pombagiras, and elebaras, all part of the hellish host. Yet that is not necessarily so.

It was most difficult to make contact with an authentic Quimbanda priest. We traveled all over the city of Salvador seeking one out. After all, I had made contact with the other three great spirit traditions: the Kardecists, the Umbanda, and the Candomble. I was not about to leave Brazil without learning also of this tradition, considered so despicable that other priests claimed to have nothing to do with it.

I was told in Salvador by the newsperson Teresa de Correa that in some parts of Brazil the Quimbanda was outlawed. It certainly was socially outlawed by the other religions.

I had a young friend, Beto, a Kardecist, who spent some time trying to track down a Quimbanda terreiro, but without luck. One night he appeared at my house, and by midnight we were in the care of a friend, Carlos de Moraes, trying to locate the house. We found the house, which turned out to be an Umbanda terreiro. Quite a disappointment.

Undaunted, we continued our search, and the following weekend, we had a lead. I was told that in Cachoera, an inland city, was an authentic Quimbanda Pai who was still practicing, more or less openly. You can't look into the Brazilian Yellow Pages under "Devil Priests" and expect to find an address, so the next weekend, Carlos, Beto, their families, and I all packed into a car for the drive to Cachoera, the first capital of the empire of Brazil. It was a wonderful town to visit, and after leaving the children and wives in a nice hotel, we went off on the devil priest hunt. Our search ended in front of a small house on a hilltop. Nothing identified it as the home of Pai Barbossa, an ancient black who worked the Buzios in the name of Quimbanda.

Pai Barbossa was not willing to tell me anything about the religion, as seems to be the practice. He did, however, read my fortune and told me to come back in a few days for an interview. I also obtained permission to film our interview.

The session was an odd one, fraught with difficulties. When I entered the chapel, his candle, placed in front of the exu, went out. That created quite a stir, as there was no breeze in the room and the candle had been burning for hours with no problem. The Pai called for his acolyte to relight it, but mysteriously, it sputtered and went out again. Another candle was brought in and we began the session.

At times the Pai would fall asleep for a moment. At others he would go into a trance state, his eyes would roll up into his head, and he would speak in a slightly different voice. It was hard for us to communicate in his dialect, but through the able assistance of Carlos, we finally got our messages across to each other. However, while the session was interesting, I had learned nothing. I still had no further knowledge of Quimbanda. Incidentally, I was later told that after I left, the stubborn candle was relit and burned perfectly.

Over the next few weeks I researched this religion in the Center for Afro-Studies at the University in Salvador. The professors were devoid of information and would tell me only what I already knew; Quimbanda is considered the religion of demons and is used to invoke their favors by those who seek gain.

Quimbanda is a proscribed religion, having the weight of the law levied against it. Of all the spiritistic and initiatory religions, this is the most veiled, its secrets shrouded even from those who seek its aid. Though Quimbanda is often attacked or avoided, its altars may be seen on many street corners, at important crossroads, and even in the marketplaces. I often came across statues of the dark exu with hundreds of offerings placed before them. No one dares interfere with the public altars; they are places of great respect and inspire great fear. Most Pais with whom I discussed Quimbanda warned me against investigating it.

Quimbanda is a lineage of Umbanda, using magical rituals and invoking the lesser evolved spirits—the exu, pombagiras, elebaras, and others—with the goal of satisfying man's basest desires.

According to one small report, it is not uncommon for these spirits, incorporated in their priests, to approach and solicit sex from devotees. The elebaras are often homosexual spirits and solicit other men who are present. Women who come to the practices are also solicited for sexual favors, and the cult services often end up in orgiastic practices. I must admit that I have only read this but not seen it myself.

Yet it is not clear whether these forces are "dark" or merely branded so by uninformed practitioners and followers of other sects. Remember that as Christianity spread over Europe, the local deities and pagan gods and goddesses were often branded as demons and their images often blended into the composite devil.

After speaking with several professors of the Afro-Brazilian religions, I began to arrive at some questions. The figure of the exu, the head of the hierarchy of Quimbanda spirits was a fertility figure. He was also classified as a source of chaotic and dynamic actions, especially powerful in the forests and the places where indigenous peoples resided. He was a libertine, and his cults were often frenzied sessions which ended in orgiastic rituals.

Lapassade and Alvez confirm this in their investigations of Quimbanda:

> The whirling dancers strike an aspect of licentiousness and sexuality. The dance becomes a theater which symbolizes inner desires for sexual and social liberty. The gods (Exu) who reign at these festivities encourage the dissolution and breakdown of rules and order and the renunciation of oneself to the burning ecstasy of emotional and sexual release practices. (24)

This has many precedents in our cultural traditions. We have experienced this before in the rites of Bacchus, or Dionysus, and of Apollo, in the secrets of Eleusis, and in the older Middle-Eastern cults of death and resurrection. Might it not then be that the feared and hated Quimbanda is the relic of some long-abandoned tantric tradition, one which practiced some sacred sexual magic still being instructed in special temples of the East? Could not the pombagiras be what is left of the ancient temple prostitutes of Astarte and other mother-goddesses? Might not the exu itself be the degenerate form of the once mighty Ba'al, or Moloch, or other deities who ruled the pre-Judaic world?

The symbolic interpretation of the Umbanda hierarchy may be of some value in understanding Quimbanda. The chain of axe would place Olorum on the top, followed by the orixas, the falange members and finally the exus of Quimbanda. Placing this order over the human body, we find that we are faced with three energy zones: the positive, the neutral, and the negative. Further, placing them over the spinal column we may surmise the following correspondence: Olorum is the top of the head, containing the glands of illumination such as the pineal, the pituitary, the hypothalamus and the highest chakra. The orixas would occupy the cervical vertebrae. The falange membership would occupy the greatest amount of thoracic vertebrae, and the Quimbas (exus and assistants) would represent the lowest lumbar vertebrae, sacrum, and coccyx.

The answers may not be forthcoming, for even in the Brazilian centers of investigation, no conclusions have been drawn upon this religion. That it has not been completely forgotten is significant in itself. That the exu, pombagiras, and Elebaras still hold a distinguished, if despicable, place in the pantheon of Umbanda deities is indicative of something. That the Pais and Mais still invoke these beings in secret means that they are still considered to be powerful sources of wisdom and energy.

Perhaps, one day, the veils which hide the sanctuary will be rent asunder and the dim lights flickering upon the altars of Quimbanda may for an instant burst forth and reveal to the world its untamed secrets and powers. Then the hidden teaching might be revealed as one which uses the lower energies to liberate the souls from its clasps of prohibitions and taboos which bind it to obsessive and comforting limitations.

It is taught in Hindu and sacred anatomy that it is there, in the lowest part of the spinal system that the kundalini hides. This febrile energy, as it passes through the cerebrospinal system, destroys all impurities it encounters, thus preparing the practitioner for illumination.

My own sense is that the Quimbanda, after stripping away centuries of fear and illusion, may yet turn out to be that very kundalini source for the other spiritistic religions. Within the African religious culture, Quimbanda may be a school of special Tantric wisdom.

Chapter XXVI
Babalorixa Pai Nivardo

Salvador, Bahia

"You have to come with me Thursday night," insisted one of my friends from the vegetarian restaurant. "This Pai is different. He does things differently. He worships the saints."

"So what is so different about that?" I asked him. "All of them do."

"Just come," he insisted. "Pai Nivardo is different."

My friend was a devotee of Umbanda and not given to the Candomble. But he was enthusiastic about Pai Nivardo, though, he insisted, he was not going to join his group.

The next day I telephoned the terreiro and was invited to come for an interview on Wednesday afternoon. Then, if I was accepted, I could come to the Thursday evening worship.

On Wednesday afternoon, I set out by myself through the oldest and supposedly the most dangerous part of the city, walking up one hill and down another till I found myself near the monastery of Saint Francis. I made my way up some steep steps and searched out the address. There was no name, nothing to indicate that this was a terreiro, but I knew this was it.

I went up the two flights of steps and arrived at an iron door. I rang the bell and was greeted by an interesting fellow, a weight lifter.

Surely this cannot be the Pai, I thought. *Too young and too healthy looking.*

It wasn't. It was one of the fellows who lived at the center and was studying to be a sacred drummer. He invited me to sit down. When he learned that I was American, he asked me a thousand questions about the United States.

His interest put me at ease; I was feeling a bit relieved about coming here. I saw no altars covered with animal bits nor blood splattered on the walls, as I had been warned of. On the contrary, it looked like a great big old house and nothing more.

Pai Nivardo's institute, I learned, was the Spiritualist Center of the Immaculate Conception, so called because it was founded on January eighth, the day, according to the Roman Catholic calendar, of the Immaculate Conception of Jesus Christ. January eighth is a day of celebration of the Virgin Mary, but in the Candomble, actually refers to Yemanja, the Candomble Mother of the orixas.

My contemplation of the old house was interrupted by the Pai's secretary. I introduced myself, a bit nervously perhaps. I had never been involved in anything so secretive before.

"Yes, we were told that you would come," the secretary said. "Please sit down, and the Pai will interview you in a while." The secretary left the room, and I turned back to chat with my muscular friend about life in the United States. Soon I heard someone coming. I stood up as was customary.

It was Pai Nivardo. My companion ran over to him, bent down, and kissed his hand. That is also custom, though not one of mine. I extended my hand. We shook, then sat and talked for quite a while.

I was surprised to see that Nivardo was Portuguese and not Negro. Many of the African priests of the Candomble inherited their congregations. But the fact that there are also so many non-African European Pais is something else. Without exception, each converted to Candomble from some other form because of some "miraculous" event in their lives.

Pai Nivardo was also unique in that he was quite well versed in the holy books of other religions, especially the Bible. His understanding of his adopted religion differed somewhat from that of the majority of other Pais, in that Pai Nivardo used the Bible a lot, interspersing his sermons with scripture and showing the practical similarities between the rites of the ancient Hebrews and the modern Candomble. He was also quick to criticize the degenerate behavior of other Pais and the misuse of their powers.

I began the questioning:

"First, please tell me how you see your center as different from the other Candomble terrieros."

Our center is a combination of mediumistic practices, including Umbanda, Kardecism, and Candomble. But I no longer consider myself any of them. My personal story is very long. At six months old it all begins. I lived on my parents' farm. There was a black man, who was also like a member of the family, who lived there.

One day I fell into a type of trance. Everyone thought that I was sick. I was unconscious. He began to sing, to hit me, and do other things.

At one year old I had a spontaneous incorporation of Yemanja. The black man told my family that this was not sickness, but mediumship. My family was Catholic and knew nothing of these practices.

They believed him and at seven years old I began my obligations as a future priest of Candomble. I was unconscious when I incorporated . . . the family told me all of this.

At seven years old I was chosen and began to work with the spirits. Then I acquired other "sons" of the saints. There are about fifty sons presently. I travel a lot. I have one in Miami and one in Switzerland.

"Your story is incredible. You had an incorporation of a deity with whom you had no previous personal experience or knowledge. This experience has obviously left you open to many opportunities and alternatives?"

Yes. I never consider that I know everything. Even as a Pai, I cannot make that assumption. The universe is great and has too much to offer. I have to keep myself open to receiving more, as well as giving much.

"I hear a lot about the exu. In the Candomble he is the closest to the Christian devil. In Umbanda they tell me the exu is evil and terribly powerful. What is your opinion?"

For me the exu is an orixa. He is not the Christian devil. He accepts offers, he carries messages, he governs oracles. The exu participates in all things. He never was a devil, nor is he a full god. He is the Son of Yemanja . . .

The African slaves weren't accepted in the white Catholic churches. They worshipped at their own altars with their own gods. But they put the Catholic saints on top of the altar to fool the white men. Under the altars they placed their ancient gods. Correspondence then occurred between their gods and saints to fool the whites. The exu in this way was related with the devil. But there is no relationship between one and another.

"Can you explain some of the cult practices which I find in all Umbanda and Candomble terreiros, such as touching the ground, water, and incense?"

In the cult practice, the people touch the ground to identify with the earth energies . . . below this special tile there is some power object interred. It is something related to the presiding god. This informs the entity of his ownership. Outside of the temple, there often are other god's houses for the different deities and where they are welcome. Incense is used for cleaning. It is combined with leaves, water, salt water to purify the environment. Water is prepared with herbs and leaves. It is left in the air for a certain time to purify it. Water in the cult represents Oxumare: a goddess/god of water. Six months he is man, the other, woman. Six months he resides in water, six in the stars. The water in the basin is homage to him/her.

"In speaking with various Pais, it seems that the number of orixas varies from the north to the south. How many are there and how do you see them?"

There are twenty-one orixas or divinities, each had an infinite "falange." The falange is composed of the orixas who serve and obey a principal orixa or chief. The main orixas are preexistent beings. Before earth they lived. The Bible uses a plural word for God: Elohim. These are the orixas or the Powers that created the universe. The orixas are Christs.

The falanges are divinities but are obedient to the chiefs. They are like secondary angels, obedient to the archangels. The gods are energies. The falanges are heavenly beings like the devas. The reason why there is so much confusion regarding the orixas is because as a rule it is difficult to find an educated babalorixa.

"It appears that you are quite universal in your spiritual outlook."

Yes, that is so. I am a spiritualist because I use parts of all traditions. For me, God has no names. He is identified with nature, so pure, so infinite, without any name. One cannot help but be universal.

"Let me ask another question about the exu, of whom I have been reading all that I can. It seems that the exu is similar to the deity Shiva of the Hindus. Destruction is a necessary part of life, to make space to prepare for the coming of the new. Is that also part of the work of the exu?"

It can be that the orixas are characteristics of the one God. Especially the exu is beautiful but receives bad publicity. The people don't understand. The sects don't comprehend him . . . The egun do evil to mankind. Not the exu. The exu are very great and do much good . . . The exu destroys so that the new may have space . . .

We are energy and attract other types of energy . . . Man may transform energy to light. But energy exists at the command of God. This energy is the exu, transformation. We are rational beings . . . but we also have irrationality. We are both positive and negative . . . analyzing this, the exu is part of us.

"A lot has been written concerning the sacred dance. The idea of dance is universal to many traditions; all of the native traditions use it, plus the Sufi, the Hassidic Jews, the Hindus, and other great traditions. In the Candomble it is called the 'gira.' "

The gira can't be danced consciously . . . it is spontaneous and must come from the deepest levels, because it is a preparation dance for the orixas . . . together with songs, the medium enters into trance and the orixa incorporates. The gira is a discipline of preparation. The students develop their mediumship by dancing. All men and women may dance until they begin to dance freely without programs.

The mediumship religions existed long before Jesus. All that we do today has its origins in the distant past. Saul of the Bible, the first king of Israel danced to prophecy. David danced before the Ark of the Law and was criticized for it.

"I know that you don't charge for your services. How do you maintain the center and what else do you offer?"

"It is interesting how we acquired the center. We rented here for many

159

years. The owners of this building, who are Catholics, told us that they were going to sell it and we would have to move. I became very worried because the rent was very little and we have little money to spend.

I went into trance and Yemanja appeared to me telling me not to worry, that she would take care of it.

In a few days the owners came to me and said that they were *giving* us the building. I asked why. It seems that they had a dream in which a luminous lady appeared to them. They identified her to be the Virgin Mary, who is, of course, the counterpart of Yemanja. The Virgin told them that it would be meritorious in God's sight to donate the building to us. So they did, even though they are Roman Catholics.

This should not surprise you as the people here are respectful of other religions. The orixas have always protected us. Therefore, we charge nothing here for our services. We never live off of our spiritual work.

Besides the cult worship, I am training my "sons" to become priests. We have a program of spiritual education and studies concerning other religions as well. Then we have our services for those who need financial help and counseling. We don't have much income here, being a rather poor center. But we have activities to help out those who ask us for help. Then we also have mediumship training and classes for the initiates. But I cannot speak of them to you. [He smiled, then laughed out loud.]

"One last question. You are called a babalorixa. What is that?"

A babalorixa is a male archpriest. An iolorixa is a woman. There are higher levels of priests and many titles but I am not stuck on them. It is the spirituality of the person that is more important.

Pai Nivardo invited me to come the following Thursday to attend the "cult of the saints," as he called it. The purpose of the cult was to allow people to receive axe from the saint(s) who appear at the dance. Only those who are initiates may dance. Other participants maintained themselves in an attitude of expectation and readiness to receive the bestowal of grace in their lives.

I found the dancing to be very exciting and sensual in a way that was different from that in other centers. Pai Gerardo's dancing was youthful and idealistic; Mai Zelinda's was purposeful; Mai Neusa was somewhat mechanical. The dancing here was "soft" and quite feminine, probably because the patron saint is the Mother of All, Yemanja.

When Pai Nivardo entered the room, everyone stood up. There were about eighty people present, and the entire group chanted a hymn. I sat in the back of the room with some other men, as I had come in a little bit late. I met a young man who was attending for the first time as well. He was a little bit nervous at being there. He was a university student, concerned that his presence might adversely affect his academic career. Of course he should have been there!

The energy generated during the dancing can only be described and experienced as an admixture of complete joy, heat, and sensuality. In the Candomble, there are none of the taboos of Christianity. This is an ancient pagan religion that celebrates the animalistic joy of being alive. It is the worship of nature and its presiding forces, and is expressed in the wild and sometimes chaotic movements of the dancers.

Several of the young women were whirled around quite rapidly with their eyes closed. That they were spinning so fast for over twenty minutes without rest was something to see. Also remarkable was that in the chaos, none of the dancers ever bumped or brushed up against any other of the twenty or so mediums dancing. It was as if they had a special sight. Pai Nivardo explained to me that the whirling is the expression of divine movement, the movement inherent in all things. It is the dance of the atoms, the planets, the flow of the All.

The energy became so intense that I felt I was being affected. But if I was, then the young man sitting next to me certainly was, too, for in the next moment he scared me almost to death.

Imagine. This very timid-looking young fellow sat quietly in his chair, watching the flurry of movement that was the dance. Suddenly, he screamed and seemed to be thrown off of his chair. Gaining his feet, he ran down the aisle as if possessed (he was possessed). The young man was thrown down on the sacred dance floor and began to leap and whirl around himself. Within moments, he was dancing with the most sensual movements I have ever seen. His eyes were completely closed. He was beautiful to watch. Those of us present knew in whose company we were standing; the energy he emitted was that of the Mother. After about a half hour of dancing, he stopped as suddenly as he had started. When he opened his eyes he looked confused, as if wondering what he was doing there. He told me later that he had no recollection of his participation in the service.

When the dancing finished, some six mediums went into deep

161

trance. Those of us who wished to receive healing came forward. The mediums made sharp sounds as they touched us, like birds. These sounds, I was told, are primal sounds, as the orixas do not speak as we understand speaking.

The entire room was warm and electric with energy. The mediums ran their hands down my body and around me to restore and balance my energies. I felt nothing strange nor different during this encounter, but I can't imagine anything being any more invigorating and exciting.

I began to attend all of the giras held in this center. During one in particular, I was standing up against a wall, watching, when I suddenly felt hands pushing me into the center of the dance floor. I looked to both sides of me to see if anyone was jokingly pushing me out. But no one was there. The pushes seemed to be coming from the sacrum and were like gentle reflexes which would thrust my spinal column outward. My inner voice informed me (big surprise!) that something was occurring.

I looked across the room and saw Pai Nivardo standing there, smiling at me. I prayed, "Dear Mother Yemanja, please don't make me do this. I can hardly walk, let alone dance. I would hate to fall flat on my face in front of these people." Perhaps an unusual supplication to the goddess, but she decided to let me go.

After the session, Pai came up to me. "I saw that Mother was standing behind you trying to get you to dance. It seems that she has claimed you for herself."

I then told him what I had prayed. "Of course, from a logical standpoint you can't dance well. I also have a bad leg. But when the Mother claims you, she dances through you and ignores any disability. When I dance I do not even know that my leg is weak!" Still, I was glad that Yemanja had let me off the hook.

At a later meeting with Pai Nivardo, I asked if I could film some of the dancing to show at the university in the United States. His immediate answer was a resounding and definite *no*. Then, strangely, he recanted and said, "Well, we have never allowed it. You know that people will not treat the gira with respect. . . . But let me consult the others."

A few days later he sent me a message: "We consulted the orixas, and they are willing to grant your request. Come next Thursday night to film. We will cooperate in everything."

The night's taping went smoothly. We got much interesting footage to show back in the States. However, an even more interesting occurrence finalized the evening's events.

At the very end of the evening, we entered into the god's house, which is in a separate room behind the sanctuary. We intended to contrast the silence of the god's house with the chaos of the trance dancing. There was no one present in the sanctuary.

We filmed the final five minutes of tape there. But when we played back the film, something of paranormal proportion had occurred. From the minute we entered the god's house, the film became congested with the sound of the buzzing of what seemed like hundreds of bees. The sound surrounded and engulfed us, though there was nothing on the tape to be seen but the sanctuary. When we filmed the video, there was nothing to be heard but the sound of silence.

When we showed the tape to Pai Nivardo and asked him to listen, he stated quite matter-of-factly, "Oh, that is a special sound of the orixas. They are blessing your work."

Why they should do that is beyond me, but all of the spirits were putting in their part. I would gladly accept any blessings on hand!

Chapter XXVII
Brasilia

Sooner than I would have wished, it was time to take leave of my many friends in Bahia and continue my trip to other parts of the country. I was also to separate from my traveling companion, Marvin, who wanted to head directly north, while I wanted to visit the capital. So we parted with the idea of reuniting in Costa Rica. My students and friends gave me a send-off party with tears and promises of meeting again before we all died. Reluctantly, but filled with new experiences and friendship, I boarded my plane to the Federal District.

I wanted to visit Brasilia for several reasons. I had heard that it was a city completely planned down to the most minute detail and that the architecture of its buildings was quite novel for Latin America. I had also learned that the leading religions had their offices there and there would be interesting temples to be seen. I had heard of an interesting spiritual community which was mediumship oriented, and I wanted to stay with them awhile. Finally, I wished to visit the International Holistic University, of which I had heard so much.

Arriving in the capital, I found a small guest house to stay in. It was located in the downtown area near the bank and next to a magnificent crystal cathedral. I spent the first day doing the tourist thing, going down to see the Federal Palace, the lake, and the National Catholic Cathedral, built to represent an inverted Eucharist chalice. It was very large and quite beautiful, as is most of the capital. It was also a welcome break from the rest of the country.

From the air, the capital appears to be an airplane itself. It is divided into two extensions which represent the wings of the plane. Then there is a crescent-shaped lake that surrounds half of the capital. The lake

164

was built to keep the city cool in the summer. It doesn't seem to work, however and the politicians flee on weekends to their native states.

Walking around Brasilia is an experience in and of itself. Once one has the hang of it, one is amazed by what must be the most beautiful and well organized city in all of Latin America. I was told by some esoteric students that Brasilia has seven pyramids in and around it and that I should visit the most beautiful of all, O Templo do Boa Vontade ("The Temple of Good Will"), which is the mother temple of this interesting religious sect.

On the second day, I visited a Buddhist temple located not far from the banking district. All of the major temples were built on land allotted to them by the state. All were placed in certain positions to beautify the city. The Buddhist temple, which belonged to the Pure Land Sect, was open to all Buddhists. Their representative told me that Tibetans, Zen, and others also used it for their practice.

A sizable portion of the Brazilian population practices Buddhism of various types: in the capital there are five Zen groups, one Tibetan group, and, of course, the Nicheren people, who have their own temple. The Buddhist temple is red and black, built to reflect Japanese tradition. It is surrounded by gardens and is quite lovely.

After wandering around there for a few hours, I decided to walk the pleasant paths to view The Temple of Good Will.

The temple is located on one of the outer streets of the city. It sits atop an artificial rise and can be seen from about a mile away from several parts of the city. However, the crow-flight distances in this city are very deceptive; I was deceived by my view of the temple and decided to walk to it. Much to my chagrin, it was considerably more than a mile. But the beauty of the temple was so overwhelming that by the time I arrived, it was all the more worth the effort it took to visit.

For a person who has visited as many beautiful temples as I, I had to admit that this building was a complete and utter surprise. Every detail of the temple was noteworthy. The quiet sector in which it is located added to the strangeness and majesty of the place. I was not accustomed to such cleanliness and order that I saw in the interior of the temple. I was told the day before that a visit to the temple would be a real treat. It certainly turned out that way for me.

The temple itself is a seven-sided pyramid, topped with a very large amethyst crystal. One enters through an underground passage, which is kept in darkness. Once entry is gained, however, the opposite is seen. Past the portals, the temple is bathed in light, as the bright sunlight coming in through side panels was gently diffused by the lavender light passing through the amethyst on top.

The temple is truly marvelous. The sanctuary is uncluttered, and each room is beautifully appointed with Oriental carpets and art work. An art lover will find the temple flooded with many examples of fine art. There is also a gallery where various programs are held.

Restful music flows through the building, calming the mind and soul. On the lowest level of the building, a meditation chapel contains the remains of Zahur, the founder. On the walls of the mausoleum is a dramatic scene of the final battle between the light and the nonlight, in which the angels of the Lord battle the evils of this world. There is other art work, well placed and very costly. There is also a warmth to this room, which is womblike and calm and made me want to remain there a long time.

There is another wonder here as well. The workers in the temple are quiet, courteous, and very eager to help out. The activities in the temple were explained to me by one of these extremely friendly volunteer guides. Worshippers walk a spiral path, designed into the floor of the sanctuary, until they arrive at the center of the building, directly under, he said, "the largest crystal in the world." Here they raise their hands upward and remain for a while, receiving the healing magnetic light of the sun.

Whether or not the amethyst is, in fact, "the largest crystal in the world" is perhaps open for debate. But the Brazilians, living in a large country, tend to make everything of cosmic proportions, like Texans in the United States. Their men and women are more attractive and their crystals are bigger than anywhere else. Everything is better; at least that is what they believe. And I love them for it.

The quietude of the temple, if you can imagine it, was loud and exhausting, and I needed a break. I entered the chapel to find a pew upon which I might rest my body and meditate for a while. As I settled into a comfortable position to prepare myself for the meditative experience, a loud voice, that of the Zahur, founder of the Legion, blared out these words: "Let's talk with God." I really didn't want to talk with anyone, but who has a choice as a guest in someone else's church?

It was hard to find a quiet room to meditate in. There was an "official" room below the main floor, and I hurried to take refuge in it. But there was a policeman guarding it, and I couldn't get back in the mood to let go anyway. The message, which was recorded, played on and on, accompanied by trumpets and other celestial instruments. Apparently, it played automatically every hour for the benefit of those who wished to pray in the sanctuary. Finally I became despondent and left. However, despite the annoying intervention of taped messages (which obviously doesn't affect everyone in the same way), this temple has never closed its doors to anyone, day or night, since it was dedicated. Anyone can go there at any hour for meditation and find the building staffed with the eager guides to help them.

The Temple of Good Will has about five million members in Brazil, with other chapters situated in other countries around the world, including the United States (not to be confused with Goodwill Industries). Members of this religion, which is universalist in nature, may also be members of other churches and mystical societies. This, of course, satisfies the inimitably eclectic nature of the Brazilian worshipper.

The teaching of the faith is based upon "the new commandment" of Jesus Christ, that ye love one another. That is the central and fundamental teaching. This religion often calls itself the "religion of the new commandment," and every other teaching and practice stems from this basic tenet.

According to Zahur, the founder of Boa Vontade, Jesus, who is one with God, sent messengers to earth to teach love. It was difficult to determine if he meant the historical Jesus or the mystical and less-well-understood Christ Consciousness. Buddha, Krishna, Mohammed, and even Baha'u'llah were incarnated to do this work, as well as Jesus Himself. Jesus holds the position of organizer of our planet and originator of all religions in the East and the West and, to this day, continues to send more modern-day prophets.

As described by Boa Vontade, a Christian is a person who follows the new commandment and loves. Therefore, neither Christianity nor salvation is limited to "official" Christians, but to all who love. If an atheist loves, then he is considered a Christian, a concept which would upset orthodox Christians around the world.

For any student of comparative religions, it is obvious that Zahur was not very knowledgeable of the great religious traditions of the world, yet was aflame in his mission to unify all the divergent religions. Similar to the Baha'i faith, the Legion's teaching stresses unity. And, like the Umbanda and Candomble, Boa Vontade has had its difficulties developing a doctrine which would unify its factions.

Still, the message is the thing; any religion that stresses love rather than sectarian divergences is well worth assisting. Brazil abounds in religious groups. Some, if comical, are highly original, involving flying saucers and plans for evacuating the earth. Extremes aside, the Boa Vontade combines its equally original focus with an apocalyptic message; Jesus will return at any moment. He will divide the true Church from the false and set the world aright.

This teaching is common to many Christian-based groups: the Mormons, Adventists, the Witnesses, and Pentecostals. All stress that "something is about to occur" and have done so since their inceptions. So "The End is Near" message is actually not all that new.

Even so, the temple and its message are quite moving, despite its apocalyptic bent. Zahur stressed the need to place Jesus' commandment to love your neighbor at the center of the new Christianity. He said that the Christian churches never practice this command and that the New Teaching must be practiced in order for a "new world" to be ushered in. Since I have never found a perfect religion anyway, I think that for its emphasis on love, one can overlook any theological sloppiness that pervades the Boa Vontade, its doctrines, and the language of its books, which are written in sensational journalese. One English translation that explained the apocalyptic role of the Legion in the Christian cause read like a tabloid newspaper. I was given many such books, which I diplomatically handed back.

If the Legion chooses to call all people Christian, be they Jews, Muslims, or Buddhists, so be it. That is nothing new; the Koran itself call all true believers Muslims. If Jesus stands at the head of all religions, even those that never mention him or were founded before him, so what? It should not bother us. In truth, it is works, not subjective theological jargon, that are important.

The organization is renowned in Brazil for its many charitable projects. One such project is a mission called "Perpetual Christmas," on which, each night, members in larger cities where poverty abounds go into the streets to dispense necessities to the poor. The Legion is also known and for its leader, who to date has not been known to rob money from church funds—a truly unique philosophy among religious leaders! Alongside the Quakers and the Unitarians, the Boa Vontade stands as one of the brightest and most universal of Christian expressions and I, for one, applaud them.

I decided to include The Temple of Good Will in my adventures, even though it is not, properly speaking, a mediumistic religion. There is no spiritistic activity of which to speak. Still, I enjoyed my visit to their temple. If I lived in Brasilia, I would go there once a week to let my eyes feast upon the play of colors, of light and darkness, and to float in the reverie like a soul wandering between worlds, dying to itself and coming into a new life. I wish this religion, O Templo do Boa Vontade, birthed in love and based in service, every success. May it prosper through its services to the one true race.

Chapter XXVIII
Vale do Amanecer, D.F. Brasilia

I returned home quite enthusiastic from my visit to the temple. I still hadn't met any mediums in the capital but decided to let things flow. I tried to find the location of the Valley of the Dawn and the International Holistic University, but without success. I didn't understand the layout of the telephone directory and found no listing for either institution. I thought that maybe it was not meant that I should make their acquaintance.

That night, while watching television in the guest house lobby, the husband of the owner asked me about my activities. While we talked he gave me his card, upon which he had written a name.

"This is a friend of mine who lives at the Dawn community," he said. "I think that you would enjoy visiting them, and my friend can help you get settled." I was delighted, of course, and made plans to go there. Another unsolicited answer to my prayers.

My second day in the capital had been a desperate one. I had been traveling for five months. I had left my traveling companion and my new friends in Bahia behind, and though beautiful, Brasilia was relatively cold (in the emotional sense) and expensive. I felt very lonely and decided to meditate for guidance. As my meditation ended and I opened my eyes, my vision alighted upon the television tower, the highest structure in the city. It had an observation deck for tourists near the top and was not far from my hotel. Immediately I decided to hike out to see it, thinking that if I saw things from a different perspective, I might also feel different.

A half hour later, I was standing at the tower, which was closed for repairs. However, there was a fair nearby. I was attracted by the noise and the colors and went in. I walked around, and seeing everyone else talking and having a great time, my loneliness returned. This was not making me feel any better. I was about to leave the grounds and go back home when I noticed a tent displaying Krishna T-shirts. I went in to examine them and perhaps purchase one, but there was no one present when I entered. As I turned to leave, I bumped into the owner, a fellow about my age.

"Are you initiated in any type of spiritual work?" he asked me, first thing, outright. No pleasantries, no prattle.

"Well, sort of." I answered. I explained what I was doing there. Like me, Carlos was interested in the practice of Zen, in which he was an initiate. We began to talk, and before we knew it, hours passed while we enjoyed our conversation. He introduced me to some of his friends, and invitations were soon extended to vegetarian homes outside of the city. To be sure, a cure for my loneliness.

I returned to see Carlos before I was due to leave for the Valley of the Dawn. I didn't want to leave without saying good-bye to him. During our visit, Carlos informed me that he had a friend who lived at the Holistic University and gave me a telephone number, suggesting that I might like to visit them. I now had contact with the university.

I raced home and called the university. I was invited to stay there and observe for three days. Once again, the cosmos provided me direction when I had none. I was thrilled that I would be going to there, but first, I was off to the Vale do Amanecer ("Valley of the Dawn"). It was here that I would encounter one of the most interesting forms of mediumship practice I have ever seen.

The valley itself is located in one of the driest areas of the Federal District. The community is located just down the highway from the town of Alto Plano, a nondescript place, miserable, hot, and dusty. The community is reached by bus service, which is actually quite good, over a decently paved highway.

The bus from Alto Plano stopped in front of Temple Square, the "downtown" of the Valley of the Dawn community. Everyone left the bus but me. I looked out the window and saw what appeared to be a Hollywood set designed for cowboy and Indian confrontations. I couldn't believe it. I half expected the people to be walking around in Texas boots and cowboy hats. Wondering if I had arrived, I asked the bus driver if this was, in fact, the famous Valley of the Dawn. He told me yes, this was indeed the valley.

171

I stood there, mouth open, somewhat paralyzed, with an incredulous look on my face, ready to sit down again and run for the capital. "This is *the* valley," the driver again assured me. I gathered my belongings and got off the bus, but not without reservations.

I just couldn't believe that this was *the* Valley of the Dawn. I couldn't believe the heat and dust in the place. I couldn't believe anything I was seeing. But I was to learn, as I stayed on in the valley, that there would be even more outrageous things that I couldn't believe.

The various precincts of the valley are delineated by white posts, the passing of which indicates that one is now entering on special ground. There are about four to five thousand people living in the valley. The Temple Square contains a fountain, a few stores which sell sacred objects and uniforms (owned by members of the Family), a souvenir store, and an artist's studio. The artist, a very talented person, specialized in painting the invisible patron spirits, selling his work to members of the community and others. He was not actually a member of the community. He became involved through his acquaintance with Tia Neiva, who asked him to paint her message so that people might understand it through art.

The valley isn't exactly a valley in the proper sense. It is more like a slight indentation with a large hill rising above at the furthest end, which looms up with a large symbol. This was later explained to me to be a keyhole through which spirits are sent to other worlds. The land is dry, brown, and cracked from long exposure to the hot sun. Some original members of the community told me that years ago, this was not so. The valley was originally filled with shade trees and greenery. But the managers of the community slowly cut down every living thing there.

I immediately sought the shady protection of the stores in the square. Inside I asked where I might find the name of a certain doctor whose address I had been given. The people looked at me as if I had just gotten off a spaceship (a not improbable stance here) or like I was an invading exu. The valley people love evil spirits because without them they have no purpose for living. You see, these people believe it is their mission to convert evil spirits to good angels and send them hither and thither. They assume that all evil spirits want conversion, though they probably never asked one personally. I was now being sized up as a possible evil-spirit convert. Alas, I was only a tourist.

No one answered me. Apparently, none of them had ever heard of the settlement's only medical doctor, who, incidentally, was also a director and one of the most active members of the community and had lived there since the inception of the Valley. I could have resented the way they looked at me, but I attributed it to a case of collective massive sunstroke.

I was getting tired, encrusted in hot dust and angry with these people. I wanted to wop someone with my crutches, but the evil Exu Dennis became the Compassionate One instead. I repeated my request to the group in the store. Silence.

Then someone's eyes lit up. They did know that doctor. They took their son to him just the other day. He lived about five streets over. Good. I had made a beginning.

It was now three o'clock in the afternoon. I had a large backpack on, and every inch of my body was crying for relief, but I controlled myself and asked, "Five streets over from where?" Silence. The eyes went dull again.

Since no one offered any additional assistance, I hoofed it (devils have hoofs you know), eventually finding the street and the house. When I rang at the door, the doctor greeted me, took my card of introduction, and sent me on my way, telling me he would seek me out later. He never did. But that was also typical of the people of the valley.

What now? Not knowing where I was going, I began to walk back the way I came. I stopped a passing youth, who agreed to guide me to the headquarters of the organization. The sun was the hottest it would get, and I thought that I was living in Death Valley. We walked all the way back to where I had entered the valley. I had made a complete turn of the place, and this youth didn't even offer to carry my backpack. We finally arrived at the headquarters' building, but there were no leaders to be found. Disgusted, I was ready to leave my body and ascend to the next world.

I was ultimately dropped off at the door of the temple and left to fend for myself. Thereabouts I found a kindly lady, a medium (I was to find out later that all members of the Valley of the Dawn are considered mediums), who sent out a few messengers to locate some decision makers. I was sent the message to settle myself in a hotel, and later that night I would be visited by an English-speaking community member

173

who would serve as my guide. I was taken to a guest house and rented a room there.

About seven o'clock that evening two young men came to speak with me. One of them, Silvio, had lived in the United States. He told me a little about the village, where he was a high-ranking initiate. He would return in the morning to guide me around. We became friends, and Silvio later used his position to help me get a look at some of the deeper aspects of the community.

The Valley of the Dawn consists of a residential community and a series of exterior temples, which in other cities also exist under the name of the Vale do Amanecer. It was founded about twenty years ago by a Brazilian medium who was affectionately referred to as Tia Neiva. Tia means aunt, but Tia Neiva was no ordinary aunt. She was considered to be a seer of top quality, an excellent spirit summoner and healer. The password in the community is *salve Deus* ("God saves" or "I greet God"). Most religions in Brazil use such passwords. Umbanda and Candomble use *Sarava,* which has a similar meaning. Salve Deus was given to Tia Neiva by the spirits to use as a mantra. Wherever one goes in the valley, one is greeted with this password, unless one is not an initiate. Then you are lucky if you are even spoken to.

As my guide and I became friendlier, he expressed doubts concerning the leaders, the Holy Family, and the general ignorance of the members. He is one of the few university-educated members who is rising through the organization's hierarchy. Members, he said, have total freedom to do what they want. They chain smoke, eat whatever, wear earrings, etcetera. There is a liquor prohibition but most drink anyway, and the village is full of sexual activity. However, not being able to snoop around long enough, I can't verify this.

The community runs an orphanage, which is in terrible condition. It also has an addiction center, which, Silvio informed me, overflowed with members who were drug and alcohol addicted. However, many of the younger men in the valley were cured of their dependency by the attentions of the foundress, Tia Neiva.

Tia Neiva herself suffered from poor health and poor education. As often is the case, she was sick from her earliest years and came close to death several times. Her own diet, like that of her followers, was sloppy. Her own health, like that of many of her followers, was poor. Her own level of literacy, like that of the majority of her follower, was also low. Apparently, none of this changed after the founding of the Valley of the Dawn.

Tia Neiva reported that once, while in a coma, she was (astrally) transported to Tibet, where she learned some of the philosophical bases of the religion she would later found. This was an interesting point, for Tibet is a Buddhist nation and Tia Neiva knew nothing of this religion. She claimed to have studied in the astral with a high-ranking lama, who apparently failed to mention to her the vegetarian dietary practices of these monks. It is interesting to note that had Tia Neiva, now deceased, adhered to Tibetan dietary practice, her health would certainly have been improved, and she might even still be alive.

Tia Neiva, everyone assured me, was a special woman. She was quite pretty and had the distinction of being the first woman truck driver in Brazil. She was known as a healer and a counselor to businessmen, who rewarded her for her efforts. Several of them continue to contribute to her work, especially to the orphanage. Since her demise, however, they no longer attend the community.

In the Valley of the Dawn, everyone claims to see invisible spirits, demons and extraterrestrial ships. Belief is a very personal thing, especially in spiritistic circles. It is hard to say what is occurring and what isn't. I do not consider myself to be an especially sensitive person. This means that while I do feel things, which in these circles are called vibrations, I don't easily see spirits and invisibles. I often doubt the claims of the hundreds and even thousands of others who do say that they see these invisibles everywhere.

The people here believe that the universe is inhabited by an enormous number of malevolent spirits, which they interestingly call the exus. The exus and other entities attach themselves to weak-minded individuals and lure them into low spiritual conditions, which produce problems, sickness, and poor luck. Some of these evil spirits work on a worldwide scale to bring about destruction. It is the mission and purpose of the Valley of the Dawn to save the world and its inhabitants from these evil creatures. But it is difficult to imagine how they will accomplish it.

The people didn't look too happy with their lives. They were almost pathetic in defense of their religion, which they used as an excuse for many things. The first thing that struck me, however, was just how little these people knew about their own sect. In fact, any real knowledge is

175

discouraged. Tia Neiva downplayed the role of education, citing it as a barrier to gaining spiritual knowledge. The members of this sect, of which there are a reported two hundred thousand to three hundred thousand members, seem to agree and try very hard to prove the foundress correct by getting the least amount of education and culture possible.

On the first day, I was guided around the village by a young man only six months a member of the community. I questioned him about certain doctrines of the church, but he could not or would not answer my questions. Rather, he would apologize and explain to me that he was new and his knowledge was therefore limited.

Another day I asked a medium a question about the organization. She acted as if I was Satan incarnated. She wanted to escape me and told me to ask her superiors. That was the usual answer to any substantial question in the Valley of the Dawn. It took four or five days before I could find a "superior" willing to speak to me. By then the word was out that a stranger, and a North American at that, was wandering around the village asking questions. Finally, a high-ranking member, an archon, invited me to his home to explain some of the contradictory doctrines of the community. I will recount our conversation later.

The temple where the general membership worships is itself rather a ramshackle affair, constructed of natural stone and a tin roof. An insignificant edifice, it looks more like a storage barn than a temple. In fact, it is quite ugly from the outside. As ugly as the building is on the outside, on the inside there is a corresponding level of awe and confusion. The interior of the temple is an esoteric student's delight; it is a museum and a madhouse combined. Psychologists (both Freudian and Jungian analysts) would have a field day inside the temple.

One finds inside many religious icons and artifacts; there are Stars of David, crosses, images of saints, candles by the hundreds, and everyone is dressed for Hollywood. There are at least a dozen private chapels, each one dedicated to some orixa, preto velho, or other spirit, for here all these entities are worshipped. This religion is the ultimate spiritistic experience. Everyone has space in it. In all that I have seen in my travels, I never saw anything like this.

There you find an Indian saint, a past life reincarnation of Saint Francis, who guards the sanctuary. Down the aisle there is a life-sized Jesus on the cross. In front of Him is the representation of the Deity

Orixa Yemanja, the Goddess Mother. In front of her are a gigantic Star of David and a menorah. As I said, there is something here for everyone.

The temple is a mixture of the three great Spiritist traditions of Brazil: the Kardecist, Umbanda, and Candomble. Add to this the flying saucers and a plethora of evil demons, and you have Disneyland for the discriminating theologian.

The members of the Valley of the Dawn believe that if the rituals that abound in this organization were to be suspended for even a day, the entire world would be destroyed by the evil powers that are even now attacking it. The entire purpose of the valley religion is to capture a certain amount of evil souls per day, submit them to the Valley of the Dawn salvation program and thus purify them enough so that they might pass through the lower prison worlds into the world of light.

Simply stated, the purpose of this religion is to save souls who are already in the other world. How they go about this process is the most complicated part of the valley system. I am not at all sure that I understand all of it. I was to learn that because it was so complicated, their own initiates comprehended it even less than I.

My English-speaking friend, Silvio, took time out the next day to give me a thorough tour of the temple's interior and to explain what it was all about. The mediums in this sect work in pairs, usually one male and one female; one of these mediums is called the "incorporator" and the other, the "indoctrinator."

The incorporator, sits down to work; the purpose of the incorporator is simply to see, grasp, and hold an evil spirit prisoner until it is freed of its evil intentions, which is the work of the indoctrinator, who stands in back of the seated incorporator and breaks into his/her aura at the critical moment, opening up a "hole" from which the evil spirit is thrown (against his will, mind you) into the world of light, where he is forgiven and turned into a nice spirit.

The reader must forgive my cynicism, please, at the ego of humankind and its compulsive desire to make everything over in its own image. I was given a book written by Tia Neiva's husband that explained the condition of the evil exus. These exus, during their lifetime, were educated, cultured, and even well-meaning beings, but had one fault—they did not believe in Christianity. They were like noble savages, noble pagans, of good heart but without salvation. Because of their sad condition, after death they were trapped in the lower astral planes, unable to ascend.

Apparently numbering in the millions, at some point each of these miserable spirits will be grabbed by a medium and forcefully educated in the inner truth of "true" Christianity and baptized. They are then called "baptized exus," who, now being nice spirits, respond to the beck and call of any who may summon them. Of course these are the ordinary, minor exus, who now trade their cultured background to become slaves of the valley people. Not surprisingly, the official opinion regarding education may play a significant role in maintaining the negative image the exus have among community members.

I was present one day during the *mesa blanca* ("white table") ritual, when all the mediums worked at full tilt. In full swing, the temple sounded like a Pentecostal church. The ritual was begun with prayers to Jesus, to *Seta Blanca* ("White Arrow"), to Yemanja, and to the foundress of the valley, Tia Neiva. The mediums then paired up, incorporator and indoctrinator.

The incorporators sat at the table and the indoctrinators stood behind them. These mediums work unconsciously, which means that they remember nothing. Each incorporator went into trance, opening and closing their fists. This was indicative of the strength and energy of the cultured, evil exu, who doesn't want to be forced into Christianity. Some of the mediums cried out, squirmed in their chairs, pounded on the table, and otherwise acted to illustrate the fight going on within themselves and their heroic effort to hold on to the evil spirits.

The indoctrinators, standing behind them, slash down with their right arm into the aura of the medium shouting "*O-ba-ta*" (a Candomble name for "God"). This invocation should release the evil ones into the higher worlds. It doesn't always do so. In such cases, the process is repeated over and over again until the medium calms down.

It was quite an impressive show to see the process at work. I sat on the sidelines, cheering on the exus! One spirit in particular was resisting conversion. The indoctrinator slashed at it, but the medium, filled with the spirit of the evil exu, only laughed her head off. The exu also spoke during the incorporation. It told the indoctrinator what foolishness this ritual was. As I listened I had to keep myself from laughing as well.

The medium told the spirit it had to change, to be baptized and become a Christian. The spirit laughed at this and remarked at how uncultured these people were and that he was not going to cooperate at all. A supplicant was then brought before the medium, but the spirit laughed cruelly and would have nothing to do with her!

The spectacle got even more entertaining. the medium ordered the spirit to attend to the client. The spirit answered, "There's nothing that I can do for her anyway; she's crazy like all of you here." The indoctrinator, a young and inexperienced person was beside himself trying to control the spirit. He yelled to the exu that he had an obligation to help, but the spirit only laughed at him. The young indoctrinator made the sign of the cross over the incorporator's head, as if trying to subdue a stubborn dracula, but the spirit only laughed louder. I had the impression that this spirit was a follower of Voltaire.

Eventually the spirit took off, and the great show was over. I tried to speak to the incorporating medium, but she refused to talk with me and referred me to her superior. I told her that she wasn't on trial and that I only wanted her to answer a few questions. She admitted to me that she remembered nothing of the session and that she traveled to some other "place."

I was privileged to speak with a spirit, a preto velho, later that same day; however, my interview with the spirit was less interesting than the mesa, blanca. I was called to sit down and give my right hand to the medium, who muttered a Catholic blessing over me and agreed to answer some questions. The problem was that the questions were out of her area. She told me that these answers could only be revealed to initiates. Unfortunately, I was not an initiate, so I will have to wait a while for my answers.

After being at the valley for several days, Silvio arranged my appointment with the archon, who invited me to speak with him. An archon is one of the highest positions in the community. As I understood the Greek term "archon," as used by the ancient Gnostics, an archon was an evil governor, or a governor of the entrapped worlds. Here, an archon is a high-ranking governor of the community. He explained many things to me, among them the following:

Mediums, as we already know, work in pairs, doing the main work which goes on daily in the temples. This is not standard for most spiritistic groups. The incorporative medium specializes in using certain chakras, especially the solar plexus energies, to catch a wandering spirit and hold it within his aura. The indoctrinating medium then uses the crown chakra to teach the spirit. The incorporative medium gives up control of his abilities, the second retains full control. The unconscious medium enters into deep trance while the other remains fully awake to direct the situation.

At the appropriate moment during the capture/education process, the indoctrinator slices into the other medium's aura, invokes the highest god, and opens up a channel through which the captive spirit may leave the aura of the medium and enter into the world of light.

The theory is that the spirit is expelled against his own will but for his own good. These spirits would otherwise invade the world, cling to people in vengeance and fantasy, and wreak havoc upon civilization. They would continue torturing the living for past karmic debts. They practice hate until, for their own good, they are caught up in the valley and indoctrinated into the Living Gospel. There is no other way to save these souls. It would be otherwise hopeless for them.

At almost any hour of the day or the night, you will encounter the mediums walking the streets of the village, in groups of seven or more, invoking the gods and shouting out prayers to entrap the poor spirits who had the misfortune to stumble into this place. If the people are not on the street, they are in the temple, drinking the holy water and asking the principal spirit, Seta Blanca, to fulfill their expectations.

The incorporative medium is in great danger, because he might attract a powerful soul that he can't control and must then be treated to expel the spirit. The job of the indoctrination medium is to protect the other from this situation. Protective spirits are invoked in these cases. The energy bestowed upon the temple comes from these beings. Some of these entities are spirits and others are extraterrestrials from other planets. They come daily to the temple and deliver these energies by focusing a ray upon the building.

As an aside, while most members knew others who have seen the extraterrestrials, very few say that they themselves have seen them. The reason that I could see none of these processes going on around me was that I was not an initiate.

The extraterrestrials come in spaceships. As they pass the moon, they go through a type of "visibility warp" and become invisible to everyone except the most sensitive mediums. They are changed from material visibility to spiritual invisibility.

During the day, I was told, extraterrestrial energies are centered upon the community and the temple itself. Especially at three P.M., a cone-shaped energy pendulum appears over the temple, bathing all in the community with protective energy. I couldn't see that either, but everyone else could see it swing back and forth over the community. I was bathed in nothing, but again, everyone else was.

There are many rituals in the valley and its associate temples, of which I was told there were seven. Of interest is the daily sundown service in the pyramid. An artificial lake was constructed with a pyramid on one side of it. The lake serves as a prison for the powerful spirits who can't be managed by the regular mediums. Extraterrestrials come and take these away.

Within the pyramid, certain energizing rituals are enacted. The people wear quite colorful and nicely made robes. Looking like princes and princesses, they group at one end of the lake at sundown and proceed to the pyramid, chanting, and disappear inside. I wasn't allowed to be present for these, as I was only a visitor. The archon did not feel obligated to explain them to me.

There are other rituals which can only be conducted around the lake. I participated in one of them. It cannot be explained, as it is a secret initiatory ritual, and I am obligated to abide by their wishes. Let it be said, however, that it involves calling upon every god, spirit, angel, and extraterrestrial in the universe. Conducted in the afternoon sun, it is, to say the least, unbearably hot work. At break everyone runs off to the store to drink Coca-Colas and smoke cigarettes.

The principal deity of the valley is Chief White Arrow, whom I repeatedly called White Cloud, a name I subconsciously seem to prefer. It seems that there is a mushroom with the same name. The chief, who appears as a benevolent guardian spirit, is represented as an Indian in flowing robes, holding an arrow pointing to his left. People come to the chief with all types of problems concerning marriage, health, and money, as well as for protection from other spirits. They congregate at his statue, intoning the correct invocations, and leave their written petitions in a box in front of the statue. Dirty water gathers at the feet of the statue, which the supplicants drink. Many take bottles of it home to drink, but one medium told me that he would never even touch the water, let alone drink it. I didn't either.

The Temple Square comes alive about nine in the morning. Before that, the doors are closed and only the pigeons choose to make the scene. The patio before the temple slowly fills up with a few faithful who ask you to buy them coffee or to give them cigarettes. The men are dressed in the traditional rust-colored pants and black shirts. They huddle together in the cold of the early morning, discussing the miracles they saw occurring the past few days. All rub their hands against the cold and puff on their newly acquired smokes. A few shake out their capes and clean up their badges and regalia.

Coffee and cigarettes are consumed with abandon here. I thought that I should open up a coffee bar and offer a cigarette and coffee deal. I would become very rich, for there are many addictions here.

As the sun rises, more members enter the square. They bow to other people and mumble "salve Deus." Then they approach you, offering a notebook to be signed. Others take the books and sign in them.

This is the "Prison ritual." The prisoners are those with notebooks, reincarnations of unjust souls who have "unsolvable problems" in their lives, which they believe are caused by karma and spirit possession. In some time past life they committed a misdeed against another being. The injured soul is now requiring repayment for that injustice, and the prisoner must balance the debt. Payment is made in the form of spiritual energy. The prisoner must collect a specified amount of energy to transfer to the injured soul, who will then be satisfied and stop its persecution of the prisoner.

The prisoner approaches others and asks them to donate some of their energy reserves. An agreement set, the donor signs the notebook and returns it to the petitioner. I signed quite a few of them, probably overdrawing on my own account. Then I was told that I could withdraw energy from other people's accounts, and I started signing away the energy of many people whom I didn't especially care for. I made up a list of some people and signed their names for everything, a type of spiritual forgery. I wonder if it worked? They probably didn't even notice!

Male prisoners are very ordinarily dressed in dark colors, but the females wear long granny dresses of many colors. Actually, for prisoners they dressed quite well. This ritual seemed to me to reflect the Roman Catholic concept of penance, though in a more complicated (and comical) way.

All members of the valley must go through this ritual once in their current existence in order to evolve to higher planes. All, that is, except for the families of the presidents and archons, and notably the children, who are free from such karmically trivial matters. They have inherited the kingdom by birth into these families.

All of these rituals were given by Tia Neiva, a poorly educated woman, but a powerful medium. It is reported that Neiva could see into other levels of reality and produced many great cures. The people believe in her completely and blindly. But what, I wonder, did she believe in? Her cosmology is so complicated, the way to salvation so abstract, the rituals so confusing, the level of education so very low. What have you created, Aunt Neiva? Is it a view of heaven which you had or the borderland of confusion?

The Valley of the Dawn was one of the most interesting communities that I had ever come across. I had originally planned to stay for three days, but I ended up staying a week and a half. It was well worth the visit. I wonder if Silvio is still there?

Chapter XXIX
I Take a Breather

I needed a haven of peace and calm, and I found it at the International Holistic University, located outside one of the satellite towns of the Federal District. The university was authorized by the governor, and the job of creating it fell into the hands of Dr. Pierre Weil, a European residing in Brazil for many years. The university hoped to offer many fields of study in the future, training all of its professionals from the holistic point of view.

While in Salvador, Bahia, the name of Dr. Weil was mentioned to me because of his investigations of the Oriental teachings and the spiritistic experiences of Brazil. I was coming from a similar viewpoint in my research. Though I was invited to stay only three days, the visit was extended to a month, as I was drafted into service at the school.

The university is located upon a very large piece of land, donated by the state for this purpose. There are several large buildings, which serve as classrooms and offices. There are also dormitory buildings and a cafeteria that serves only vegetarian food. It was nice to be there and to step outside of the spiritistic culture for a while. I was quite saturated with phenomena, and as I would soon head back to another world, I felt that this was a positive transitional move. I especially liked to go to the house located next to the waterfall, where I could meditate whenever I wanted to.

The main part of my visit was involved in teaching and taking classes during an intensive week-long experimental holistic seminar, in which we meditated, touched, released emotions, and frustrations, and other things. I think that we all came out of the experience clearer on our life's goals.

I was soon making new connections in and through the university.

One day I was asked to invite Dr. Claudio Caparelli to visit the students. Dr. Caparelli had been in the Brazilian navy and was now retired. He is known around the capital district as an unusual Pai do Santo of the Umbanda, his particular sect called Esoteric Umbanda.

We drove out to visit his terreiro in one of the outlying areas of the district. His attractive home and center were situated in one of the driest and rockiest parts of the area. We were given a tour of his place and explanations of his Umbanda practices.

Esoteric Umbanda is a basic, less African form of the religion, doing away with many of the rituals that I encountered in other tendas. Dr. Caparelli feels that Esoteric Umbanda is the real Umbanda—other forms being deviations or derivations of it. His idea is that there is an essential core of Umbanda practice, derived over thousands of years and experienced under many names on many continents. This essential kernel was embellished by the cultures through which it passed, becoming "African" Umbanda, "Native Indian" Umbanda, "German" Umbanda, "Hindu" Umbanda, and so on. Esoteric Umbanda, then, takes the inner Umbanda teachings, separates them from their cultural overlap, and therefore presents a simpler form and practice, which is accepted as valid among the other Umbanda forms.

I later attended one of Dr. Caparelli's services, held in his very attractive and unusual octagon temple. I immediately noticed some of the more obvious differences. First, the altar was covered with "natural" representations of the orixas instead of the more exaggerated cult statues seen in so many tendas. There were crystals, stones, plants, and water and other representations. I found it new and aesthetically quite pleasant to the eye, compared to the other Umbanda centers I had visited. There were few African source symbols present; this was obviously the Aumbanda of which Tantredo spoke in his book.

Another main difference was the absence of sacred dances during the cult worship. Chants were sung, but also were Brazilian hymns. The number and intensity of rituals were kept to a minimum, but the work was the same; people were being dispossessed of disruptive spirits.

Following the service, we were given the option of having private consultations with the spirit guides. It was my understanding that in these sessions I could ask the spirits questions about themselves; however, when I attempted my first question, the spirit told me that this was not the purpose of the interview, but rather to discover meaningful information about oneself.

I was not, at that moment, interested in delving into my dark past, but I did wish to ask a few questions that were related to some of my observations. I wanted intellectual discussion, but the spirit wanted to counsel me. I gave in, hoping that we might do both.

Actually, the interview was surprisingly rich in advice. The spirit, speaking through this medium, was a female who was a slave during the Portuguese conquest, a preta velha. She gave me a very accurate summation of my life and hit upon a point that had actually been annoying me for quite a long time. It was a very intimate and sensitive point, and I was quite surprised that she picked up on it. I told her that while she had said many valid things, I needed more time for us to talk about it. Only twenty minutes was granted for the interview, and Dr. Caparelli was looking over his shoulder at us to tell me that my time was up.

I quickly asked the spirit permission for one personal question. She grudgingly agreed to my request.

"I have finished traveling all over Brazil, visiting and interviewing many spirits. I have an idea that I would like to share with you. My feeling is that spirits have disguises, like human beings, and that the same spirit often takes on different masks and appears to different groups as they would visualize it. Are you really a preta velha? Are you also wearing a disguise? Is this presentation a disguise of your deeper reality?"

There was silence for a few seconds. The spirit then answered:

It is true, that we appear in disguises appropriate to the gathering. In this moment I appear as the spirit of an old black female slave. But I am not that.

I pursued. "I understand that you are pure spirit and not the mask which you are presently wearing."

That is true.

The questioning was getting interesting.
"Have you ever appeared in other places as orixas, foreign spirits, exus, etcetera?"

I have.

"Could you drop your present disguise and appear to me in a form that is more culturally suitable for me, let's say an English-speaking North American spirit, so that I could relate to you better? Or could you show me your true face without the disguises?"

I could do that if it was appropriate.

"I would like to see you as you really are."

Do you know how much energy it takes to hold together this form? If I let it go, then I wouldn't be able to communicate with the others here. I feel that you ask this question out of ego.

"I ask this out of a search for the true spirit and not the dramatics which are presented in the name of the spirit world."

As I looked into the eyes of the medium, I felt indecision there, as if the spirit might agree to the request. For six months I had been visiting all types of spirit beings. They seemed to believe in their own identities as much as most incarnated humans do. Were these spirits not aware that they were not realities but reflections of the One Spirit?

In the tendas of Umbanda, the people thought that the caboclos, pretos velhos, and orianzas were literally that. In Spiritism they thought that if a spirit said he was Uncle Jack, he was. In the terreiros, the spirits which called themselves orixas were believed to be such. This was my last chance to speak with a Brazilian spirit. What was really going on?

I experienced an intense energy, a combination of frustration, apoplexy, and even some anger coming from the medium. Then my thoughts were brusquely interrupted by Dr. Caparelli, who said, "This is not the time for such discussions. We are here to give advice."

The doctor was not happy with the line of questioning that I had followed. He indicated that I had been presumptuous and not humble. Be that as it may, the question resounds. What would really occur in the universe if all of us, humans and spirits, took off our masks? Would the revelation of pure spirit bring about the night of Shiva and a new day of Brahma?

I thanked the spirit for her time and energy and gave my seat to someone else, who wished to find out why life was not going the way he wanted it to.

Dr. Caparelli, himself of Italian descent, attracted a great many educated Brazilians from the capital district. One of them told me that he likes Umbanda but prefers the esoteric understanding better than the rituals. That is why he likes this temple. Personally, I enjoyed the spirit and sensuality of the dancing and thought that the service was dull without it, though the teaching is fine. Esoteric Umbanda approaches the Kardecist religion closer than the other lineages.

As a side activity of the center, the doctor allowed his facilities to be used for a children's school. When I was there, he had a type of Sunday school going, where the students and teachers were obviously enjoying themselves.

One afternoon we went to the terreiro to see the pyramid. We were told that the pyramid was one of the seven in this Federal District. We were invited to participate in a cleansing process before entering the pyramid. The treatment takes place outside the structure.

First, after taking off your shoes, a fumigacao is performed, followed by passes made over and around your body while you stand in a circle made of white gravel and girdled with crystals. These energy passes are the same as seen in all spiritistic centers. Then you are invited to enter another area, a rectangle with a tubular pyramid structured over it. The tubes form the outline of the pyramid, which is low to the ground. Lying inside, you receive a shiatsu massage, which opens up your meridians, deblocking your energy. Then you are taken down into the base of the pyramid itself. The massage was an entirely new idea, one I had not seen in the terreiros I previously visited. I liked it!

The pyramid was built of cement and had massive walls, which were cracking. A large crystal was mounted on the uppermost point. The walls of the inside were covered with natural wood. It was somehow similar to a military bunker. In here you lie upon a table with certain light colors directed at you, and a medium administers the correct treatment. I was told that the pyramid sits upon several tons of crushed quartz crystals. Water is pumped through the crystals, which energizes it for use in healing. Our group found all this very interesting and asked questions about the work. We were told that some very unusual cures were obtained through the therapies here. Soon we were offered some cool refreshment and the doctor invited us into his house.

We were directed to the second floor, where an extra treat was waiting for us: an orgone box, built large enough to hold a person sitting within it. Orgonomy is a science developed by the psychiatrist Dr. Wilhelm Reich. The box is used in cancer treatment. I have never experienced one before and was allowed to sit in it for twenty minutes. It became plain to me that many mediums in Brazil were quite well educated in psychology, especially in the humanistic, experimental, and transpersonal areas.

Finally, feeling refreshed, I bid Dr. Caparelli farewell and wished him the best of luck in his work. He had certainly given me a new focus on Umbanda and his energetic therapies.

Chapter XXX
Off to the Amazons

I had about three weeks left to my visa. Brazil allowed visitors only six months to stay in the country. I could then leave and return for another three months, but leaving Brazil involves great distances. I decided that when my six months were up, I would travel up to Colombia and stay with friends there.

I was as sorry to leave Brasília as I was to leave Salvador. I had met some very fine people and felt that part of my heart stayed with them. A group of friends took me to the airport, where we hugged until the plane came.

The flight to Manaos was longer than I expected. Living in Central America so many years led me to expect short flights between capital cities. I am amazed at the amount of land which falls within the national boundaries of Brazil. I am even more amazed at how a small country like Portugal could have conquered so much. It was explained to me that the Portuguese did not conquer the existing country. It was the work of a pope who, working with an inaccurate map, sliced South America in half, giving one half to Spain and the other half to Portugal; that other half is modern-day Brazil.

I had several reasons to fly to Manaos. First, to journey to Brazil without visiting the Amazon state is like going to France without visiting Paris. It just is not done. Second, I wished to see how the mediumistic religions flourished in this isolated state. Third, I wanted to meet the author and philosopher, Dr. Carolos Tinoco. I had read one of his books and wanted to discuss some points with him.

I had a fourth reason; perhaps I might be able to experiment with narco-mediumship, specifically, the sacred beverage of the São Daime.

I had never heard of the São Daime or of its holy drink, the *ayuasca,* until I arrived in Brazil. My hosts in São Paulo told me of its benefits and how it was becoming quite popular among the New Age people of that country. In Salvador, Bahia, I spoke with people who had experimented with it and told me of their experiences. The same was repeated in Brasíflia and in many other places.

I was happy to observe that many of the young people of Brazil are turning to its native peoples as a source of inspiration. After having their origins invaded and defiled for centuries, a flourishing Candomble serves as a bridge for millions of Afro-Brazilians to return to their roots and ancient spiritual greatness. The rituals and practices of the Indians still connect other millions with their origins as well. Brazil is large enough for everyone, and every teaching is welcomed there. I found the mystical East represented throughout the nation, as well as the esoteric lodges of Europe. The field of medicine is somewhat more diverse than in other Latin American nations, with its homeopathic, chiropractic, massage, and natural therapy schools. At the same time that millions of people are accepting ideas from other societies, they are linking up with their own past. I see this as a positive sign.

When I arrived at the airport, I signed up immediately for a tour up the Amazon river. No visit to Brazil is complete without it. The tour guide helped me to get a room in a clean and inexpensive hotel near the river in the old port section of the city.

Manaos is a large city of about two million inhabitants. It sits upon the littoral of the Rio Amazonas. It is a bustling place and very hot. Its inhabitants are Portuguese, mulattos, native peoples, and lots and lots of foreigners. Many tourists skip the rest of the country to spend their limited time boating up the Amazon.

After getting settled in my hotel, I tried to call Dr. Carlos Tinoco at his home and office but had no luck reaching him. That would have to wait until my return.

I, a young Dutchman, our guide, and the boat crew plodded upstream for three days to see the Amazon and inhale its pure oxygen. It is true that the Amazon basin is the lung of the planet. The air is rich in the smells of the ancient jungle, the sounds of its creatures, and peace of its waterways.

We fished for piranha during one day and went out to see the crocodiles that night. I swam in the warm waters of the river and felt the tensions of the past five and one-half months melt away as my body and soul came alive with the caresses of this primal river. We hiked through parts of the jungle as well, but that was not the easiest thing for me to do. With help, I did well and enjoyed it. When, in three days, I returned, I had lost many wrinkles and tensions. I was feeling great.

The morning after my return, I made contact with Dr. Tinoco at the University of Manaos. "I am lucky," he said, "because the university is on strike. So I have time to sit around with you."

He gave me his address, and I set off to visit him at his home. As it turned out, Dr. Tinoco and his wife were vegetarians and had a vegetarian store. They invited me to sit and eat with them. Refreshed, we went upstairs to his office and rooms where he teaches yoga, the only yoga instructor in Manaos. At the university, Dr. Tinoco was the head of the department of mathematics. He had been the head of the physics department, but because of his involvement in "mystical" investigations, he was asked to leave the chairmanship. He had no such pressure as a mathematician.

Dr Tinoco had changed, he told me, from his days of mediumship investigation to now. At that time he had been deeply involved in the investigation of the inner states of consciousness experienced in mediumship trance. He worked for a time with Dr. Hernani Andrade and wrote a scientific follow-up to Dr. Andrade's book, *O Modelo Biologico Organizador* (*"The Biological Organizing Model"*), which deals with the spiritual side of organizing the body's information.

A few years ago he had the opportunity to travel to India, where he became aware of the ancient Vedic explanation of the universe. He converted to the study of inner states of being through his involvement with Oriental meditation and Yoga, enabling him to present valuable information from the scientist's point of view.

Up until this moment, Dr. Tinoco and I spoke in generalities. I had not told him that I was trying to discover the sacred beverage and to use it before I left Brazil. I didn't know exactly how to broach the subject with, and at that moment I was wondering if I would ever discover it.

Our conversation had come to a momentary lull, when Dr. Tinoco asked me, "Have you ever tried ayuasca?"

"Do you mean the sacred drink of the Indians?" I asked, trying to disguise my glee. "No, I haven't. Do you have a contact?"

"Yes. My wife, children, and I have participated in São Daime several times with positive results. I will make arrangements for you to try it. It would be a positive way for you to take leave of our Brazil."

I didn't have to say yes. It was understood that a few hours later the doctor would call me at my hotel and give me details. After a good vegetarian meal, I walked to my hotel and waited for the call that was not long in coming.

The following night, my last in the Amazon, was to be my initiation in the sacred drink.

"You actually drank it?" many of my friends asked me. I did indeed, and it affected me for several months, not always positively. But as I look back upon my experience with ayuasca, I can't help but feel it was worth it.

I had never considered the hallucinogenic experience to be a form of mediumship. Yet after attending a conference about the sacred drink and hearing the lecturer, who was a medium, speak about its superior mediumistic results, I began to wonder.

The three main mediumistic religions use the vehicles of prayer, meditation, dancing, and rituals to enter into the trance state. The native peoples of the world often use substances to do the same; peyote, marijuana, tobacco, mushrooms, and ayuasca are used to affect certain parts of the nervous system, shutting them down to allow the other parts to take upon themselves more responsibility. This seems to produce greater sensitivity and psychic awareness.

I had previously read of *soma,* a sacred drink of the Hindus, *haoma,* used by the Zoroastrians, as well as the ancient uses of special wines in the Greek and Roman cultures. It was not strange to me that the native peoples of the Latin American continent should use substances as well to communicate with God, gods, or the spirits. After all, had I not experienced a period of inner peace and compassion towards everyone after using mushrooms?

The long awaited night of ayuasca finally arrived. I was quite excited about it. Ayuasca is made from the bark of two trees. It is alkaloid and quite toxic, so don't try it without proper supervision. It must be prepared in a special way and fermented for a period of time.

The fermented liquid was thick, brownish, and heavy looking, kind of like crude oil. I didn't especially like the looks of it, but upon swallowing it, I found it didn't taste as unpleasant as it looked. I was told the day before that after swallowing the drink, there might be a need to throw up the unsuitable substances for about an hour. Thinking that it would be better to keep them down, I fasted for twenty-four hours and felt no need to vomit, though I suffered from an upset stomach and acid condition for several days. I had to drink a lot of aloe vera and eat yogurt in order to normalize my system after that. I was told that the shamans who use this liquid often tend to develop stomach problems and cancer. "But why do they use it?" I asked. "It heightens their powers. The healers can look into the body of the afflicted person and see their sickness. Then they can cure them. Also, they can see the gods."

We began by meditating, saying some prayers and listening to a tape of Sanskrit mantras, Eventually feeling ready, I drank the glass of liquid placed in front of me. Dr. Tinoco stood by for any contingency, with paper and pen to ask me questions as planned.

My stomach initially warmed up and I felt myself at ease, not realizing that anything was occurring. After about fifteen minutes, my eyes began flashing and I felt that the earth was beginning to move under me. It serves little purpose to relate all the details, common enough to any hallucinogenic experience. Lights were flashing on and off around me; things appeared to be clearer when I realized that my eyes were open. What I next realized was also very interesting.

It seemed that as I was staring out in front of me, my attention was drawn to a point in the air. As I observed that point, it enlarged and appeared to become a good-sized opening, rather ovoid but not uniform in its dimensions. What happened next was even more interesting.

Beings were coming out of the oval into my universe! None of them were paying any attention to me. I then understood this opening to be a type of doorway between worlds. The entities going in and out of the portal were of humanoid appearance. They used the aperture as easily as anyone else would walk in and out of any open doorway.

As I sat there, fascinated by this bizarre scene, I thought of the story of Jacob's ladder, wherein the patriarch had a dream of a ladder reaching up into heaven and saw angels walking up and down, going about their celestial business. In a sense, that is what I was watching.

I eventually realized that the beings going in and out did not recognize me because they were not perceiving me! I was just as unreal, as nonexistent to them as they were to me. I chuckled at this revelation; as I did, one of the beings came through the portal and stopped a moment. He looked directly at me. I saw a big smile on his face, as if he too were in a trance and could see me in my dimension. He stood there for a while, both of us looking at each other and smiling. I for my part felt no fear or nervousness at this perception. Was he a figment of my mind? or I of his? Each of us the other's hallucination? In any case, I wondered if he was thinking the same thing I was. With a wave of the hand, he ducked back through the doorway and disappeared from sight. I tried to follow him, but found myself incapable of moving.

My attention was drawn to another phenomenon. My extradimensional friend quickly became an experience of the past as the area around me was suddenly infused with strong white light, permeating, penetrating into everything. I looked around and noticed that the trees were moving back and forth in a type of universal rhythm. Also the leaves on the ground were moving around, very much like inch worms. Even the ashtray on the table seemed to be moving; everything appeared imbued with life.

While I remained incapable of physical movement myself, and not, I was aware, in very good control of my senses, a part of my mind remained clear and detached, the consummate observer. My inner voice, peeping up from deep space asked me, "Which of these perceptions are truly real? Are you more aware now than before? Of what? Is it perception which makes things real? Is this the essence of mediumship, a shift in perception affecting ordinary reality, creating new reality?"

"Quiet!" I hissed at my mind. "Not now, not now. I'm enjoying the ride."

After a time, I don't know how long, for I was no longer conscious of time, I began to normalize my condition. My experience had lasted about four hours. At the end, I found that I could bring myself back to normal by the force of my will. However, there was no willpower during the experience. I drifted any way that the energy took me and was content with the wonders I had been shown. I was served some tea and bread, which helped to stabilize me, and after profuse thanks and farewells to the Tinocos, I was driven to my hotel.

The next morning I was taken to the airport, where I boarded a small plane to Tabatinga, the frontier border town. With a deep sigh and a pocketful of new friends and experiences, I walked across the border to Leticia, Colombia.

Appendices

A. The Special Role of the Exu

According to the teachings of Umbanda, and Quimbanda, its darker sibling, the exus represent what the Catholics and Protestants call demons or evil angels. In the Spiritist doctrine of Allan Kardec, they are called possessive spirits, usually invoked in black magic rituals. According to the teaching, their name was first uttered by God during the celestial revolt against his authority. The Archangel Lucifer and his followers attempted to usurp his rights and prerogatives. Named a traitor to Heaven for his opposition to God, Lucifer and his company were cast out from the Heavenly Kingdom to earth, which would remain his domain forever.

The exu became the source of all evil afflicting the children of Adam and Eve, exercising dominion over their progeny in accordance with the Law of Karma. God allows them to prove humankind. In the struggle, the spirit guides and orixas fight against them to free individuals from their grasp and from any obstacles that prohibit their progress into higher spiritual conditions.

Not all exus stem from the original celestial battle but are spirits who, in previous incarnations, committed atrocious acts. They are now obligated to do evil once again and suffer within themselves its consequences. These spirits need help more than any other being, as they are closest to us and therefore depend upon us for their own progress, much as we depend on those positive spirits who are superior to us. We must learn to communicate and work with them in order to assist them in their evolution. Even though they are low spirits, there is the possibility of their salvation. They can evolve, for nothing in the universe is lost.

A very few exus have voluntarily decided to do benevolent deeds in order to renounce their former evil ways. They are known as the "baptized" exus, the product of the community of the Valley of the Dawn. The majority, however, continue to do evil, committing acts which are considered inadvisable for spiritual progress. These are often called "pagan" exus, or Kiumbas (Quimbas); they infiltrate society with the goal of spreading confusion and fulfilling mankind's lowest destructive desires.

An exu appears as proud, authoritarian, and asks for food, drink, candles, etcetera. The medium has an obligation to convert the exu from an agent of evil to a practitioner of good. When a medium is spiritually well educated, the exu is told that he will receive nothing. The medium then explains that, being a low spirit, the exu should try to progress to higher levels. In order to evolve, it would be explained, he must stop doing the terrible things that continue to aggravate his spiritual situation. It is important that the path of evolution is explained to him.

The explanation above is a literal understanding of the exu. As in all religions, however, there is an inner and outer understanding. It was explained, upon gaining the confidence of some of the Pais do Santo that I met, that deeper perceptions of the exu exist.

Mai Vera, a famous priestess of the Candomble, in Salvador, Bahia, said that the average devotee of the Candomble and the Umbanda does not understand the true role of the exu. She feels that people often take doctrines upon faith instead of testing them. When I asked her about the differences of orixas and exus, she answered:

These are not single spirits. They are parts of one whole, one unity though they appear as individuals. All entities are different names but ultimately they are expressions of the one Spirit.(7)

The exus came to earth without physical desires and needs. The exu is considered evil, but he does the work of the orixas. There are exus who are very high. Some exus are called elibaras (male) and others, pombagiras (female), who live on other spiritual levels. These are incorporated in ritual services and acquire characteristics. Mai Vera finalized her explanation:

The understanding of the exu depends upon your own criteria . . . The

198

exu is a force containing both negative and positive energy. If you are negative, your negativity will expand. If you have a positive magnetic energy, he will expand it also. What you are he reveals more of. (7)

Another priest, Pai Nivardo, also of Salvador, Bahia, holds a more enlightened view of the exu:

For me the exu is an orixa. He is not the Christian devil. He accepts offers, he carries messages, he governs oracles. The exu participates in all things. He never was a devil, nor is he a full god. He is the Son of Yemanja. The African slaves weren't accepted in the white Catholic churches. They worshipped at their own altars with their own gods. But they put the Catholic saints on top of the altar to fool the white men . . . a correspondence then occurred between their gods and saints to fool the whites. The exu in this way was related with the devil, but there is no relationship between one and another. (7)

During another interview, Nivardo said:

Especially the exu is beautiful but receives bad publicity. The people don't understand. the sects don't comprehend him . . . The exu are very great and do much good . . . The exu destroys so that the new may have space . . . We are energy and attract other types of energy . . . Man may transform energy to light. But energy exists at the command of God. This energy is the exu transformation. We are rational beings, but we also have irrationality. We are both positive and negative . . . analyzing this, the exu is part of us. (7)

It must be remembered that the exu is part of the Candomble legacy. In the northern state of Bahia, the homeland of Candomble, the exu is still recognized as an orixa and less identified with Satan. In the southern states of Rio and São Paulo, an environment that is more white and Christian, the exu is more active as the agent of evil, identical to the traditional role of the devil.

The exus are primordial, free, amoral, and powerful. The elibaras are their male forms, often viewed as street characters, such as drug pushers, pimps, etcetera who have made it economically. The pombagiras are the female forms identified as enticing, sensual prostitutes; but among both groups are very aristocratic cultured spirits. Tia Neiva, the foundress of the Valley of the Dawn classifies the exus:

Very handsome, highly educated men and women who resist conversion to Christianity. They may have committed no other sin and have actually helped other people, but their pride in rejecting the claims of Christianity make them pagans.

The devil has often been used as a symbol of protest and as a declaration of rebellion against the established order. The African slaves experienced suffering at the hands of Portuguese owners, who followed a religion headed by God, Jesus, Mary, the saints, and opposed by Satan. Thus the orixa exu took on a more exalted position as leader of the dispossessed and suffering. In the minds of many today, he is the symbol of liberation from society's taboos and restraints. He has become a type of Prometheus, who struggled with the gods to bring light to humankind and was expelled from heaven for doing so.

The images of the exu, as seen in the sanctuaries of Umbanda have horns, tails, and the trident of Poseidon, the ancient god of the seas. Pai Roberto Caldiera explained to me that its three points represent the positive, neutral, and negative polarizations of life. The exu is an orixa, that group of elevated souls that have important tasks in the universe dictated to them by Olorum, the great God. He is Mercury, carrying messages from the other orixas to humanity. He punishes and often rewards. He is feared and reverenced, and all Umbanda services must begin with the opening prayer dedicated to him. This invocation is usually said with the sanctuary curtain closed; at the finish, the acolytes open the dividing curtain between the initiates and the viewers.

Also, many sanctuaries will have an exu figure at its entrance. He, like the guardian demons of Tibetanism, protects the temple against the entrance of scoffers and the profane. The symbols often are imbued with powerful irradiations of energy. The first encounter that I had with an exu protection symbol was quite powerful. I had heard of them but never experienced one. I asked the priest of the sanctuary if that was an exu. He asked me why. I explained that a coldness and a sense of foreboding seemed to emanate from it. It was, of course the guardian exu.

The exu stands between the gods and mankind. His primary function is to initiate. He seems not at all concerned with the process, which is to catalyze. Be it good or bad, he is delightfully oblivious. He is a mechanical transformer. All of the chemicals of life are present, but when the exu interacts with them, processes are initiated. In this sense the exu represents the vital life force that penetrates all existence, making it dynamic, a force which is amoral and nonethical.

It is even present in the other orixas. In themselves they can do nothing until the exu is present. They cannot communicate with humanity if the exu doesn't carry their messages. The exu does not judge which message to deliver, he merely fulfills his obligations. As a force, he is like electricity; he can illuminate or destroy. The exu is potential, latent in all things. This potential flows through the cosmos maintaining all things in movement. In the body, the exu is often blocked and not flowing. This interruption causes problems such as sickness and premature ageing. Appropriate therapies must then be applied in order for the force to be redirected and the blocks to the original flowingness restored. For this reason the exu is approached for healing work.

As the vital force, the exu is expressed especially as sexuality, abundance, fertility, and unfoldment. It is believed that these forces, being blocked, build up massive quantities of repressed force, which, upon being liberated, produce impressive impact. This is the power of the orgasm, the energy of spiritual ecstasy, the power in the hands of the healer, and other forces that are experienced as released highs. The dances dedicated to the exu are Dionysian in character to awaken this orgiastic energy.

The exu are catalysts and produce catharsis. Nothing may be perceived or experienced without their presence. The exu holds primacy in all cult venerations as the initiator. He is present in the healing herb, releasing its beneficial properties, and is likewise present in poisonous substances.

Exu has many parallels with Oriental traditions. The exu as energy is neither male nor female. But like the cathartic energies of Hinduism and Buddhism, they are often represented in female form; in the East, they are called Shakti, in the exu tradition, pombagiras. Shaktis and pombagiras have similar functions—to activate a relation between primal energies and the initiate. Yet this envisionment of energies as female is for the facilitation of the initiate, as the pombagiras are no more female than the elibaras are male; they only appear so. The pombagira is understood by the common devotee to be an evil spirit, sensual, entrapping, to lead a male downward into the domain of evil. She is believed to be a prostitute spirit in the astral who sucks the energy of her human subjects. Yet, even Kali, the terrible Hindu goddess of destruction, has her other side as the Mother Creator. Similarly, the pombagiras also serve a higher purpose.

I propose that the exu tradition has a Tantric side to it. I view its purpose as facilitating communication between the physical and the spiritual worlds by harnessing the orgiastic energies within the body as fuel so that the devotee may enter into union with the Absolute. Thus, through the destruction of certain structures, the way is open for the energies of the cosmos to enter into the human experience. In our world, the traditional domain of the exu, he stands as its supreme energy. There are no fixed limits where the worlds divide, and it is here at the fluidic borderlands of astral and physical, visible and invisible, that the exu reigns supreme. Like the Greek god Charon, who carries the dead across the dividing river of Styx into the afterlife, the exu carries the power of the gods down to the worshipper as well as the energy of the worshipper up to heaven.

The nature of good and evil is compared to a spit of land that stands at a point between two currents that alternately wash over it—one minute sweet water, next, salt. Is the spit part of the salty or part of the sweet? In the same moment, the exu carries the swimmer from one shore to another. Is he then within the physical or the astral?

It is here at the borderland of morality and experience, at the limits that are constantly fluctuating, sometimes withdrawing, sometimes advancing, at this dynamic border that the exu is present to fulfill the highest experiences of those who have arrived.

The individual finds himself standing on the spit (morality), trying to decide between the oceans of good and evil. It is not until his awareness is awakened that the duality of good and evil is vanquished and the tormented soul finds peace. But this only occurs through the efficiency of the exu and his destructive path.

Just his name strikes fear into the heart of popular Umbandists. The exu is feared because his work is essentially destructive. He is, along with his legions of elibaras and pombagiras, intent on the destruction of all things in his path. Exu is the supreme destroyer of matter, constantly consuming the old in order to provide space for continual renewal.

It is important to realize that the lower spirits, led by the exu, are intent on a destructive work that heralds the processes that might bring us closer to illumination. Most of the great traditions complement this. Christianity claims that a death must occur before one can enter Heaven's Kingdom. Saint Thomas's Gnostic Gospel speaks of an "undressing." The Bardo spirits, as envisioned in the Tibetan Book of the Dead, present us with frightening masks that appear to destroy us so that we might awake. Often it is through destruction that one enters into new spaces.

The ego, which separates man from his true state of Nirvana, must be destroyed—either through knowledge and will or through fear and suffering. The exu, his spirits, and his falange, the realm of the lower spirits, prepare the ego to experience enough suffering and destruction to make the quantum jump into consciousness. Very few is the number of souls that walk the Path for its own sake. The majority are forced into the light by suffering experiences.

The exu is the great destroyer of time, the breaker of limits, and the corruptor of fixed and programmed self concepts. How many people in their living dream-state are satisfied with their personal Tower of Babel, erected In the middle of a desert, constructed with blocks of confusion, and resting on a foundation of self-delusion? It was necessary for an awakening to occur through the agency of an angry and destructive god, who sent a thunderbolt to destroy the tower that was proposed to reach all the way up to Heaven.

It is no mistake that in many of the Tarot decks, the Tower, which is being tumbled by a mighty thunderbolt, is the powerful card of transformation. For whatever has been raised upon temporary foundations, like a house built upon sand, must also come crumbling down. The destructive force that upsets the foundation of illusion is also the exu. He enacts karma and maintains the law of impermanence. The exu, as the lord of the limits, is the eternal energy of conveyance, of destruction, which returns all things seen and created to the All, which is God.

Visit a Buddhist shrine, and you will meet the exu there, this time disguised as monstrous gods. These guardian demons keep the superfluous away. Superficial seekers will be scared by the horrid faces and postures. These dharma guardians work to destroy the superficial in each soul so that a pearl of wisdom might be realized. When the breakthrough in consciousness occurs, then the demon is no longer seen as evil but as a savior. He is the other face of God.

As Mai Vera stated, it is according to your criteria that the exu is understood. To a person of depth, the exu becomes the friend, not the foe. He is the initiator of destructive processes, which prepares the way for the coming of illumination. At first, like Asreal, the Sufi angel of death, he appears to be a slayer. Soon he is discovered to be Israfil, the angel of light. Thus, the exu as Lucifer is redeemed as the light bringer, and Prometheus is once again unbound.

The spirits of the inferior world also have their lineage; they have personal characteristics and names. Among some of the more powerful and more popularly invoked exu are: the Exu of Seven Gateways, Exu Old Galo, Exu World Vira, Ze Pelintro, John Caveira, the Hairy Exu, Exu of Mud, Exu Ze of Covas, Pombagiras Mary Molambo, Mary Quiteria, Diana, Mary Padilha, Cigna, and Queen Gira.

The elebaras are exus who perform the function of corroborating a person's karma. They, too, are identified by a name which best characterizes its personality. They bring problems such as material suffering, ills, disasters, and spiritual collapse into the lives of individuals, which provide them opportunity to balance their existence and thus eliminate karmic debt. Using such "tools" as misery, vice, suicide and insanity, they offer the opportunity of educational experience.

It is not strange, therefore, that elebaras are seen as the causes of problems instead of their actual role as the collectors of debts left over from previous incarnations.

B. Ritualistic Practices in Umbanda

Umbanda is an initiatory religion. Through the use of its magico-Gnostic rituals, the devotee is empowered to attain the knowledge that will ultimately effect his spiritual progress and lead him to a condition in which he can effectively channel and use axe. The proper use of Umbanda ritual will enable him to erase any karmic debts, thus eliminating the need to reincarnate upon earth. Then he will enter into the falange and serve as an instrument of charity to those upon the earth.

Umbanda magic is divided into two categories: propitiatory magic and gnosis. Propitiatory ritual concerns the invocation of forces to satisfy personal needs. This is the most sought-after type of ritual in the tendas of Umbanda. The majority of worshippers consult the Pais to gain favor concerning mundane problems with money, relationships, health, and so on. Many Pais complained to me that perhaps out of every thousand people, only one or two come for spiritual advancement.

The Sacred Gira

The gira, or sacred dance, runs through the great religious traditions of the world. I have participated in Native American dances, indigenous Brazilian dances, and I have danced with the Sufis of Islam and with the Chassidim of Judaism. I have participated in Pentecostal and charismatic services, where the people begin to move as if in dance. At some of the lesser Christian movements, such as the Shakers, dance was employed regularly.

In Brazil, the Candomble and Umbanda utilize the sacred gira as the principal psychotechnical instrument for inducing altered states of consciousness. The purpose of the dance is to prepare the medium for the incorporation of his spirit guide. Incorporation, as explained in my other works, is that alternate state in which a separate spirit entity takes over the personality of the medium, thus giving him a different persona. Inherent in the gira is the ability to upset the normal brain functioning. Once a certain pitch of ecstacy is reached, a psychological space is created in which the spirit may enter into intimate communication with, and direct the communicative activities of, the medium.

The Kardicist religion accomplishes this phenomenon without the gira, as does the Esoteric Umbanda. The gira requires special dance steps coordinated with specialized pontos and rhythms in order for the trance state to be invoked.

As the medium submits more fully to the experience, he forgets about himself and loses the concept of time. His conscious mind is ultimately enjoined in the ecstatic submission to his patron deity. Whereas in other traditions, such as Sufism, Hasidism, and Pentecostal, the god figure itself is channeled into the devotee's body, the Umbanda priest is taught that in such a state, he is open to receiving his spirit guide, or some other member of a falange.

At the height of ecstatic pitch, the medium may fall upon the ground, jump in the air, scream, shake, or demonstrate other "abnormal" behavior, which indicates that the spirit has occupied his mind space. Immediately the medium will incorporate the several physical characteristics of the occupying spirit: voice, facial expression, stance, and other habits that might be traditionally identified with him. Many of these characteristics fall into the domain of stigmata, a word usually identified only with the marks on the hands and feet of Catholic saints and mystics that resemble the nail punctures of Jesus on the cross.

As part of the priestly training, acolytes are told legends and stories and given descriptions of the lives of their own African and native saints, so the stigmata that they demonstrate would naturally manifest as slave and Indian traits.

I found it very difficult to understand the pretos velhos' archaic Brazilian slave dialects as much as the dialects of the Amazonian and western caboclos. The walking sticks, the smokes, and drinking of the native cachaca palm liquor are also included among the stigmatic characteristics.

The end of the gira marks the beginning of spirit possession. The spirit is greeted by disciples with embraces and kissing of the hands. The spirit then demands a piece of wood or floor space and a piece of chalk with which he will draw his ponto, the emblem of his lineage. This coat of arms will indicate which power is working through him and his source of axe. In Umbanda, the ponto is a series of cabalistic lines by which that spirit may be invoked and with which he identifies himself. The ponto will remain until the spirit disincorporates, when it is erased.

An important part of the gira is the use of cantos, or sacred songs. Each deity and spirit requires a special invocation and hymn. These are usually written in Portuguese or an African dialect. They are usually rhythmic and declare the special characteristics of the gods.

The cantos, which are often quite beautiful and hypnotic, serve as mantras. When constantly repeated to the accompaniment of the drums, rhythmic clapping, and dancing, they often induce altered states of consciousness. I have observed devotees ecstatically crying and smiling, as if they had experienced divine beatitude. The following are examples of cantos, the first one dedicated to the goddess Yemanja and the second to the goddess Oxun:

To Yemanja

A estrela brilhou	The star shines
La no alto do mar	In the heights of the sea
Quem ven nos salva	Who comes to save us
E nossa Mae Iemanja.	It is our Mother Yemanja.
Sejos benvinda	Be welcome
Nossa Mae de muito amor	Our Mother of infinite love
Venha nos salvar	She comes to save us
Pelo cruz do Senhor.	By the cross of the Lord.

To Oxun

E la e flor de maio	She is the May flower
E la e flor de maio	She is the May flower
Se a minha mae	Is my mother.
E linda flor de maio	The pretty May flower
Aleleu	Hallelujah
E flor de maio.	She is the May flower.

The gira is a magical ritual utilized in Umbanda to manifest spirits through the possession of its cavalhos or mediums. The gira unfolds itself through three steps: the preparation, the opening, and the closing. The preparation involves all of the necessary indicated works so that the spirit may incorporate or possess the medium with complete security and follow within the precepts laid down by Umbanda. Included in the preparation phase are these prescriptions: the temple must be physically cleansed as to be spotless; the physical purification of the participating mediums; the magical preparation of the mediums, which usually consists of meditation and concentration exercises; the completion of the energy current needed for the possession; a talk on the importance of the spirit's incorporation; the *defumacao* (incensing of the sanctuary) in order to eliminate the bad entities which may be present; and finally, the opening.

The opening of the sacred space occurs when the chief priest, a *babalao,* uses incense in the defumacao and invokes certain orixas to the bless the rituals that are to follow. Then the opening commences with the appropriate hymns dances, which invoke certain entities to take possession of their mediums, often called the *aparelho* ("apparatus"). At this point the spirits incorporate and begin their works of charity, which consist of healing, counseling, and other acts of service.

After completion of their charitable works, the closure begins. This consists of parting hymns and prayers of thanks to God, Jesus, the saints, and other entities for participating in the work. At this time, the spirits part from their mediums. Finally the guardian of the lineage is acknowledged in a song, and the final hymn and dismissal is given. Some slight procedural variations occur from tenda to tenda, but most Umbanda centers follow this general procedure.

One of the most popular rituals in Umbanda is the *fumigacao,* ("fumigation"), which is both magical and symbolic. As to its magical side, it clears the sacred space and the people within that space of negative energies, usually in the form of evil entities: eguns, exus, and other low spirits. It is said to work on all types of negative thought forms as well and is often employed in depression, despair, and when incorporation, voluntary or otherwise, takes place.

The presiding Pai swings the incense container back and forth in the four principal directions, sanctifying the limits of the four principal directions, sanctifying the limits of the sanctuary. Then the doors and windows are sealed with the smoke. Finally, each acolyte visitor is fumigated until the purification is complete. It has also been suggested that the ritual of fumigacao symbolizes the expansion of the spirit in its evolution from center outward in all directions.

Other purifications are enacted with a sacred dust, ash, or talc, which is poured into the palm of the Pai or an assistant and then blown in the four directions. This signifies the purification of the air. The dust is often perfumed, and the room then has the fragrance of flowers. Another purification includes the use of blessed water. In the lineages of the Orixa Yemanja, the water may contain some salt, in others, it may be sweet water. This water is sprinkled upon the altar and the heads and hands of those who are participating in the gira. The water is often magnetized by the incorporated mediums beforehand and saved for the next meeting. The magnetized water is also given out in small bottles to the suppliants for the cleansing of their homes and for use as baths to cleanse their own vibrations.

Magnetic Passes

The magnetic pass is the principal healing mechanism in Umbanda services. Special nights are dedicated to healing, when certain spirits are invoked. Then the suppliant takes off his shoes, enters the sacred area of the sanctuary, and either sits or bows in front of the incorporated medium.

At that point, the medium makes light passes over the body, especially dedicating additional time to those areas which appear to be magnetically off balance. The medium often does not touch the patient's body with his own hands, preferring to use some ritual object such as a crystal, feather, or large piece of chalk.

These objects are cleansed after each patient. Magnetic passes are a contribution of the Kardecist religion and were incorporated into the Umbanda service from the beginning of this movement.

Ritualistic Clothing and Colors

White is the traditional color worn in the Umbanda service. I was informed that white signifies ritual purity and is the color of the supreme guiding spirit of Umbanda, Jesus Christ. Traditionally, white is also the color used among the African tribes that were invaded by Muslim missionaries. Tribes, like the Houssa, brought Islam back with them to the state of Bahia. Due to the lack of Islamic activities, those Africans were absorbed into Catholicism, but the use of white pants, white turbans, and white robes was incorporated into Candomble and Umbanda cult practice.

White is used in the Umbanda sanctuaries: the altar cloths, candles, and clothing. The sanctuary itself is usually painted in white, as is often the floor.

Part of the typical ritual clothing are the beads worn to differentiate among the grades of initiation. The more beads worn, the higher the grade through which the initiate has passed. The color of the beads identifies the particular lineage and deity. Let us take a brief look at the various colors and their meanings.

The colors of the orixas vary in Umbanda and often between the various traditional nations. For example, the Angolese Umbanda might utilize a completely different color to invoke the same deity that a Malu Umbanda uses. As it is impossible to give all the differences, I will try to give a general survey of the more popular colors and the orixas which they represent.

1. *Exu:* Black and deep red are the colors of these entities. This is because they are spirits who are not very evolved and therefore live in darkness. Deep red indicates those spirits who like to fight and shed blood. The pombagiras are often represented by yellow, in addition to black and blood red.

2. *Ogum:* There are several colors related to this being. Some centers use green, blood red, and white. Green represents the countryside and the herbs which grow there; deep red represents the blood spilled in wars, for Ogum is a warrior deity. As the knight guardian of the deity Oxala, he also carries white.

3. *Oxossi:* This orixa's color is dark green, which represents the grasses and herbs, where he reigns and where native peoples live. He is the head of a large falange of caboclos.

4. *Xango:* He is represented by maroon, since he is an ancient orixa and is identified with Saint Francis of Assisi, who is also dressed in this color. Sometimes he is also identified with white, which makes him one of the greatest orixas, just under Oxala.

5. *Yemanja:* Her colors are transparent tones, reflecting the waters of the oceans. Transparent white is used because water is crystalline. Green is used to represent the plants that grow in the water. Her devotees often use sea shells instead of beads, as she is the deity of salt waters.

6. *Oxala:* This is the highest of the orixas, second only to the great God Olorum. His color is milk white, the symbol of his purity. He is the father of all the orixas, and his color represents peace, love, and forgiveness. Some sanctuaries also honor him with red, since he is identified with Christ, which signifies his sufferings.

7. *Nana:* Nana is normally associated with lilac, which signifies pain and acceptance of suffering and because she is the eldest of the deities.

8. *Iansa:* controls fire and lightning rays. Her color is usually blood red because of the wars in which she is often called upon to participate.

9. *Ibeji:* is represented in Umbanda by the only Brazilian orixas, Cosme and Damien. These two beings are crianzas, child-like spirits and therefore are identified with angels. Their colors are light green and rose. Oftentimes they are dressed in rose colors, as their correspondent is the Catholic Our Lady of the Angels.

10. *Pretos velhos* are the old black slaves and are considered to be secondary orixas in Umbanda. They use white and black, white because upon death they intervene in the prayers of those who are passing to the land of light. During their lifetime as slaves, they were clothed in white rags. Black is used because they are Africans.

11. *Obaluaie* is the protector of cemeteries. His colors are black and white. He uses white because he is of high rank. Some priests link blood red with him because of his identification with the deity Iansa. Black represents death.

The Buzios

Many traditions have an oracular process which divine the future and is often used to dredge up forgotten events of the past. The *buzios* are sea shells, quite small ones, which are thrown in a certain manner to explain the direction of life. A look at the rituals of Umbanda would not be complete without the mention of this important rite. The oracular ritual is the means of communication between the faithful and their understanding of God's will. The priest who throws the shells has the responsibility to reorient the life of his student, harmonizing his personal life with that of the flux and movements of the cosmic life. The student is told about his past and future actions so that he can minimize the consequences of disagreeable events that will conflict with universal laws. The buzios, then are related to the Tarot, I Ching, the Egyptian Book of Destiny, the oracles at Delphi, and other divinatory processes.

The shells are thrown on an *opanifa* (an eight-sided board inscribed with sixteen signs). One sign represents the universal masculine principle, another, universal femininity. Seven of the remaining signs represent the male orixas and the last seven, the female orixas. Each of these orixas represent certain divine characteristics:

211

Oxala - peace and just men

Xango - mature, business-minded persons

Ogum - the military personality and people related to conflict

Oxossi - physicians, chemists, healers, seekers of spiritual and material things

Omolu - aged people, illness and fear

Oxum - mother, housewife, the sincere woman

Iansa - a woman given to intrigues

Yemanja - dreamers, pacifists

Nana - counselors and advisors

Ibeji - children

Exu - evil men, enemies

Pombagira - evil women

After some ceremonial chanting, candle-lighting, and incense-burning, the priest throws the shells and relies upon his intuition for the interpretation of the haphazard landing. The priest often dresses in his liturgical vestments, which include some symbols upon his breast and right shoulder.

There are, of course many other rituals in Umbanda, which are revealed only to those who have advanced to certain levels. To become a priest, for example, the acolyte must submit to certain rites, among them purification by having their heads shaved like those of monks, the carving of certain symbols cut into the scalp, certain symbols painted on, and monastic laws imposed for a period of time. These rituals are revealed only by word of mouth and are reserved only for the initiates and not given to the profane. It is my purpose only to introduce those most commonly demonstrated in the Umbanda centers.

Pontos

Pontos are ritual chants used in the magico-invocation practices of both the Candomble and the Umbanda. They are generally directed to the orixas and sometimes to the falange members. They are songs to establish a rhythmic musical environment in which the medium(s) might enter into trance state. The pontos appear on the left in Portuguese and in translation on the right. I tried to capture the beauty of the language whenever possible.

YEMANJA

A estrela brilhou	The star shines brightly
La no alto do mar	Over the heights of the sea
Quem vem nos salvar	Who we see saves us
E nossa Mae Iemanja.	It is our Mother Yemanja.
Sejas benvinda	Be Thou welcome
Nossa mae de muito amor	Our mother of so much love
Venha nos salvar	Who has come to save us
Pelo cruz do Sehnor	By the cross of the Lord above.

INHASSA

Inhassa chegou no reino	Inhassa has entered her kingdom.
Chegou, con chuva e com vento	She's come with rain and wind.
Ela i dona de Jacuta, veio sarava	She is the Lady of Jacuta, Hail!
Os seus filhos Ino Gonga.	From your children of Ino Gonga.

OXUM

Ela e flor de maio	She is the May flower
Ela e flor de maio	She is the May flower
Sea minha mae	She is my Mother.
E linda, flor de maio	She is lovely, the May flower
Aleleu	Hallelujah
E flor de maio.	She is the May flower.

XANGO

Eh . . . Xango Maior.	Oh . . . Ancient Xango
Xango da lei maior	Xango gives the ancient law
Na canjera de Umbanda	In the holy dance of Umbanda
Inda ioio, Xango da lei maior.	Inda ioio, Xango gives the ancient law.

213

OXOCE

E Zambi quem governa o mundo.	It is Zambi who rules the world.
So Zambi pode governa.	Alone Zambi is able to rule.
E Zambi quem clareia os estrelas;	It is Zambi who brightens stars;
E quem clareia Oxoce la no Jurema.	Oxoce who is of Jurema.

OXALA

Oxala nosso Pai	Oxala our Father
Ele vem nos ayudar.	He comes to our aid.
Ele vem con sua luz.	He comes with his light.
Ele traz sua pax.	He brings his peace.
Oxala nosso Pai, a bander vem	Oxala our Father, who
A bander vem nos fermar.	cares for us when we are ill.

Glossary of Terms

Axe: divine grace, power, the energy which animates all things, the power of God Olorum, which must reach all beings to heal, to harmonize and to produce happiness.

Candomble: Afro-Brazilian religion, brought over by the slaves, bases its cult upon the worship of the orixas. It has been called the secret national religion of Brazil.

Caboclo: a native Indian who suffered under the Portuguese and through suffering gained wisdom and spiritual evolution. In Umbanda he belongs in a falange as a spirit guide.

Crianza: a child who has died in innocence, has not sinned, and therefore serves as a spirit guide to others on earth and works within falanges.

Falange: a lineage based upon the rituals, teachings, and guidance of one of the principal orixas. Members are pretos velhos, caboclos, crianzas, and other positive souls who merited entrance through personal evolution and good spiritual qualities.

Fumacao: fumigation or smoking, using incense prepared from special barks and graces. Used to purify the person, place, or object and protect it from attacks of evil spirits.

Gira: the sacred dances dedicated to the orixas and used in Umbanda and Candomble as the primary psychotechnology to prepare the medium for incorporation.

Incorporation: the condition which exists when a medium voluntarily allows a spirit to possess it for some purpose, such as healing, counseling, writing, etcetera. There are two types of incorporation: conscious, where the medium

215

maintains some type of awareness, and unconscious, where there is no personal knowledge of what the spirit is doing. Unless there is incorporation, there can be no trance or paranormal activity.

Mediums: those people gifted with the capacity to communicate with spirits and establish a relationship with them. They demonstrate paranormal talents, such as spirit writing, healing, painting, etcetera.

Olorum: the Supreme Deity, God Almighty in the Candomble and Umbanda religions.

Orixa: the deities of Candomble, sometimes said to be twelve, twenty-two or hundreds in number. During the years of Portuguese dominion, these gods were hidden under the names of Roman Catholic saints; today they still have a double personality as both Roman and Candomble saints.

Pai do Santo (female: Mai do Santo): the priests of the Umbanda and Candomble traditions. They have been initiated into the mysteries of their corresponding orixa or saint.

Preto velho: a onetime black slave who through meritorious deeds or suffering now serves as a spirit guide in the Umbanda and works through the falange.

Quimbanda: the religion which pays special reverence to the lower or "dark" forces, often called Dark Umbanda, a form of black magic.

Quimbas: the lower spirits, exus, elibaras, pombagiras, vampires, etcetera.

Spiritism: the movement founded by Allan Kardec and based upon his investigations with thousands of mediums throughout the world. Its teachings are called the Doutrina or Codificacao ("Doctrine" or "Codification").

Spiritualism: the movement initiated in the middle 1800s, based upon the belief in a spirit world and in communication with spirits. The first recorded spiritualistic activity began with the Fox sisters who communicated with an entity through table rapping. The movement soon spread to Europe.

Santeria: the religion based upon the adoration of the Orishas; brought to the island from Africa, it shares many similarities to the Candomble of Brazil and the vodoon of Haiti; the three are cousin religions. Cuban santeria is well spread within and without Cuba, especially in the large Latin centers of Miami and New York.

Terreiro: the place where the Umbanda and Candomble priests meet with their congregations and spirits. Terreiro ("Paio") refers to the land between the slave quarters and the main house where the Portuguese dons and the slaves could mingle, the slaves dancing and relaxing.

Tenda: a store where ritual objects are sold; a place where the Pai attends to the public consulting, healing, et. al. Often used to designate an Umbanda chapel.

Umbanda: the Afro-Brazilian religion, which integrates elements of Spiritism, Candomble, and Roman Catholicism with African native spirit practices. Umbanda seems to be the only true Brazilian religion, started by de Moraes in that country.

References

1. Baha'u'llah, *The Seven Valleys and the Four Valleys* (Wilmette, Ill.: Baha'i Publishing Trust, 1968).
2. G. Meek, *Healers and the Healing Process* (Wheaton, Ill.: Quest, 1982).
3. S. White, *The Betty Book* (New York: Berkley Publishing Corp. 1939).
4. T. DaSilva, *Umbanda* (Umbanda Federation of São Paulo, 1946).
5. D. Boyd, *Mystics, Magic and Medicine People* (New York: Paragon House, 1986).
6. G. L. Playfair, *The Unknown Power* (New York: Pocketbooks, 1975).
7. J. Dennis Trisker, "Observations of Incorporation of Brazilian Mediums," Master's Thesis: Atlantic University (Virginia Beach, Va.: 1992).
8. F. Louiza, *Umbanda e Psicoanalise* (Rio de Janiero: Editora Espiritualista, 1971).
9. *Umbanda* (São Paulo: O Planeta, Special Edition 1 & 2, 149-C).
10. O. Cacciatore, *Diccionario dos Cultos Afro-Brasileisos* (Salvador Bahia: Centro Dos Estudos Afro-Orientais, CED Press).
11. H. G. Andrade, *A Reincarnacao em Brasil* (Federacion Espirita do São Paulo).
12. J. Klimo, *Channeling* (Los Angeles: J. P. Tarcher, Inc., 1987).
13. Ken Wilber, "A Developmental View of Consciousness" *Journal of Trans-personal Psychology*, 1979, vol. 11, no. 1.
14. E. C. Mendes, *Personalidade Intrusa* (São Paulo: Editora Pensamento, 1980).
15. A. Kardec, *Al Estudo da Dounina Espirita* (São Paulo: Lalce, 1972).
16. C. A. Perandrea, *A Psicografia a Luz da Grafoscopia* (Curitiba: University Spiritist Research, 1990).
17. E. Armond, *Mediumidade* (São Paulo: Spiritist Press, 1971).
18. W. Viera and Xavier, *Mecanismos Da Mediunidade* (Brazileira, Rio: Fed. Espirita, 1990).
19. H. G. Andrade, *As Tres Faces da Parapsicologia* (Julho: Boletin Medico-Espirita #4, 1986).
20. W. Barnstone, *Gospel of Thomas, the Other Bible* (San Francisco: Harper & Row), 1984).
21. *Espirito, Corpo Espiritual e Corpo Fisico* (Julho: Prieto Press Boletin Medico-Esperita #4, 1986).
22. *Journal of Spiritist Medical Association* (São Paulo, 1988).
23. *Journal of Spiritist Medical Association* (São Paulo, 1987).

24. LaPassade and Alves, Centro Dos Estudos Afro-Orientais, *Quimbanda* (Salvador, Bahia: CED Press.
25. C. A. Tinoco, *Biological Organizing Model* (Curitiba: Grafica Veja, 1982).

Bibliography

Lyra, A. *Psychiatry, Parapsychology and the Phenomenon of Spirit and Demon Possession* (São Paulo: Spiritist Medical Review #2, December 1984).

Dr. A. Sech, *Spiritistic Obsessions as Related to Other Mental Pathologies* (Spiritist Medical Review #2, December 1984).

Gil, A. M. *Reflections on Obsession* (São Paulo: Beletin Medico-Espirita #2, December 1984).

Ram Dass, *Be Here Now* (Lama Foundation, N.M., 1962).

Brazil Puts Its Faith in Spirits, São Paulo: Veja Magazine, April 10,

J. Andrea, *Dinamica Psi* (Petropolis, Brazil: F. V. Lorenz Press, 1990).

Dr. W. Ferreira de Melo, *Das Obsessoes* Ibid.

A. Kardec, *El Evangelio Segun el Espiritismo* (Buenos Aires: Editora Argentina, 1991).

Encounter of the Nations of Candomble (Salvador, Bahia: Center of Afro-Oriental Studies, CED Press, 1981).

J. Andrea, *Energetica do Psiquismo* (Petropolis, Brazil: Soc. Espiritualista, Lorenz Press, 1990).

Pro. Henrique Rodrigues, *A Ciencia do Espirito* São Paulo, Brazil: Casa Ed. O Clarim, 1985).

A. Kardec, *The Spirit's Book* (São Paulo: Lake, 1972).

221

W. M. Gonzalez, *The Santeria Experience* (Englewood Cliffs, N.J.: Prentice-Hall, 1982).

A. Kardec, *The Medium's Book* (Brazil: Lake, 1972).

S. Bonder, *The Divine Emergence of the World-Teacher* (Clearlake, Ca.: Dawn Horse Press, 1991.

F. Jose de Mello, *Spiritism and Critical Judgement* (São Paulo: Spiritist Medical Review #2, December 1984).

Itkak Bentov, *Stalking the Wild Pendulum* (New York: Dutton, 1972).

W. Valente, *Sincretismo Religioso Afro-Brasileiro* (São Paulo: Companhia Editora Nacional, 1977).

Ailton Paiva, *Similarities and Differences Between Kardecism and the Afro-Brazilian Religions* International Spiritist Review, (São Paulo: February 1974).

W. M. Gonzalez, *Santeria* (New York: Harmony Books, 1989).

D. J. Carlat, *Psychological Motivation and the Choice of Spiritual Symbols: A Case Study* (Journal of Transpersonal Psychology Vol. 21, #2, 1989).

E. C. Mendes, *Personalidade Hiperconsciente* (São Paulo: Editora Pensamento, 1988).

V. Mansfield, *Looking into Mind, An Undergraduate Course,* Journal of Transpersonal Psychology Vol. 23, #1 (from: The Notebooks of P. Brunton).

A. Guillermoprieto, *Letter from Rio* (The New Yorker, December 2, 1991).

R. Lucio, *O Homen Sadio: Una Nova Visao* (Belo Horizonte: Hospital Espirita "Andres Luiz," 1989).

L. Trindade, *Exu: Power and Danger* (São Paulo: Icone Editora Ltda., 1985).

H. G. Andrade, *Espiritu, Perispirito e Alma* (São Paulo: Editora Pensamento, 1984).

E. C. Mendes, *Personalidade Subconsciente* (São Paulo: Editora Pensamento, 1988).